Lost in Transition

Lost in Transition tells the story of the "lost generation" that came of age in Japan's deep economic recession in the 1990s. The book argues that Japan is in the midst of profound changes that have had an especially strong impact on the young generation. The country's renowned "permanent employment system" has unraveled for young workers, only to be replaced by temporary and insecure forms of employment. The much-admired system of moving young people smoothly from school to work has frayed. The book argues that these changes in the very fabric of Japanese postwar institutions have loosened young people's attachment to school as the launching pad into the world of work and have loosened their attachment to the workplace as a source of identity and security. The implications for the future of Japanese society – and the fault lines within it – loom large.

Mary C. Brinton is Reischauer Institute Professor of Sociology at Harvard University. She has also held professorships at the University of Chicago and Cornell University. She is the author of *Women and the Economic Miracle: Gender and Work in Postwar Japan*, the editor of *Women's Working Lives in East Asia*, and the co-editor of *The New Institutionalism in Sociology* and *The Declining Significance of Gender?* Her work has appeared frequently in journals, including the *American Journal of Sociology*, *American Sociological Review*, and *Sociology of Education*.

Lost in Transition

Youth, Work, and Instability in Postindustrial Japan

MARY C. BRINTON
Harvard University

CAMBRIDGE
UNIVERSITY PRESS

CAMBRIDGE UNIVERSITY PRESS
Cambridge, New York, Melbourne, Madrid, Cape Town,
Singapore, São Paulo, Delhi, Tokyo, Mexico City

Cambridge University Press
32 Avenue of the Americas, New York, NY 10013-2473, USA

www.cambridge.org
Information on this title: www.cambridge.org/9780521126007

First published 2011
Reprinted 2011

A catalog record for this publication is available from the British Library.

Library of Congress Cataloging in Publication Data

Brinton, Mary C.
  Lost in transition : youth, work, and instability in postindustrial Japan / Mary C.
  Brinton.
    p. cm.
  Includes bibliographical references and index.
  ISBN 978-0-521-19914-8 (hardback : perm paper) – ISBN 978-0-521-12600-7
  (paperback : perm paper)
  1. Youth – Employment – Japan. I. Title.
  HD6276.J3B75 2010
  331.3'470952–dc22   2010031209

ISBN 978-0-521-19914-8 Hardback
ISBN 978-0-521-12600-7 Paperback

Contents

Figures

Tables

Preface

Foreign visitors arriving in Tokyo can be forgiven for not immediately sensing the havoc wreaked on individual lives by the economic recession and dramatic employment restructuring of the late twentieth century. The bursting of Japan's financial and real estate bubble in the early 1990s led in the ensuing decade to the highest unemployment rates and greatest economic anxieties experienced in the country since the early post–World War II years. And while the country was still struggling to recover, financial crisis hit once more in the fall of 2008 – this time striking down postindustrial economy after postindustrial economy and sending unemployment rates up once more. Even so, a walk down the street in Tokyo's central business districts reveals sidewalks full of middle-aged *sarariimen* (male office employees) rushing to their next appointments. A stroll past upscale coffee shops in Tokyo's major shopping districts provides glimpses into an elegant world populated by clusters of upper-middle-class housewives enjoying lunch and gossip together. These sights, so familiar from Japan's period of sustained economic growth prior to the 1990s, can make it seem that not so much has changed after all during the subsequent years of recession.

There is a reason these scenes mask the impact of economic recession and employment restructuring: Those most affected are not the middle-aged and not the elite. Instead, the people who have been "lost in transition" as the Japanese economy tries to restabilize itself in the early twenty-first century are people in the younger generation, especially the non-elite among them. This book tells the story of these individuals. I analyze why so many of them became lost in the transition from school to work and, in a larger sense, lost in Japan's transition to a mature postindustrial economy with a labor market ever more bifurcated between "good" and "bad" jobs.

LOST IN TRANSITION: A SOCIETY AND A GENERATION

I originally began the research for this book to answer the question of why Japan's highly praised school-work system operates so well. Many English-language reports and publications in the 1980s and early 1990s pointed to Japan's unique and efficient school-work transition process with admiration. Japan in the 1980s had low unemployment rates among youth and did not seem to be suffering from many of the youth labor market problems that other countries faced. Given my long-standing fascination with how institutions structure individuals' opportunities and constraints and lead to patterns of inequality across social groups, I embarked on in-depth research on Japan's high school–work system. Why did this system seem to be so much more effective than anything we had in the United States, especially in terms of smoothing the transition into full-time work for lower-educated youth? This group corresponded to the population in the United States for which the school-work transition was so poorly orchestrated by our existing social institutions.

One of my colleagues at the University of Chicago at the time was William Julius Wilson, a preeminent scholar of the working poor in the United States. The research of Wilson and others pointed out the severe difficulties faced by American urban high school graduates and dropouts in trying to find jobs.[1] They lack assistance from their schools or from public policies that help match new graduates with employers. In contrast, Japan in the 1980s looked remarkably different, and well worth understanding better.

In my initial research I focused on urban public high schools in Japan that had traditionally sent large numbers of students into the labor market. I visited twenty low-ranking public high schools one after another in two urban areas of Japan – the densely populated Kawasaki-Yokohama area bordering the southwestern edge of Tokyo, and the much smaller city of Sendai in Miyagi prefecture, two and a half hours north of Tokyo by bullet train. In those twenty high schools I conducted long, semi-structured interviews in Japanese with the *shinro shidōbu no sensei*, the teachers in charge of advising and guiding students into jobs or into higher education.

---

[1] See particularly William Julius Wilson, *When Work Disappears: The World of the New Urban Poor* (New York: Vintage, 1997).

Fourteen of the schools I visited are general academic high schools and six are vocational ones. None of them send very many graduates to university. Instead, they are schools from which large numbers of graduates have traditionally entered the labor market, through the coordination of the *shinro shidōbu* (the school's guidance department), local employers, and the *shokugyō anteijo* (local public employment security offices, about which I will have more to say in Chapter 2).

What I discovered in these interviews and in accompanying research in Japan in the mid-1990s was so fascinating that I continued the research over several years, moving back and forth between Japan and the United States. Much of what I heard in the early interviews with Japanese high school teachers and principals surprised me. At one school I was taken in to meet the principal, who had been assigned to the school only recently. He introduced himself and gave me his old *meishi* (name card), with the name of his former high school crossed out and the name of his new high school written above it. As we talked, he explained that he had previously been the principal at one of the top high schools in Kanagawa prefecture. Now, he said ruefully, it feels like "I have descended from heaven into hell."

Of course, the existence of high schools in Japan where discipline problems are difficult and teachers and principals experience considerable frustration is hardly new, and should not be surprising.[2] But as I visited more and more high schools in the mid-1990s I sensed that there were new phenomena emerging that were not yet being fully discussed in Japanese society. That is, not only were the English-language writings that praised the effectiveness of the Japanese school-work system becoming out of date, but the increasing frustration of teachers and students at low-ranking high schools seemed to be almost invisible within Japanese society as well.

When I was invited to present my research at a number of Japanese universities and research institutes in the mid-late 1990s, I discussed the results of the interviews I had conducted with high school guidance teachers. Many members of the highly educated Japanese audiences at these seminars looked at me as if I were talking about the moon rather than Japan. My audience reacted as if I were talking about a place so foreign that it could not possibly be Japan. This made me realize that I was seeing and describing things that did not sound familiar to them.

---

[2] In his classic *Japan's High Schools* (University of California Press, 1983), Thomas Rohlen discussed a range of discipline problems in two of the five schools in Kobe where he conducted ethnographic research.

What I described were high schools where as many as 30 or 40 percent of graduating seniors went into neither jobs nor higher education (nor did they become *rōnin*, students "sitting out" to study for an additional year before university). I visited schools where teachers coached students intensively on how to interview for a job but where, after two or three failed interviews, students simply gave up and took themselves out of the running for either jobs or higher education. I described schools where teachers faced a classroom of students sleepy from having come to school from their nighttime *arubaito* (part-time jobs) at local *conbini* (convenience stores, ubiquitous in urban Japan) or other workplaces. I discussed schools where teachers said things were going well if they were able to cover even one-third of the pages of the required curriculum.

While scholarly Japanese audiences were surprised and even shocked at what I described, the schools I had visited did not fit the images of Japanese high schools that average Americans hold either. One such image is that of a high school full of students intent on getting into a top-ranked university. In that image, students who are not in the forefront of the university exam competition enthusiastically turn to participation in school club activities, pursuing judo, baseball, or debate practice. Another common image that occasionally appears in the American media is Japanese schools where bullying among students is so rampant that some students simply reject school entirely and refuse to attend.

The Japanese high schools that started me on the path of writing this book do not neatly fit either of these two stereotypes. Instead, they fall somewhere in between. They are in the middle or lower one-third of the ranks of public high schools in their districts. Their graduates have a variety of destinations – some graduates go directly to university or junior college, some to *senmon gakkō* (specialized two-year training schools), some into full-time jobs. But increasingly over the past fifteen years, some students simply go – they are out of school and out of work. They are not in full-time jobs or even part-time jobs that have a clear future.

When I first saw the situation for non-elite Japanese young people in the mid-1990s as it was beginning to get worse and worse, my vantage point was mainly through the eyes of the teachers with whom I spoke, teachers who were increasingly worried about what awaited their graduates in the labor market. It was their narratives that so surprised my Japanese audiences. Later I realized that what I was hearing was a prelude to what would develop by the early twenty-first century into a frenzied public discourse in Japan about unemployed youth, part-time employment, job-hopping, so-called parasite singles (young people who remain single and live in their parents' household into their late twenties or early thirties), and NEET (young people who are in neither education nor employment). But terms such as NEET were not commonly used before 2000, and neither the teachers nor I had any language we could easily call upon to describe the troubling phenomena that were appearing.

As we reach the end of the first decade of the twenty-first century, the situation that developed in Japan during the 1990s' "ice age of employment" may still not be immediately visible on the streets of Tokyo. But it is highly apparent when one walks into a Japanese bookstore. In the past several years the poor employment prospects for Japanese young people, especially the least-educated among them (particularly high school and junior high school graduates), have become a topic of intensive study and discussion in the media and among prominent Japanese economists and sociologists. So too have discussions of *kakusa shakai* ("unequal society"), NEET, and, most recently, the *wākingu puā* (the "*working poor*," a term borrowed from the books of sociologist William Julius Wilson and others who write about American urban poverty). The media attention in Japan being showered on these phenomena is staggering.

This book explains how and why a disproportionate share of the non-elite among Japan's younger generation has gotten lost in the transition from school into the workplace. This transition on the individual level mirrors the larger transition of the Japanese economy into a mature postindustrial economy with more insecure employment relations than were dominant in the high-growth period of the 1960s to 1980s. The young people I focus on are the ones who did not go to top high schools; who didn't enter an elite university such as Tōdai or Waseda or Keiō on the first try; who didn't become *rōnin* (high school graduates who could afford to study an extra year or two for the university entrance exam) in order to make it into even a second-ranked university of their choice. Instead, they finished high school and tried to enter the economy in the decade of the 1990s. In the process, many of them became lost in the transition from school to work. Having left the security of their high school, they are no longer students but neither have they moved on to the next set of affiliations that have traditionally defined Japanese adulthood: secure employment and marriage. One has only to talk to the "man on the street" and to read media and government reports to see how young people's lack of successful transition into these situations – what I will call in this book *ba* or social locations – troubles older Japanese and policy makers.

I do not deny that young university graduates have also been hard hit by economic recession and employment restructuring, nor even that some middle-aged Japanese have lost their jobs as well. Even young Japanese who graduated from top-ranked universities in the 1990s and experienced a relatively smooth transition into the labor market are facing a much different set of realities from what their parents faced. Their everyday work lives and their patterns of transition among jobs are deeply affected by how Japan is changing. Underneath the difficult transitions facing all younger Japanese as individuals is a fundamental transition in the very fabric of Japanese society. It is no longer the case that people's lives get played out in a small number of secure *ba* or social locations. The very idea of a secure *ba* has begun to vanish.

In November 2008 I added my voice to the cacophony of viewpoints offered by Japanese scholars and the media on the roots of economic insecurity in the young generation by publishing *Ushinawareta ba o sagashite: 'Lost generation' no shakaigaku* ("Searching for the Lost Place: The Sociology of the 'Lost Generation,'" NTT Press). The present book is significantly revised from the Japanese in order to provide more context and background for American and other English-speaking readers and to present a more theoretical framework for a scholarly audience, but my analytical approach is basically the same as the one I used in the Japanese publication. I employ a comparative and distinctly sociological perspective and set of methodologies, placing me somewhere between the labor economist who argues from numerical data on large numbers of people and the ethnographer who does intensive study of one site such as a school or a workplace. The book explains how and why youth employment problems in Japan have become so severe and analyzes the implications for youth themselves and for Japanese society. Using information and viewpoints from high schools, employers, and young people, I analyze how Japanese schools and firms have become disconnected from one another and show how young people are trying to make a successful transition from school into the next phase of their lives.

Why have high schools traditionally been such a pivotal launching pad for Japanese young people into their adult lives? What unique issues are being raised for Japanese youth and for Japanese society itself as the ties between high schools and employers crumble? I report what high school teachers have to say about changes in the Japanese system of launching young people into the labor market, and I tell the stories of individual young people to show how their work lives are forming as they enter their twenties and move through them. Are they landing on their feet by the time they are thirty, even though they finished school during the ice age of employment? Who is having a soft landing and who is having a hard landing? Why?

I argue that the possibilities of entering an economically secure social location or *ba* are disappearing in the lives of many young Japanese. We can see this as we watch the relationship between schools and the workplace undergo a transformation. Youth are caught in the context of a fundamental realignment and reorganization of what I have elsewhere called Japan's distinctive "human capital development system."[3] This is the system of institutions within which individuals develop their skills and abilities. This institutional transformation has produced new economic and employment problems for youth, as well as psychological problems related to how they develop their sense of identity and their ability to trust society. These are not just problems for individual youth. They are developing into central problems for Japanese society as well.

More than my previous research, working on this book has unexpectedly led me to think more deeply about my own society. While Japan and the United States are in many ways unlikely cases for comparison, the fact remains that the close relationship between the two countries means that many Japanese continue to look to the United States to see how things are done here. And the fact also remains that no matter how cosmopolitan this author may think herself to be, American society is ultimately the one she knows best. With these provisos in mind, I hope readers will understand why the book occasionally utilizes some comparisons between Japan and the United States. I turn to such comparisons especially in the analysis of job search strategies and levels of interpersonal trust – two areas that have profound implications for how young peoples' lives play out.

Note on Japanese names: Consistent with common practice, Japanese names are listed with surname first and personal name second except in cases where reference is made to Japanese scholars' publications in English. In that case, American usage is followed, with first name preceding the surname.

---

[3] This is developed in my work on gender inequality in Japan. See especially "The Social-Institutional Bases of Gender Stratification: Japan as an Illustrative Case," *American Journal of Sociology* 94 (1988): 300–334; *Women and the Economic Miracle: Gender and Work in Postwar Japan* (Berkeley: University of California Press, 1993).

Acknowledgments

Most social science books follow a circuitous path that leads out of the author's imagination and into a rocky terrain filled with arguments and stories that ultimately are built into a finished piece of research (although it goes without saying that scholars almost never feel "finished" with anything). So it was with this book. Along the path where I collected the many sources of data from which I draw in the following chapters, I received tremendous help from several people. Hirata Shūichi of the Japan Institute of Labour Policy and Training deserves my deep thanks, as he was charged with the difficult task of making cold calls on my behalf to the high schools in Kanagawa prefecture at which I would show up to do in-depth interviews. Hirata-san helped write the letter of introduction for me from the Japan Institute of Labour Policy and Training and thus helped break the ice before I set off on the train to various urban and suburban locations in and around Kawasaki and Yokohama to meet high school teachers, many of whom were initially puzzled and nervous at the prospect of meeting a foreign researcher. The mutual feelings of nervousness virtually always dissolved within the first ten minutes or so, and I am deeply indebted to all of the teachers who shared their insights and experiences with me. Some of them did so during multiple visits over the years, and I appreciate their time and patience in opening up their knowledge base to me. I especially appreciate the help and friendship of Arita Yoshie. I thank Professor Akinaga Yūichi for providing introductions to high schools in Sendai. My graduate students at the University of Chicago were tireless in the tasks of coding the job-opening announcement data used in Chapters 4 and 5 of the book. (You all have jobs now so I won't embarrass you by mentioning your names, but I want you to know how much I appreciated your help.) Zun Tang, then at Cornell University, was an outstanding research assistant and was instrumental in implementing my theoretical ideas in the crafting of the network analysis discussed in Chapter 5.

I was fortunate to receive funding from several sources to support the research reported in this book. An Abe Fellowship from the Center for Global Partnership funded my initial year of fieldwork on Japanese high schools as well as comparative work on high schools in Seoul, South Korea. I benefited greatly from being able to devote part of the year I spent at the Center for Advanced Study in the Behavioral Sciences at Stanford University working on the initial framing of the book. A Spencer Foundation Mentor Network Award helped fund some of the data coding and interview transcription costs, and later a Spencer Foundation Grant was instrumental in the collection of survey data from a sample of high school graduates in the Yokohama-Kawasaki area and in Sendai. This survey, introduced in Chapter 3, also helped generate a subsample of young men to be interviewed in depth. Additional time in Japan was supported by a grant from the Social Science Research Council and, most recently, by a Fulbright Research Fellowship. I am deeply grateful to all of these funding sources for making it possible to initiate and delve deeper into this research over time.

The first version of this book was written for a Japanese audience. Although I wrote the original text in English, I did so with the explicit purpose of finding a Japanese translator and publisher as soon as I finished the writing. The audience to which I addressed my thoughts, arguments, and explanations was not so much an academic one, but rather the broader reading public interested in contemporary social issues. Through support from the Japan Foundation's Center for Global Partnership as well as Harvard University's Reischauer Institute for Japanese Studies, in March 2007 I held an author's workshop to get comments and suggestions from a small group of scholars on drafts of the first five chapters. It was an international and interdisciplinary group that included Fujihira Shinju (political scientist, associate director of the U.S.-Japan Relations Program at Harvard), Genda Yūji (economist, Tokyo University), Hirao Keiko (sociologist, Sophia University), David Slater (anthropologist, Sophia University), and Yamamoto Yoko (educational sociologist, Brown University). I am very grateful for the input I received from these colleagues, all of whom read my draft chapters with care and contributed valuable suggestions that helped me refine my arguments as I completed the book.

The biggest gift of all from the book workshop was the opportunity to receive input from Genda Yūji, who inspired not only me but also all of the others in the room to move forward in our respective projects with intellectual passion. I am extremely indebted to Genda-san for taking it upon himself to shepherd my manuscript into the world of Japanese publishing by introducing me to the translator Ikemura Chiaki and to Miyazaki Shino, my editor at NTT Publishing. It is only because of their guidance and care that I was able to publish the Japanese book. Because I had wanted very much to share my research with a broad reading public in Japan, I endeavored to produce a book that used less academic jargon than the scholarly books American social scientists (including myself) usually write. I am grateful to have been able to realize that goal. I will be doubly satisfied if readers find the present volume even slightly easier and more interesting to read as a result.

I am very grateful to Lew Bateman at Cambridge University Press, who so skillfully shepherded the book through the acquisition process. Margarita Estévez-Abe was the reader for the final draft I sent to Cambridge. She pushed me to undertake yet more revisions and to reorganize and bring to the forefront the theoretical ideas that I had underplayed in the more "popular" version published in Japan. Her advice was extremely helpful. My faculty assistant at Harvard, Laura Thomas, turned data tables into figures and was relentless in checking and rechecking every detail there and elsewhere. Working with her was sheer joy.

As I finished the final editing of this book, I realized that I have never thanked in writing two of the professors who first inspired me to pursue a PhD and join the community of Japan scholars. Susan Hanley and Kozo Yamamura, I thank you after all of these years. (Kozo, I still think I was right to spend additional years in graduate school studying sociological theory and methods. I hope I've changed your mind on this by now. If not, it will never happen.)

Finally I want to extend apologies and great thanks to my daughter Emma and the rest of my family for putting up with my work on this seemingly interminable project, and to my friends – especially those in Five Fields – who were never too tired of the project to ask me how it was coming along. It's done now. At least I think so.

Lost in Transition

I

The Lost Generation

"People in my parents' generation seem to remember the world as having been a more energetic and lively place when they were in their thirties. It's different now. Even though everyone says the economy is recovering, there is no feeling of energy – just kind of a gloomy atmosphere."

– Twenty-eight-year-old male graduate of a low-ranking public general high school

Kakusa. NEET. Furītā. Parasaito shinguru. Hikikomori. Wākingu puā. Net-café refugees. Shōshika.[1] Japanese newspapers, magazines, and books are filled with terms such as these, emblematic of a society undergoing transformation and grappling with new and bewildering social problems. To comprehend these phenomena requires an understanding of what young Japanese experienced in the 1990s when they entered adulthood. The Japanese labor market was changing under their feet, undergoing important structural transformations that made their choices and opportunities fundamentally different from the choices their parents had faced. Although young people's work and lifestyle preferences were changing as well, more important were the changes occurring in the institutions in Japan that had supported the prior generation's movement from school to work and into adulthood. The breakdown in school-work institutions

---

[1] The translations of these terms are as follows: *kakusa* (economic inequality); NEET (young people who are neither in school nor employment); *furītā* ("free arbeiter" – young people who freely move among jobs and take time out of the labor force); *parasaito shinguru* (young people who live with their parents and rely on them financially); *hikikomori* (extreme social isolates, the large majority of whom are men in their twenties or thirties); *wākingu puā* (the working poor); *net-café refugees* (homeless people who live in Internet cafés); *shōshika* (the declining birthrate).

and in employers' guarantee of secure employment to large numbers of new graduates produced a "lost generation" in the 1990s, a cohort of young people unable to gain a stable economic toehold from which to embark on their adult lives.

Lost in the transition from school to work, the lost generation is a reflection of a deeper transition in Japanese society – a transition away from social institutions that helped guide individuals from one life stage to another. These life stages have been deeply connected in Japan to what we might call the "social locations" in which individuals find security and a sense of identity. The rupture in the social institutions guiding individuals into such social locations has profound implications, as it requires individuals to master new sets of skills to navigate what have become rocky and at times lonely transitions. The costs of these recent institutional changes in Japan have been borne mainly by the young, especially the least educated among them.

A story from my fieldwork at Japanese high schools will illuminate the idea of "social locations" and will illustrate how young people's movement among social locations was more or less smoothly orchestrated by social institutions prior to Japan's economic crisis of the 1990s.

SHAKAIJIN AS KAISHAIN

"A success is when we find a company for the student." This is what a teacher in the guidance section of a low-ranking academic public high school in Kanagawa prefecture (outside of Tokyo) told me when I asked him what the school considers a "successful outcome" for a graduating senior.[2] When I asked why, he replied simply, "*Anshin dakara*" (because it is safe and secure, or literally, "because it gives peace of mind"). Such a definition of success indicates that the school had fulfilled its task of placing the graduating senior into a company. The most important thing was to find a good organization (a social location or *ba*) for each student to move into in the next phase of his or her life. Success was not defined in terms of helping students find the type of work to which they were best suited. Indeed, across the twenty high schools in which I conducted

---

[2] As will be discussed more thoroughly in later chapters, the first important "fork in the road" in Japanese students' educational careers is application to high school. While not compulsory, more than 90 percent of young people matriculate to high school. Throughout the book I will distinguish between academic or general high schools, attended by more than three-quarters of young people, and vocational high schools.

in-depth interviews of teachers, such a definition never surfaced. As one teacher commented dryly, "We talk about young people becoming *shakaijin* [adult members of society], but what we really mean is that they become *kaishain* [company people]."

The well-managed transition of individuals from school to company is a microcosm of the distinctive way that postwar Japanese society was organized before the 1990s. It was important for individuals to be attached to a *ba* – important for their material success in life and important also for their identity and sense of well-being. The concept of *ba* is difficult to translate into English, as the nuances go beyond such neutral terms as "organization" or "institution." The concept was so central to sociologist Nakane Chie's analysis of Japanese society and social structure as to merit explanation at the beginning of the first chapter of her classic *Japanese Society*.[3] Translating *ba* as "frame," Nakane wrote: "*Frame* may be a locality, an institution or a particular relationship which binds a set of individuals into one group: in all cases it indicates a criterion which sets a boundary and gives a common basis to a set of individuals who are located or involved in it" (Nakane 1970: 1).

Scholars studying a foreign culture often suffer the occupational hazard of declaring certain terms untranslatable into English, and Western scholars of Japanese society are as likely as others to fall prey to this. But the concept of *ba* is just such a term. "Frame" denotes the bounded quality of *ba*, the idea of a line defining the "groupness" of a collection of individuals. But frame remains an awkward translation. Nor does "organization" quite capture the quality of *ba*, as the term organization evokes neither a sense of long-term membership for individuals nor the way in which *ba* shapes and reinforces individuals' identity. For these reasons, I prefer the term "social location." I will use *ba* and social location interchangeably to denote an organization or bounded collective to which individuals belong and from which they derive a sense of identity and security. "Social location" has the additional advantage of capturing the sense in which such membership also defines or categorizes the individual in the eyes of others standing outside the situation. For example, the role

[3] The late economic historian Murakami Yasusuke extended the idea of *ba* in his writings (with Kumon Shumpei and Satō Seizaburō) on "Japan as *ie shakai*." Murakami traced the historical evolution of *ba* as an organizing principle in Japanese society, and asserted that this principle of social organization is more efficient under certain environmental conditions (such as *sakoku*, or a relatively closed society as exemplified by Japan during the Tokugawa period from 1600 to the middle of the nineteenth century) than others. For a summary of the argument see Murakami (1984).

of "wife" defines a woman as a member of the *ba* of family, identifying her to those outside the marriage as being in the "state" or "social location" of marriage.

Although Nakane has been strongly criticized over the years by foreign anthropologists and sociologists for depicting a stereotypical and elitist view of a homogeneous Japanese society and downplaying the significant boundaries between social classes or between ethnic Japanese and ethnic minorities, the validity of her emphasis on the importance of *ba* or social location for individual identity and psychological and economic security remains largely intact. Nakane contrasted the importance of *ba* as an organizing principle of Japanese society with the importance of individual characteristics or attributes in societies such as the U.S. She depicted the U.S. as a society where individuals move more frequently between *ba*, depending less on attachment to a particular *ba* for their identity and well-being and more on the individual characteristics they carry from place to place.

The Japanese high school teachers with whom I spoke clearly viewed the purpose of their assistance in students' job searches as finding a social location or *ba* for graduates. The process was not fundamentally about what these young people wanted to do in their lives. Rather, it was about the *ba* they would become members of. In a sense, this *ba* would be the organization that would turn them into full-fledged members of society. The *ba* would turn them into adults, or *shakaijin*.

This idealized process whereby Japanese young people move out of the status of full-time student and into the status of worker or adult has been heavily predicated upon the availability of full-time jobs in *shokuba* or workplaces (note again the *ba* built into the term). What happens, then, when fewer and fewer employers recruit new graduates into full-time jobs and thereby bestow upon them the status of full-fledged membership in the workplace? What happens when schools are no longer the important *ba* that help connect young people to this next stage in their lives? In broader terms, what happens when social institutions falter in their ability to help young people make the transitions that society tells them are the principal ones they must successfully pass through in order to become adult members of society?

In 1990s Japan, all of this came up for grabs. But the most immediate manifestations of the breakdown of Japan's finely-tuned mechanisms for moving young people from school into the labor force at first belied the deep underlying systemic changes. What was most visible instead were the new lifestyles of young people: greater movement across jobs and a greater propensity to move in and out of the labor force; an ever-lengthening period of time, often into one's late twenties or early thirties, residing in the parental household; and a seeming lack of interest in getting married and having children – the two hallmarks, along with full-time employment, of "responsible" Japanese adulthood.

FURĪTĀ AND "PARASITE SINGLES"

Social concern over changing lifestyle patterns among Japan's youth was fueled by the publication of sociologist Yamada Masahiro's *Parasite shinguru no jidai* (*The Age of Parasite Singles*) in 1999. Yamada argued that Japanese young people hold fundamentally different values and preferences from their parents' generation. In his view, young people can afford not to take work seriously because they are able to rely on their parents financially while continuing to reside with them. His book portrayed a symbiotic and unhealthy relationship between two phenomena (although unfortunately providing little hard evidence for either of them): young people's loss of the "unique" work ethic that had characterized postwar Japan, and the parental generation's tendency to pamper youth and permit their selfish twenty-somethings to remain economically dependent far into adulthood. Particularly at fault, according to Yamada, were young Japanese women, whom he portrayed as selfish and materialistic, valuing luxury goods and foreign vacations over marriage and motherhood.

As with any stereotype, Yamada's portrayal of dilettantism among young Japanese contained some grains of truth, though these grains had scattered by the late 1990s. During the "bubble economy" of the late 1980s to early 1990s, labor demand soared and many young people – especially university graduates – had their pick of jobs. The term *furītā* came into common usage, denoting a young person who moved in and out of jobs and even in and out of the labor market in order to pursue a fulfilling lifestyle. *Furītā* as a term came from the combination of *furī*, the *gairaigo* (defined as a foreign word with Japanese pronunciation) for "free" and *arubaito*, the *gairaigo* for the German word *arbeit* (labor or job).[4] High levels of labor demand made it possible for some university

[4] The Ministry of Health, Labour and Welfare (MHLW) defines *furītā* as individuals aged fifteen to thirty-four who are not in school and who are either working as part-time or temporary employees, are unemployed and searching for part-time or temporary employment, or are not working but are willing to accept part-time or temporary work. In the

graduates to move in and out of work and to experience a more mobile
and free lifestyle than the one their parents had entered at a similar stage
in their lives.

In the late 1980s the Japanese media trumpeted fanciful stories of
furītā who worked for several months, quit their jobs, and then used
the wages they had earned (generally while living with their parents) to
indulge in such adventures as three-month long surfing trips in Australia.
After such frivolities they would return to Japan and begin another job in
order to garner the savings for their next adventure. Beneath such stories
lay a mixed discourse describing the freedom, boldness, and irresponsibility of the young. Yamada's "parasite singles" rhetoric fed into this
latter stereotype of irresponsibility and frivolity, characteristics foreign
to an older generation raised in an era when such lifestyle options were
the stuff of pure fantasy, to be entertained only at the risk of near-certain
social ostracism. At the same time, *furītā's* apparent snubbing of the
stable but plodding lifestyle of Japan's postwar *sararīman*, the full-time
male employee who was at once the symbol of the country's phenomenal
economic growth and the symbol of conformity to company dictates,
was taken by a minority of observers as a refreshing sign of youthful
creativity.

By the early years of the twenty-first century a discourse emphasizing
the adventurous though spoiled nature of young Japanese began to give
way to the sober recognition that it was the 1990s decade of economic
recession and employment restructuring – not youthful exuberance and
disregard of social norms – that was responsible for rising youth unemployment and part-time employment. With the publication of Genda Yūji's
Shigoto no naka no aimai na fuan (*A Nagging Sense of Job Insecurity*)
in 2001, government bureaucrats, the media, and scholars started to pay
greater attention to the ways that employment restructuring had pushed
young people to the periphery of the labor market.[5] Meanwhile, in-depth
research by Kosugi Reiko of the Japan Institute of Labour Policy and

case of women the MHLW applies this categorization only to the unmarried; the implicit
assumption is that a married woman is supported mainly by a male breadwinner and
therefore is not considered to be at economic risk to the same degree as male or unmarried
female part-time or temporary workers.

[5] Genda is widely credited for reorienting the discourse on young people toward a focus
on how employment restructuring and job loss affected their behaviors. *Shigoto no
naka no aimai na fuan* received the prestigious Suntory Prize for Social Science and
Humanities and the Nikkei Economic Book Award. An English translation of the book
was published in 2007 as *A Nagging Sense of Job Insecurity: The New Reality Facing
Japanese Youth.*

Training (JILPT) documented the dwindling full-time employment options for young people and the younger generation's concomitant struggle to establish satisfying work lives.[6] Honda Yuki of Tokyo University's Institute of Social Science added her voice as well, first through her analysis of the historical roots of Japan's high school-work system and then through several books on the contemporary breakdown of the traditional system and the consequent difficulties for youth.[7]

Spurred by the dissemination of research by Genda, Kosugi, Honda, and others, the recognition grew in Japan that many young people who came of age during the severe economic downturn of the 1990s faced labor market conditions that rendered stable employment a mirage they couldn't bring to life even if they wanted to. *Furītā*-hood increasingly took on a hollow meaning. As I will show later in this chapter, increasing numbers of young people fell into standard categories of disenfranchisement such as the unemployed and the marginally employed. Moreover, new ways of categorizing young people's attachment or lack of attachment to paid labor emerged as well. The possibilities of entering an economically secure location or *ba* have simply been disappearing.

INSTITUTIONAL EQUILIBRIUM, DISEQUILIBRIUM, AND SOCIAL GENERATIONS

My original goal for this research was to analyze Japan's high school-work system and to better understand how Japanese high schools and employers historically came to participate in a well-articulated process of matching the educational nonelite into jobs. As mentioned in the preface, Japan's unusual school-work process was widely praised by scholars and policy analysts in countries such as the U.S. where the movement from school to work was anything but smooth for high school graduates. But the ground was shifting under my feet from the very start, with the system unraveling in the late 1990s even as I conducted my initial fieldwork on it. What began as an analysis of a distinctive institutional solution in Japan to a problem faced by all societies – how to help young people, especially the least-educated among

---

[6] Kosugi's work has appeared mainly in Japanese with the exception of several articles in the *Japan Labor Review*, the quarterly journal of the Japan Institute of Labour Policy and Training, and a recent English translation of *Furītā to iu ikikata* (*Escape from Work: Freelancing Youth and the Challenge to Corporate Japan*, 2008).

[7] In English, see Honda (2003), Honda (2004), and Honda (2005a). In Japanese, see especially Honda (2005b).

them, to make the transition from school into work – became a much larger analysis of how and why Japan's particular institutional solution was no longer working.

As my empirical research progressed I realized that I was studying an example of the problem that sociologist James Coleman regarded as being at the heart of what sociology should most concern itself with: how the macro-level context affects individual motivations and behaviors and, more importantly, how individual behaviors subsequently transform the macro-level context.[8] Coleman's strong belief was that this endeavor was best attempted with the assumption that individuals are purposive, goal-directed actors. In my particular project I was observing how the social actors involved in placing Japanese young people into the workplace – schools, employers, and young people themselves – were responding to the pressures of economic recession and employment restructuring. The responses of these sets of actors were then shaping a new macro-level landscape, a new institutional equilibrium, with a structure of employment opportunities and constraints quite different from the ones that had existed before. The challenge for young people was to figure out the strategies and resources that could help them navigate this changed landscape.

The theoretical framing I had crafted during twelve years of colleagueship with Coleman at the University of Chicago deeply shaped the direction in which this project moved – or had to move, because of the fact that my project on institutional stasis had transformed into one on institutional change. But viewing individuals as rational and goal-directed was not quite sufficient to understand the interplay between individual choices and the institutional landscape in which they played out. Why? Because institutional change occurs not only in a structural context but in a cultural context as well. Individuals respond to new opportunities and constraints against the backdrop of cultural templates of what is appropriate or even imaginable behavior. This is not typically the stuff of which rational choice theory is made. To be sure, the cultural appropriateness of particular choices or behaviors can to a degree be analyzed through an understanding of social norms, and Coleman along with other rational choice theorists in sociology and related disciplines have considered norms to be an important arena for rational choice theory. But it is harder to find within a rational-choice approach the tools with which to analyze why some choices may not even occur to individuals or why, even if they

[8] See Chapter 1 in Coleman, *Foundations of Social Theory* (1990) and also Coleman's "A Vision for Sociology" (1996).

do, individuals may not have the necessary psychological or emotional resources to act on such choices.

Understanding how institutional change impacts individuals' motives and behavior and how these in turn help construct a new institutional landscape requires an understanding of the cultural valences of preexisting institutions and an appreciation for how the range of possibilities for individual actions and reactions is constructed by these cultural valences. Individual strategies of action may be theoretically possible without being empirically thinkable or practicable when it comes to everyday behavior. But the analyst cannot understand this without knowing what went before – that is, without knowing what behaviors were facilitated by the preexisting institutional landscape.

In thinking about the issue of "what went before," it is helpful to refer back to what Mannheim referred to nearly a century ago as the problem of generations. Mannheim discussed the significance of individuals in a generation sharing a common set of social circumstances as a result of the timing of their biological birth (Mannheim 1952). This biological fact gives rise to individuals' shared location in social structure and shared predisposition for modes of thinking and experience. In Bourdieu's terms several decades later, the individual's *habitus* stems from growing up in a particular social-structural environment (Bourdieu 1977). While Bourdieu's central project was the analysis of class relations and reproduction, such dynamics occur within the larger historical context, a fact to which Mannheim drew attention. (Class dynamics enter into the story of the present book in terms of the differences in how young Japanese men from elite versus nonelite educational backgrounds have navigated the changed institutional environment of the 1990s and beyond. This is broached in Chapter 6.)

Mannheim's early articulation of the shared social-structural location and common experiences of members of a generation or birth cohort has had an enduring effect on the use of "cohort" as an analytical category by demographers and social scientists who study the life course. Sociologists of the life course have increasingly turned their attention to how the transition to adulthood is patterned by social institutions such as the educational system, the labor market, and the state welfare regime.[9]

---

[9] See Breen and Buchmann's article in a special issue of *Annals of the American Academy of Political and Social Science* (2002). This issue of the *Annals* was devoted entirely to the comparative analysis of the transition to adulthood across a range of Western postindustrial societies, particularly in Europe. In 2007 the *European Journal of Population* also

This is a rich and vibrant literature, but has two limitations with respect to the aims of this book.

First, the empirical literature on the transition to adulthood is almost entirely centered on the countries of Europe and North America, making only occasional reference to Japan as one of the countries that Gösta Esping-Andersen categorized as a "hybrid" welfare system situated between the conservative Southern European type and the liberal market regimes characterized by the United States (Esping-Andersen 1997). Second, demographers and life course researchers tend to focus on the structural conditions in which members of a cohort are born and experience the transition to adulthood. Less well-developed is the extension of Mannheim's idea that cohort members' access to particular cultural resources and tools is also influenced by the historical and social-structural circumstances in which they were born and were socialized.[10] This is expressed well in his concept of "social generations," a term that has been picked up more readily by European than American demographers and has been developed in particular by the French sociologist Louis Chauvel in his analysis of the generational divide in France (Chauvel 2007).

Chauvel points out that American sociologists and demographers tend to restrict their use of the term "generation" to discussions of kinship, preferring the term "cohort" to refer to individuals born in the same year or experiencing an event (e.g. marriage) in the same year. In contrast, the term "social generation" is more commonly used in European scholarship and refers to groups of cohorts experiencing a common period of social or economic change. Unlike members of a "historical generation," who by definition share a collective identity by virtue of having been born during a specific historical period, members of a social generation may not necessarily recognize their collective interests or identity. They are nevertheless all socialized during a particular time period distinct from the one before. They are raised by parents who may not ultimately recognize the changed contingencies, constraints, and opportunities of the current period but instead refer implicitly to the conditions in which they grew up as the basis for instructing their children on how to live.

devoted a special issue to the comparative study of the transition to adulthood. See also the work of Karl Ulrich Mayer, especially Mayer (2004).

[10] This is not unlike the concept of "cultural toolkit" that the sociologist Ann Swidler developed in a now-classic article (Swidler 1986).

Japan's lost generation is just such a social generation. Although members of the lost generation face different constraints and opportunities than the prior generation, they are nevertheless equipped mainly with the cultural tools and strategies they inherited from their parents. These tools may not be the best ones for dealing with the dramatically changed opportunity structure. This situation has produced anxiety, confusion, and disappointment among many members on both sides of the "social-generational" divide.

Mannheim's term "social generations" and what he called the problem of generations is thus highly relevant for understanding that Japanese who came of age after the early 1990s confronted a different structural reality than their parents. It is also relevant for analyzing how older people have interpreted the actions of the young. Such interpretations are filtered through the early experiences of the older generation because, as Mannheim puts it, "Early impressions tend to coalesce into a *natural view* of the world. All later experiences then tend to receive their meaning from this original set, whether they appear as that set's verification and fulfillment or as its negation and antithesis. Experiences are not accumulated in the course of a lifetime through a process of summation or agglomeration, but are 'dialectically' articulated ... " (Mannheim 1952: 287).

There is a severe disjuncture between the ways that many middle-aged Japanese experienced the transition from adolescence into their adult lives and the ways they see their children experiencing it. The chapters of this book will explore the structural location as well as the cultural resources of the lost generation, setting both against the backdrop of the relatively stable life course patterns and the underlying institutional supports that characterized Japan during its high-economic growth period from the late 1950s into the 1970s.

Of particular importance in the story I tell is that the relatively smooth transition to adulthood experienced by large numbers of young people who came of age during the high-growth period was supported by social institutions that neither required nor rewarded individuals who used ties to acquaintances (so-called "weak ties") rather than strong ties to institutions to get ahead. Schools were charged with the responsibility of helping students move into full-time positions in companies. Growing numbers of young male workers in Japan's expanding postwar economy experienced the benefits of strong attachment to a particular firm or workplace. Notably, this was an attachment to a secure social location rather than an attachment to an occupation, profession, or particular set of skills that one could carry from one workplace to another.

In my view, the combination of the postwar school-work system and the growth and stabilization of "permanent employment" for large numbers of men is closely aligned with what we might call the structure of trust in contemporary Japanese society. Social scientists have increasingly found that there is cross-cultural variation in whom individuals trust and how deep that trust is. As Yamagishi Toshio has shown in a series of innovative social-psychological experiments, Japanese in general have a lower propensity than Americans to trust strangers in the absence of a system that monitors cheating and ensures compliance with rules (Yamagishi and Yamagishi 1993; Yamagishi 2003). Consistent with this laboratory finding, comparative survey research verifies Japan's position as a low-trust society relative to many other industrial and postindustrial societies. Whereas Japan ranks high on norms of civic cooperation (e.g. conformity to laws and well-established norms of civility) its citizens are less likely than those in many other countries, including the U.S., to agree with the statement that "most people can be trusted" (Knack and Keefer 1997).

Similarly, I will argue that during much of the postwar period what young Japanese needed to do was to trust social institutions to help them move forward in their lives and to become settled in a stable *ba*. Trusting or exchanging information with acquaintances or strangers was neither the dominant nor the most effective strategy. Strong ties, generally to members of one's social location or *ba*, were what a person needed to rely on. Teachers were called upon to secure the pathway for students into the work world. Employers were subject to legal and normative provisions that made it difficult for them to shed workers, thus ensuring a strong though not always happy bond between employers and their "regular employees" (i.e. employees without fixed-term contracts). Plunging feet first into the external labor market in search of a better opportunity in mid-career was a path neither encouraged by this type of institutional environment nor chosen by most of the individuals with the best job skills. It does not take a leap of imagination to see why young people's stock of common strategies for action in these stable institutional circumstances became newly obsolete in the depressed economic circumstances of the 1990s, nor why the parental generation was initially puzzled over why this was the case.

The story of the lost generation is embedded in a larger narrative of continuing rigidity in some institutions (the system of guaranteed permanent employment and job security for a minority of workers) and unraveling in others (the school-work system). This intertwining of institutional rigidity and disintegration has necessitated new individual adaptations on the part of the younger generation. Before looking at their adaptations it is important to understand the commonly-shared life course patterns and underlying institutions that existed before the economy entered its downward spiral in the early 1990s. These life course patterns are the backdrop against which the early lives of the lost generation are juxtaposed, both self-consciously by members of the younger generation and under criticism from members of the older generation. Subsequent chapters will reveal how the institutions undergirding young people's smooth transitions across the *ba* of school and workplace have frayed during their lifetimes and will show the individual-level consequences of this institutional unraveling. An important feature of these consequences is that they are the most severe for Japan's least educationally elite young people.

LIFE COURSE PATTERNS IN THE HIGH ECONOMIC-GROWTH PERIOD: THE POSTWAR FAMILY SYSTEM

The passage into adulthood was unusually orderly in Japan for the generation that preceded the lost generation. When sociologists find common patterns of moving through life course stages across a broad range of individuals, they speak of the "standardization" of the life course. The high economic-growth period of the late 1950s to mid-1970s in Japan epitomizes a historical span when such life course standardization ruled the day. A central reason is that the postwar generation came of age in an unusually stable period, one in which the so-called permanent employment system stabilized.[11] The family sociologist Ochiai Emiko identifies the postwar period as a span of nearly thirty years during which Japanese social structure was quite stable, a period when the "postwar family system," as she terms it, came to dominate (Ochiai 1996). This system was based on a strong breadwinner ideology and on the ideal of the nuclear family. By the late 1960s, the proportion of so-called "love marriages" exceeded for the first time the proportion of arranged marriages. Moreover, women born in the late 1940s to early 1950s became the first generation of Japanese women in which housewives represented the majority. With more men able to support a middle-class lifestyle for their families because of secure employment in a growing firm in one of

[11] See Moriguchi and Ono for an excellent synopsis of the development of lifetime employment and the interplay of normative and legal forces that continue to sustain it (Moriguchi and Ono 2006).

Japan's urban centers, married women could specialize in housekeeping and childrearing to a degree unknown to prior generations.

The so-called *dankai no sedai* (clumped generation) that resulted from Japan's short-lived baby boom in the late 1940s was unusually large – about twice the size of the cohort born during the preceding twenty-five years. In Ochiai's terms, this transitional generation sandwiched between the generation coming of age prior to World War II and the generation coming of age in the 1990s "became the mainstay of postwar Japanese society, and its members have a strong tendency to base value judgments on their own group experience." She continues, almost wistfully, "One wishes they were more aware that the demographic conditions they experienced were unique, and that those of us born later could not follow directly in their footsteps if we tried" (Ochiai 1996: 67). This indeed epitomizes Mannheim's problem of generations. To the degree that the older generation views their own life course patterns as normal, it is akin to the similar tendency in the U.S. to compare contemporary lifestyle patterns to an idealized and stylized version of the 1950s with its breadwinner ideology, stay-at-home mothers, and stable households.

For young Japanese coming of age in the early 1960s to the 1980s, the path into adulthood was defined as the smooth movement from a stable attachment in one social location or *ba* (school) to stable attachment to other *ba*, notably the workplace and marriage. As I will show in the next chapter, this is also the period in which the school-work transition system became fully institutionalized. There was a narrow range of socially appropriate ages for individuals to experience various life events: leaving school, entering full-time work, getting married, and having one's first child. And there was just one sequence that these events were supposed to follow. Not everyone wanted or was able to conform to this sequence. But individuals who did conform, and did so at the socially appropriate age, were generally regarded as carrying out their young adult lives successfully. The choice of going back to school after getting married or after working for several years was, for most people, not a choice at all – it simply wasn't done. And the socially acceptable age range for marriage (and the strong assumption that everyone would marry) and for having children was a narrow one.

Older Japanese may see this standardized sequence and timing of life events as taken-for-granted, or *atarimae* (the way things are). But the normal Japanese life course was characterized by an unusual degree of orderliness when compared to other countries. A number of examples will illustrate this.

By 1960 Japan showed by far the greatest concentration in women's age at marriage across industrial countries. More than 90 percent of all marriages occurred in couples where the bride was between the ages of twenty and twenty-nine. Mediterranean countries such as Spain and Italy also showed a relatively high concentration in women's age at marriage but even so they hardly compared to Japan; in Spain a little more than 75 percent of all brides were in their twenties, and in Italy the figure was closer to 70 percent. Other European countries showed less conformity in age at marriage. The U.S. represented the extreme, with a little more than 40 percent of all brides in their twenties.

These international comparisons are indicative of the unusually strong postwar norm dictating that Japanese women marry during their mid-twenties. The norm that women should marry by age twenty-five was so strong in the mid-1980s that the analogy to Christmas cakes was frequently made ("Why are Japanese women like Christmas cakes? Because if they don't sell by 25, they are not worth much.")[12] Marriage was sometimes jokingly referred to as women's "lifetime employment" (*eikyū shūshoku*), a tongue-in-cheek analogue to the ideal of men's lifetime employment in one company. Coincidentally, a Japanese colleague reported that of all the data I included in the Japanese-language version of the present book, it was the age-at-marriage statistics that most astonished his graduate students. With many of them not only anticipating delayed marriage but anticipating that they may not want to marry at all, they were unaware that norms were so strong for the cohorts immediately preceding them.[13] This anecdote is a reminder of how much things have changed for the new generation. Indeed, in international comparisons Japan shows not only the greatest concentration in age at marriage in the 1960s–1980s but the greatest drop in concentration since 1990. This higher variance in marriage age since 1990 indicates the younger generation's departure from adherence to the strong age-at-marriage norm of their parents' generation.

---

[12] See Brinton 1992 for a longer discussion of life-course norms in Japan through the mid-1980s.

[13] Men's age at marriage was also more narrowly prescribed by social norms in Japan than in most Western industrial societies in the 1980s. For example, about 40 percent of American men who got married did so by the age of twenty-three, compared to less than 10 percent of Japanese men. Another 40 percent of American men married between the ages of twenty-three and twenty-nine. In contrast, about 60 percent of Japanese men married in the narrow age range between twenty-three and twenty-nine.

The timing of first childbirth in Japan was even more concentrated in a certain age range than the timing of marriage. As recently as the late 1980s close to 50 percent of all Japanese babies were born to women age twenty-five to twenty-nine, a percentage substantially higher than in Western industrial countries. Research by Morgan, Rindfuss, and Parnell showed that the pattern of getting married "on time" and having one's first child "on time" had been established by the late 1960s in Japan. Furthermore, rates of voluntary childlessness were very low (Morgan, Rindfuss, and Parnell 1983). People were expected to marry and, once married, were expected to have at least one child soon after. The time interval between marriage and first birth in Japan varied neither by the education of spouses nor by the age at which they married; both are striking demographic conformities. Regardless of education, the norm was strong that couples should start trying to have a child soon after marriage. This contrasted with the U.S., where the time between marriage and the birth of the first child depended on the couple's level of education and their age at marriage.[14]

It was not only the timing of marriage and childbirth that was highly normatively prescribed in pre-1990s Japan. So too was the sequencing of these events. Among highly industrialized countries, Japan has had a remarkably low rate of out-of-wedlock births over the past half-century. Here again it is strikingly similar to Italy and Spain, although rates of out-of-wedlock births even in those two countries have increased more rapidly in the past few decades than in Japan (Hertog 2009).

Full-time participation in school and in the workplace was also orderly in timing and sequencing for most Japanese in the 1960s-1980s. Up until the end of this period work was not typically an experience young Japanese engaged in while they were in school, with the exception of sons and daughters who helped out a bit in the family business (if their father was self-employed) or university students who tutored junior high or high school students for university entrance exams or did seasonal jobs such as wrapping New Year's gifts in department stores. Most Japanese high schools prohibited their students from holding part-time jobs during the school year. After graduation from high school or university one became solely a worker, not to return to school at a later

---

[14] Morgan, Rindfuss, and Parnell (1983) reported that this was true in the 1980s U.S. even if the analysis was restricted only to the white population. In other words, variance in the U.S. was not due to a more ethnically heterogeneous population with more variable marriage and childbirth patterns than in Japan.

point in one's twenties, thirties, or beyond for additional education or training.[15]

The proportion of the population in school declines dramatically with age in all societies, especially as people move through their early twenties. But the age drop-off in Japan is very dramatic compared to the U.S. Amazingly, in the early 1980s the percentage of American twenty-five- to twenty-nine-year-olds attending an educational institution was ten times the percentage in Japan; this figure increased to forty-seven times for thirty- to thirty-four-year-olds and to eighty-seven times for thirty-five- to thirty-nine-year-olds. The contrast increases further still in middle age, suggesting that it is not produced simply by more Americans than Japanese moving through professional or PhD programs in their late twenties and early thirties. More American than Japanese adults return to higher educational institutions such as community colleges and universities once they begin their working life. Some Americans leave the labor force entirely in their thirties or beyond to return to school full-time, then re-enter the labor force after acquiring additional skills. Others continue to work full-time or part-time while they attend classes in the evenings. These choices generally reflect individuals' hope that attaining additional skills will further their progress in their chosen occupation or help them move into a different occupation. Either way, the focus is on mobility in the labor market.

In contrast, until very recently many Japanese universities would not consider applications from individuals above the age of twenty-five.[16] So-called lifelong education has been oriented toward the cultivation of hobbies or cultural pursuits. Participation in adult education has been heavily gendered, with middle-class women populating classes sprinkled with only a few men – generally retirees.

The sequencing of entry into employment and marriage was also highly patterned in the decades of Japan's high economic growth. In a survey of 1,200 men and women I conducted in the early 1980s in three

---

[15] An exception was of course the handful of men at elite corporations who were sent to American business schools to "network" among the up-and-coming foreign business elite.

[16] Age discrimination has been against the law for the past thirty years in the U.S. In 1975 the U.S. Congress passed the Age Discrimination Act, prohibiting discrimination on the basis of age in programs or activities receiving financial assistance from the federal government. This covers local school systems as well as colleges, universities, and other post-secondary educational institutions as well as American workplaces that receive any type of federal assistance.

Japanese cities, more than 95 percent of all men and women who had ever worked for pay had entered the labor force in a full-time job within two years of leaving school. Less than 5 percent were married when they started working. This demonstrates the orderly sequence of entry into full-time work and subsequent marriage for the vast majority of men and women (Brinton 1993).

The norms regarding Japanese women's work trajectories in the latter half of the twentieth century increasingly broadened as women's strategies of combining family and labor force activity became more diverse. This has been much less the case for Japanese men. For the vast majority, entry into a full-time job at the point of graduation from school, marriage five to seven years later, and the event of parenthood a few years hence has constituted the pattern that marks successful embarkation into adult life. Continuous full-time employment has been the anchor securing men's journey through adulthood, and most desirable and stable of all has been continuous membership in the same firm, as I will show in Chapter 3.

In many ways, the standard Japanese life course patterns of the 1960s-1980s were emblematic of a culture of security rather than a culture of risk. There were established pathways from school to work and from work into marriage (although how work and marriage combined was a highly gendered phenomenon). One needed to do the right things, such as studying hard and mastering appropriate behaviors and ways of speaking. And parental financial assistance was key to promoting a young person's success in Japan's severe educational competition. Armed with these advantages, the path to "successful" adulthood was relatively straightforward.

Social institutions such as the school-work system supported the postwar family system and the accompanying postwar life course by helping Japanese young people move from one secure *ba* to another – from school into work and into marriage. Once there, stable membership in such *ba* was maintained through a combination of strong social norms and institutional regulations such as employment protection for full-time workers.

There is, of course, a darker side to the prevalence of such strong social norms governing the life course. First, individuals suffered social stigma if they were not able or did not want to live their lives in this orderly way. The standardized life course was a "one size fits all" model for living that exerted considerable pressure and often imposed stigma on those who either could not follow or did not want to follow the same pattern. This was especially true for Japan's rising "middle mass" in the 1970s, where success was narrowly defined. Second, the standard model for how men and women would live their lives depended to no small degree on the possibility of stable full-time employment for men. If men entered full-time employment after leaving school, they could marry. If they remained in full-time employment they could support a family and women could have marriage as their "lifetime employment." Men's successful transition from school to work was one of the bases for a typical middle-class lifestyle and, by extension, for a typical middle-class lifestyle for the women who married them. In many ways postwar Japan represented the epitome of a stable institutional and ideological equilibrium, with a strong male breadwinner ideology undergirded by social norms and an expanding body of case law precedents that made it very difficult for employers to dismiss regular (viz. full-time male) workers (Moriguchi and Ono 2006).

It is against this backdrop that Japan entered the 1990s. The dramatic bursting of the real estate and financial bubble in 1991–92 made it suddenly much more unlikely for young Japanese men to achieve the orderly life course that was the "normal" one in the 1960s, 1970s, and into the 1980s. Indeed, their ability to even embark on such a life course was sharply curtailed by employers' actions to preserve the system as best they could for the men who had been hired into implicit permanent employment in the previous decades. The culture of security, of *anshin*, was increasingly out of reach for more and more young men, even if they chose to strive for it. As employers struggled with the cost of the rigid permanent employment system that had spread throughout more and more companies during the high-growth period, by the mid-1990s they were slashing more and more full-time entry-level positions. As a result, the possibility for young men to establish a secure attachment to a work organization faded fast. If Japan in the 1960s–1980s was unusual in the extent to which people followed orderly life courses compared to many other countries, it was unusual as well in the speed and severity with which the foundation for these patterns – the availability of full-time employment for young men – disintegrated in the 1990s.

THE EMERGENCE OF NEW EMPLOYMENT PATTERNS AMONG THE YOUNG

Unemployment: Japan in Comparative Perspective. Japan was regarded internationally throughout the postwar period as having enviably low unemployment rates. But in the 1990s the Japanese unemployment rate

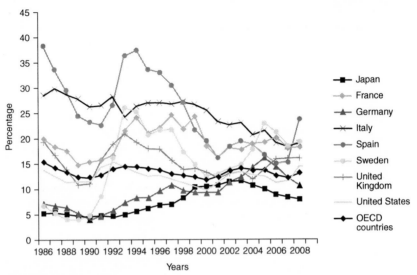

FIGURE 1.1. Change in Unemployment Rates for Young Men: Japan and
Various OECD Countries.
Source: OECD.stat

crept up. Indeed, for young Japanese men it would be more accurate to
say that the rate rose precipitously. Starting at less than 5 percent in 1992,
the year the Japanese economy entered recession, the unemployment rate
for young men (ages fifteen to twenty-four) rose to more than 10 percent
by the early twenty-first century.

Yet even with this doubling of the unemployment rate young Japanese
men remained less likely to experience unemployment than their counterparts in the U.S. and many European countries (Figure 1.1). Whereas young
Japanese males' employment situation deteriorated after the early 1990s,
their probability of becoming unemployed remained relatively low by the
standards of other postindustrial economies. A similar but weaker statement could be made with regard to the length of unemployment spells –
here again, Japanese young men hardly fared the worst among their OECD
counterparts. Long-term unemployment (defined as lasting twelve months
or more) constituted around 10 percent of total Japanese youth unemployment through the mid-1990s and then shot up, more than doubling
over the subsequent decade. But even with this increase, the proportion of
unemployed Japanese youth who experienced long-term unemployment in
2007 was almost the same as the OECD average (OECD 2009a).

In short, even though Japanese young men's likelihood of experiencing a spell of unemployment increased after the early 1990s, the

situation for young men in many other postindustrial economies was arguably worse. But such cross-national comparisons, I argue, are much more relevant to social scientists than to the people who are actually affected. Why? Because comparisons of this sort do not take seriously the idea of social generations and the implications of thinking through how the generations compare themselves to each other. Stated simply, it is unlikely that Japanese young people evaluate their employment situation with reference to the situation of young people in other countries. Such a comparative framework bears little relevance to their everyday experiences. Instead, I would argue that their bases of comparison are more likely to be: 1) the work lives of their parents' generation or the cohorts in-between their parents and themselves, and 2) the work lives of other young people around them. For those reasons, the more relevant data to consider are those internal to Japan – data that reflect the change in employment experiences for Japanese young people in the 1990s versus young people in prior decades, and data that compare the experiences of young people in the same cohort with and without higher education. If international data are relevant at all to an understanding of young people's subjective experience of work, what may be the most important is a comparison of the speed of change in Japan versus that in other countries.

Taking this feature of international comparison into account, we can briefly revisit unemployment rates and durations across countries with an eye to how much change has occurred since the mid-1980s. This comparison tells a somewhat different story than Figure 1.1. First, among the twenty OECD countries for which data are available from the mid-1980s, only one-third of them (seven) experienced an increase in unemployment among young male workers by the middle of the present decade. Japan was one of these.[17] Second, among the twenty-seven countries with data on the average duration of unemployment for youth in 1997 and 2007, Japan was also one of only seven countries where the percentage of youth experiencing long-term unemployment increased over the period. These comparisons show that the worsening employment situation of young men in Japan was not typical for young men in the majority of OECD countries. But are young Japanese men simply representative of the full spectrum of male workers within Japan? To judge this we must turn to more detailed within-country comparisons across age groups.

[17] The other countries experiencing an increase were Finland, Germany, Luxembourg, Norway, Sweden, and the U.S. See OECD.stat.

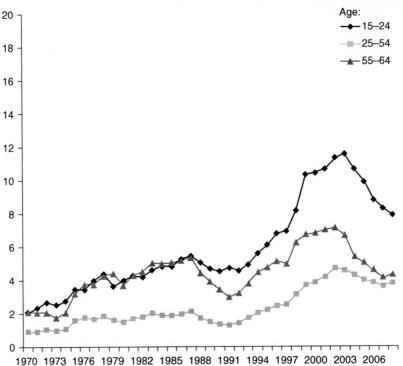

FIGURE 1.2. Comparison of Unemployment Rates for Younger and Older Men: Japan.
Source: OECD.stat

Unemployment: The Experience of Different Age Groups. Figure 1.2 compares Japanese unemployment rates for young men (ages fifteen to twenty-four) with those for men in their prime working ages (ages twenty-five to fifty-four) and in late middle age (ages fifty-five to sixty-four) over the past three and a half decades. Figure 1.3 shows the same comparison for the U.S. and Figure 1.4 shows the average unemployment rates for these age groups in OECD countries overall. Each figure demonstrates the common feature that the unemployment rate for young men exceeds that for prime-aged and older men. This phenomenon is very pronounced for the U.S. and for OECD countries overall. In both cases the state of the economy has an impact on young workers that closely mirrors but greatly exceeds the impact on middle-aged and older workers. For all age groups there are significant peaks and valleys in the unemployment rate in economic recessions and recoveries respectively.

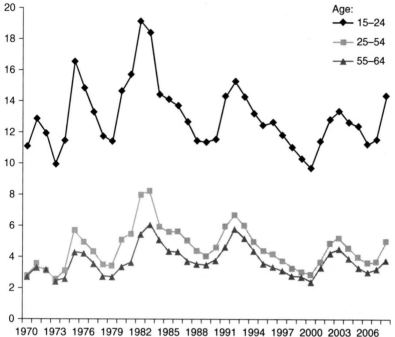

FIGURE 1.3. Comparison of Unemployment Rates for Younger and Older Men: United States.
Source: OECD.stat

But the patterns for Japan diverge from the U.S. and the OECD average in several ways. First, prime-age Japanese male workers consistently have the lowest unemployment rate, even relative to older workers. Whereas unemployment rates for prime-age and older workers are similar to each other in the U.S. and the OECD, the oldest male workers in Japan have been at considerably greater risk of unemployment than prime-age workers. A major contributory factor is undoubtedly the low retirement age in Japan. Second, the youth unemployment rate in Japan began to markedly diverge from unemployment in the other two age groups in the early 1990s, shooting up to an unheard-of peak of nearly 12 percent by 2003. Unemployment declined for all age groups in Japan with the anemic economic recovery after 2003, but remains at the level of the 1990s. Third, although comparisons have been made by some observers between the employment dislocations in Japan caused by the oil shock of the early 1970s and the lost decade of the 1990s, such comparisons do not do justice to the dramatic changes of the early 1990s.

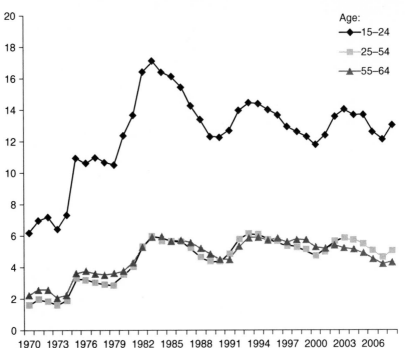

FIGURE 1.4. Comparison of Unemployment Rates for Younger and Older Men: OECD Average.
Source: OECD.stat

To wit, by 2003 Japanese youth unemployment was more than triple what it had been in 1975.

Employment Protection for "Core" Male Workers. Why has unemployment risen so sharply for young Japanese workers? A major reason is the difficulty faced by Japanese employers in trying to shed middle-aged workers. Although the employment contract between employers and long-term (so-called "regular") workers is implicit, in point of fact, Japanese labor law makes it difficult for employers to engage in layoffs.

The subject of employment protection and labor market performance has generated a small cottage industry among labor economists associated with the OECD. OECD countries show considerable variation in the extent of employment protection they offer. Moreover, countries vary in the amount of protection they offer regular (i.e. full-time) workers versus fixed-term contract workers. Some of the central questions asked by economists in this literature are whether employment protection legislation is associated with overall inflexibility in labor markets, and which demographic groups are most affected (either positively or negatively) by such legislation.

Some economists prefer to discuss employment regulation rather than legislation per se, recognizing that employment protection is affected by a variety of institutions (e.g. collective bargaining agreements) in addition to labor legislation. Employment protection consists of regulations pertaining to both hiring (e.g. conditions under which temporary or fixed-term contracts can be used) and firing (mandated pre-notification periods, severance payments, requirements for collective dismissals, and so forth). The OECD assigns countries a score from zero to six to indicate the extent to which regulations make it difficult for employers to dismiss regular employees. Japan ranks third out of twenty-seven countries (preceded only by Norway and Portugal) on this measure: It is extremely difficult for Japanese firms to dismiss regular workers. In contrast, Japan falls in the middle of the distribution of OECD countries with respect to the regulation of temporary employment or workers on fixed-term contracts. This ranking is the result of the lifting of many restrictions on companies' use of temporary and fixed-term contract workers with the labor market liberalization policies of the late 1990s (Song 2008). In short, Japan represents a case of partial deregulation, where protective regulation for core or regular employees remains strict but employment protection for temporary and fixed-term contract workers has been significantly relaxed.

Recent comparative analyses demonstrate the effects of strict regulation of regular employment on the experiences of different age groups (OECD 2009b). Countries such as Japan with stricter employment regulation for regular workers tend to have lower rates of unemployment for prime-age male workers. Stringent employment protection regulation is related to lower turnover in the labor market; in countries with strict regulation, workers tend to stay in their jobs longer and, conversely, spells of unemployment tend to be longer.

These general conclusions from the analyses of employment protection and labor markets across the broad swath of OECD countries resonate well with the experience of the "lost decade" in Japan. In pointing out the employment protection enjoyed by middle-aged male Japanese employees, Genda Yūji has argued that the negative impact of economic recession and employment restructuring in postbubble Japan was not felt across a broad age spectrum, nor did it affect men and women equally (Genda 2001). Middle-aged male workers were largely protected while the youngest and oldest male workers, along with women, suffered the

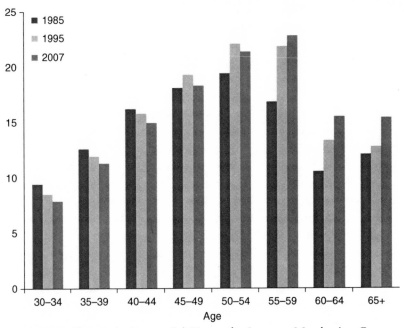

FIGURE 1.5. Changes in Average Job Tenure for Japanese Men by Age Group.
Source: Ministry of Health, Labour, and Welfare, *Chingin kōzo kihon chōsa*.

brunt of the negative impact. Even in conditions of economic downturn most Japanese employers exerted great efforts to maintain the commitments they had made to male workers hired during Japan's high economic-growth years. As Genda pointed out, many views expressed in the Japanese media and among the general public at the beginning of the twenty-first century exaggerated the risks of layoffs for middle-aged, university-educated, white-collar male employees. In point of fact, only about 2 percent of unemployed persons in Japan at the beginning of the twenty-first century were university-educated forty-five- to fifty-four-year-olds (Genda 2003). As of 2008, this had not changed.

A comparison of the job tenure (years in one firm) of Japanese men shows the different experience of younger versus older men during the past two decades. Figure 1.5 shows that the average number of years spent in one firm actually increased for older men (especially those over age fifty) between 1985 and 2007 but decreased for men under age forty-four.

The American labor market illustrates a contrasting situation. The labor economist Paul Osterman has shown that during the 1990s, job tenure fell for middle-aged as well as younger men in the United States

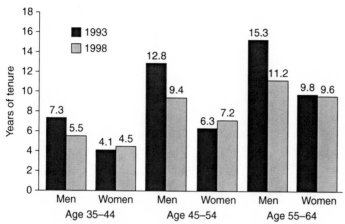

FIGURE 1.6. Change in Average Years of Tenure for American Workers by Sex and Age Group.
Source: Osterman 1999.

(Osterman 1999). While average job tenure was increasing to twenty-two years for Japanese men in their fifties, job tenure was declining to just nine years for American men age forty-five to fifty-four and to eleven years for men ages fifty-five to sixty-four (Figure 1.6). In other words, the decline in job security in the U.S. was felt across age groups – older American men were not protected from this danger. Figure 1.6 also shows that if anything, American women have fared better than men in recent years. The risk of losing one's job also extended across the occupational structure in the United States in the 1990s and into the twenty-first century. Most American economists agree that through the late 1980s, white-collar workers and especially managers faced a much lower risk of being laid off than blue-collar workers. But since the early 1990s employment security for all workers, including managers, has declined in the U.S.

The Experience of "Irregular" Work. In addition to experiencing greater increases in unemployment than other age groups and a greater decline in the years spent in one job, young Japanese have become marginalized in the labor force in another way as well: through their increasing rates of "irregular" work. Over the past fifteen years there has been an increase in most OECD countries in the prevalence of part-time, temporary, and other contingent forms of employment where employers do not make a commitment to retain a worker over a long period of time. National differences in the definition of irregular or contingent work make comparisons across countries difficult. But as with unemployment

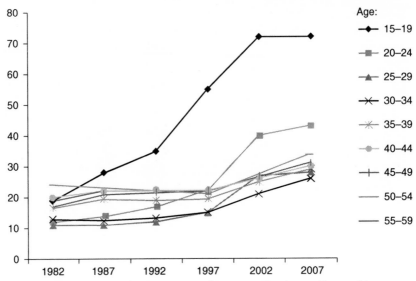

FIGURE 1.7. Change in the Percentage of Japanese Employees Engaged in Irregular Work.
Source: Sōmushō, *Shūgyō kōzo kihon chōsa*.

and job tenure, the comparison of younger to older workers in Japan tells a story of increasing disadvantage for the young generation.

Figure 1.7 shows how steeply the proportion of all employees engaged in irregular work, termed *hiseiki koyō* in Japanese, increased among the young. The proportion of twenty- to twenty-four-year-olds working as irregular workers nearly quadrupled between the early 1980s and 2007 and the proportion among even younger workers (ages fifteen to nineteen) did so as well. In contrast, the rates of irregular work in all other age groups increased over time but at a much slower pace. The heightened level of irregular work among young people contrasts with a decline in unemployment for young people since the late 1990s, as shown earlier in Figure 1.1. There is a cruel irony in this: Unemployment may be down, but among those young people with jobs, the prevalence of irregular, unstable employment has gone up.

NEET. I cannot conclude this discussion of the increasing peripheralization of young workers without mentioning NEET, a new way of categorizing workers that developed in the early 2000s. The NEET category is a sad counterpart to the freewheeling image of *furītā* that had prevailed just a decade earlier. The term NEET was borrowed from the expression used in England for youth who are "not in education, employment, or training" (hence "NEET"). NEET are defined by the Japanese Ministry of Health, Labour and Welfare as individuals age fifteen to thirty-four who are not enrolled in school, are not in the labor force (and are not counted in the ranks of the unemployed, as they are not looking for work), and are unmarried. In the typical jargon of labor economists they are "discouraged workers" or "idle," with the added qualification that they are single rather than married. NEET have either stopped actively looking for work or, in the most extreme cases, have never actively sought employment and do not express a desire to work. In 2007 the number of NEET topped 600,000, down slightly from a peak in 2004 but still much higher than the level in 1993, early in the economic recession. The proportion of NEET increases across age groups, with rates for people in their early twenties on the order of 11–12 percent but rates for people in their late twenties or early thirties closer to 20 percent.

THE NEW ECONOMIC MARGINALIZATION OF YOUNG MEN

A central purpose of this book is to explain why the labor market situation of young Japanese men has deteriorated so badly and to explore the implications for individuals and, by implication, for Japanese society. My analysis centers on a particular group of people: young men who are the educational nonelite. This is the group that particularly benefited from the school-work institutions of the high-growth period and became in turn an important engine of Japan's rise to manufacturing superpower during that period. These are not the men who graduated from top universities and entered career-track jobs in Japan's leading banks or in the national bureaucracy. Instead, this population achieved a middle-class lifestyle in the 1960s-80s by moving out of high school into entry-level career-track jobs in manufacturing, engineering, transportation, skilled crafts, and even some of the white-collar sectors of the economy.

One might assert that the hard times faced by the educational nonelite of the current lost generation bear some resemblance to the declining fortunes of America's male high school graduates over the same period of time. But this analogy does not hold up well. Why not? Because the institutional starting point in Japan was different, and engendered different skills and strategies on the part of young Japanese male nonelites than in the U.S. When the institutions unraveled in Japan, the strategies that had worked so well – strong reliance on institutional support for job searches, on-the-job training, and career development – were no longer tenable. Without the attachment to *ba* that had been so carefully orchestrated by social institutions for those Japanese reaching adulthood prior to the 1990s, the current generation has been set adrift.

Readers might question why I restrict my focus mainly to men. I have a strong reason for doing so. Although young women have also been strongly affected by economic downturn and by employers' strategy of putting more and more young workers into temporary and part-time jobs rather than career-track ones, the striking change since the early 1990s is how much this phenomenon has become a nongendered one. The big story is not just that the young have borne a greater economic cost than the middle-aged or the old, but that the negative impact has spread to men in a way unheard-of in prior generations.[18] Here is a statistic that will be particularly surprising to readers who know Japan well: The current probability that a young man is in irregular work is nearly equivalent to the probability that a married woman in 1980 would have worked part-time. Part-time work for Japanese married women became widespread during the era of the modern postwar family, and has remained a common way for women to balance work and family during their prime childrearing years But part-time work among young single men? This brings into sharp relief the economic peripheralization of young men – what we might call the de-gendering of irregular employment in postindustrial Japan.

As a scholar of gender inequality I hardly wish to argue that men's employment is intrinsically more important than women's. But in the context of a society where the male breadwinner ideology has been as strong as it has in Japan, the employment insecurity of men in their twenties and thirties has broad echo effects. The increasing peripheralization of young people in Japan's labor market is indicative of the trend toward ever-greater dualism in the employment structure – the increasing polarization of labor into "core" and "noncore" jobs in one of the world's most important postindustrial economies. This trend is particularly jarring in a country where "normalcy" came to be associated in the high economic-growth period with families where men held full-time jobs and were the primary breadwinners and women assumed the role of full-time housewives and mothers. While not the subject of this book, the sharp decline in the past fifteen years in the likelihood of young men moving into full-time jobs upon graduating from school is inextricably linked with the ever-higher average age at marriage in Japan and the

[18] The negative employment effect of the 1970s oil shock was a more gendered one, targeting women.

very low birth rate. The deterioration in young men's chances of entering stable employment has also undoubtedly fed into the heightened public consciousness of *kakusa*, or economic inequality, in the past decade – a subject to which I briefly return in the final chapter of the book.

The broader argument of this book is that Japanese society is in a state of disequilibrium, changing from a society where individual lives center on stable ties to a small set of *ba* in each life-cycle stage[19] to a society where this remains true for fewer and fewer individuals. My purpose is not primarily to make a normative claim. There were advantages to what the social psychologist Yamagishi Toshio has called *anshin shakai* or a society of security (Yamagishi 1999). One of these was a certain degree of social stability and social order that stemmed from individuals' strong identification with – and reliance upon – larger social units such as schools, workplaces, and families. The ubiquitous business cards of the Japanese corporate world, of course, bear witness to the importance accorded to a person's membership and rank in a particular *ba*. Status was measured by the prestige of the company and by the employee's rank in the standard ladder of managerial positions in Japanese companies from *kakarichō* (chief clerk) to *kachō* (section head) to *buchō* (department head). Both company name and the individual employee's status within the company were immediately apparent to anyone reading a person's business card. To wit, Matsumoto-san's card would indicate that he was not primarily an engineer but rather a *kachō* at Toyota. Likewise, Ishida-san did not self-identify as a computer scientist but as a *buchō* in Matsushita. Kuriyama-san was not a university graduate but a Tōdai graduate, and so on. Being able to identify oneself as a member of a well-recognized *ba* defined one's location in the social and economic universe, a universe that was distinctly Japanese rather than global.

The downsides of this style of social organization were many, but not all of them are as obvious as one might imagine. Only a minority of men could occupy such social locations. But also, individuals' aspirations to enter and stay in these social locations encouraged the nurturance of skills specific to each location. So-called firm-specific training tied individuals ever more tightly to the *ba* in which they had achieved membership. In lieu of encouraging social and work skills that would

---

[19] As argued earlier in the chapter, I see this for students as attachment to the school and to family; for men, attachment to the workplace and marriage; for many women, attachment principally to marriage. Stable, long-term attachment to a workplace continues to be experienced by relatively few Japanese women.

extend a man's horizons outward from the particular *ba* to which he belonged, this type of social structure encouraged the development of skills that were particular to his social location. To move away from this mode of work orientation poses significant challenges to the younger generation. One problem is that full-time, stable membership in a workplace *ba* has become less accessible because the former generation has held on to so many of the stable jobs. But a less visible and more profound issue is that the very institutional framework that guided young people into *ba* has disintegrated. The gateway into stable *ba* has become narrower and more cluttered with part-time and dead-end jobs that offer neither the chafing constraints nor the comfortable benefits of *ba*. Ultimately, what I shall call the "loss of *ba*" may prove to be a positive outcome of the current institutional disequilibrium in Japan. But it will have come at a social cost, one disproportionately borne by the young generation.

Instead of seeing Japanese young people as having unusual work behaviors stemming from their embrace of problematic values, we need to shift our vision 180 degrees and examine from the inside out the taken-for-grantedness of a number of distinctly Japanese social institutions and patterns that existed before the economic bubble burst. Only then does it become clear why the 1990s and the early twenty-first century have produced a lost generation.

Chapter 2 tells the story of how the labor market for new graduates (*shinsotsusha*) developed during the high-growth period and shows how the structures and norms supporting the transition from high school into full-time employment for Japan's large cohorts of young people became institutionalized. I examine the rhetoric used by schools and employers to describe the relationships between them, and introduce the concept of institutional social capital to elucidate how the school-work transition occurred and what employers saw themselves accomplishing by recruiting from the same schools year after year. Chapter 3 explains why attachment to a stable workplace or *ba* has been central to the economic and psychological well-being of Japanese men. Chapters 4 and 5 then look in greater depth at how high schools and firms were connected through ties of trust that facilitated the movement of new graduates out of the *ba* of school into the *ba* of the workplace. In these chapters I argue that the abundance of jobs for high school graduates in the high-growth period obscured the stratified structure of the job-matching process; when the economic recession and the "ice age of employment" deepened in the 1990s, it became much clearer which types of schools (and by implication, which students) had benefitted the most from the highly regulated recruitment system for new graduates.

Chapters 3–5 constitute the core empirical chapters of the book and draw on a range of data, the bulk of which I collected myself. I draw extensively on interviews I conducted with high school teachers and with officials at public employment security offices, the local offices charged with facilitating and monitoring schools' involvement in graduates' job placements. An original survey of nearly 130 employers provides insight into the ways employers think about the recruitment of new high school graduates; a survey of urban Japanese in their late twenties, conducted together with two Japanese colleagues, evidences the increasingly blurred line between school and part-time work and the varied level of attachment to school for vocational and general high school students. School-level data I compiled on graduates' job placement shows the highly stratified pattern of employers' attention to the range of high schools from which they can conceivably recruit new labor. Because these varied data sources reflect different levels of analysis and illuminate different parts of the institutional story of the book, I introduce each data set at the point when it bears on the story line.

In Chapter 6 I draw on in-depth interviews with three young men in the lost generation with different educational backgrounds and different personal skills and resources. Their narratives illustrate how some young people have developed the capacity to use weak ties in their search for satisfying work, despite the fact that it has been reliance on institutions that the educational system has traditionally encouraged. Through navigating the external labor market on their own, the identities of these young men have of necessity developed independently from attachment to a stable workplace *ba*. This is something on which they reflect with candor in their comments. Finally, in Chapter 7 I discuss the future of the lost generation in the context of the discourse on widening economic inequality in Japan. The book closes with reflections on the importance of the Japanese case for other postindustrial societies.

2

The Historical Roots of Japanese
School-Work Institutions

"Some schools have a good understanding of our business, and we have a very significant trust relationship with them. For us, the key elements of recruitment are close ties and trust."

– Small manufacturing company in Tokyo, mid-1990s

Along with high economic growth in much of the postwar period, Japan achieved a relatively high level of economic equality. One of the secrets to this achievement was a set of social institutions that helped even less-educated young men secure relatively stable positions in the workforce. These institutions developed under specific historical circumstances in Japan and were particularly effective during the decades of the 1960s through the 1980s.

By the early twenty-first century, however, Japan was no longer a place where most young men, regardless of educational background, moved smoothly into their adult full-time work lives. This new reality can only be understood by looking at how key social institutions have changed. Both schools and workplaces helped the prior generation acquire and utilize their skills and abilities, or human capital in economists' terms. But these institutions and the relationship between them changed during the 1990s in ways that are fundamentally disadvantageous to young people, especially the least educated. The institutional changes have not happened principally because of young people's behaviors. Rather, they stem from employers' and policymakers' decisions about how risk should be distributed across different segments of the labor force.

In the second half of the twentieth century in Japan the risk of insecure jobs was generally borne much more heavily by women than by men. But the previous chapter showed that after the early 1990s this risk extended to a particular group of men as well: the young. To put it in strong terms, many young men have in effect had their growth stunted by the combination of institutional rigidity that has protected the jobs of many middle-aged men and institutional change that has restructured many entry-level positions into part-time, temporary jobs.

Underneath both the institutional rigidities and the institutional changes are employer and government policy choices that are deeply connected to the norms and values embedded in the employment relationship in Japan, and connected as well to fundamental ideas about how the abilities of individuals should be nurtured and rewarded.

Comparative research by Japanese and foreign labor economists has shown how the Japanese employment system evolved differently from employment systems in many Western industrial economies. But it is not just the employment system that is distinctive. In earlier work on gender inequality in Japan, I used the idea of a human capital development system to conceptualize how the responsibilities for developing individuals' human capital are distributed across different institutions in society – schools, workplaces, and families (Brinton 1988, 1993, 2005). The concept of a human capital development system puts employment systems and labor market institutions into a broad societal context that includes the family and schooling, institutions universal to every society. A society's human capital development system is more than an economic construct. It consists of the division of labor among a society's institutions for developing the human capital of individuals, and it also embodies some of a society's dominant norms and patterns of interaction among individuals. The concept's utility lies in how it broadens the way we think about how social and economic institutions shape individuals' journey through their life course as productive members of society.

For illustration, consider the contrast between Japan and the U.S. in terms of their very different types of human capital development systems. The Japanese system involves parents, schools, and eventually employers as important stakeholders in developing young people's human capital. This chapter lays out some of the historical background for why this is the case. In contrast, the U.S. represents a model where, by virtue of the way its social institutions have evolved, individuals have carried greater responsibility for making their own decisions about investment in their human capital. While many American parents foot the bill for a portion or all of their offsprings' college expenses, the American higher education system and federal loan programs financially assist a large proportion of college students. In contrast, the cost of tuition and living expenses for Japanese undergraduates is much more heavily borne by parents. Once employed, young people in the two societies have also been expected to demonstrate different amounts of individual initiative with regard to their own human capital development. In particular, large firms in Japan conventionally invest more heavily in workers' skill development than their counterparts in the U.S. – and expect a longer-term career commitment from their workers as well.[1]

Germany exhibits yet a different distribution of responsibility for human capital development than either Japan or the U.S.; its "dual system" of formal vocational education in school and apprenticeships in the workplace has been written about extensively.[2]

Understanding Japan's particular human capital development system is key to analyzing the situation of the country's youth in the past fifteen years. Japan's human capital development system throughout the second half of the twentieth century prioritized the transition of young men from school into a workplace *ba* where they could continue their skill development under the sponsorship and guidance of their employer. In Japan, the centrality of human capital development processes in the workplace has meant that it is crucial for young men to gain a foothold in a company. The institutional mechanisms guiding young men from school into the labor market have been central to making this happen. A teacher in the guidance department of a low-ranking general high school put it this way, after I had answered his own questions about the high-school work process in the U.S.: "You're telling me that in the United States, high school seniors have direct contact with companies when they are looking for jobs? Wow. That really shows that the companies are treating them like adults .... The American system sounds so different from ours, where people are pulled along on a rail and as long as they stay on track, then to some extent they can automatically find a job." The gradual deterioration of this rail together with the fading possibility of stable employment

---

[1] The traits that American companies have come to value in their employees are well demonstrated by data from a 2005 survey of Fortune 1000 companies. Among these companies, only 16 percent said that "loyalty to the company is rewarded" and the proportion saying "rewards are tied to seniority" was only 5 percent. The results are from research conducted by the University of Southern California's Center for Effective Organizations, reported by O'Toole and Lawler (2006).

[2] For recent discussions of the German system, see chapters by Mayer and Solga, Hillmert, and Dustmann and Schoenberg in Mayer and Solga (2008). Also see Thelen (2007).

during the 1990s constituted crucial breaks in what had essentially constituted Japanese society's social contract with young men.

I have explored elsewhere how Japan's human capital development system has disadvantaged women as a group, privileging instead the human capital development of men.[3] The historical development of Japan's educational system as well as its infamous long-term employment system (with long job tenure, seniority-related wages, and on-the-job training) have been written about extensively and there is no need to review such histories here. Instead, this chapter focuses on the part of the Japanese human capital development system that is especially key for understanding what happened to youth in the 1990s: the transition from school to work.

The history of Japan's school-work transition system provides a central backdrop for understanding how the 1990s produced a lost generation of young men. Why? Because the system had reinforced Japanese young people's reliance on their schools to aid them in searching for their first posteducation job. The expansion of the system and its smooth operation during Japan's high-growth period of the 1960s-1980s paradoxically rendered its unraveling in the 1990s even more destabilizing for young people's entry into the labor market. The deterioration of Japan's unusual school-work system has made it glaringly obvious that young people are now having to develop new types of skills in order to navigate in the labor market.

Before turning to how school-work institutions developed in postwar Japan, some international comparisons will illustrate the differences between Japan and other countries in terms of where the responsibility for human capital development lies.

Figure 2.1 shows the proportion of upper secondary (high school) students enrolled in vocational curriculum tracks in Japan and a number of other OECD countries. The bar for Japan at the far left-hand side of the chart shows that relatively few Japanese high school students are in vocational education tracks. This is similar to the southern European

---

[3] The responsibility of Japanese parents to privately carry most of the cost of their children's education and the responsibility of employers to bear the costs of workers' skill development result in greater overall investment in Japanese men's than women's human capital. Japanese women have typically been assumed to be impermanent members of the labor force, leaving at some point to devote themselves primarily to household and family responsibilities. This assumption has resulted in a larger wage gap between Japanese men and women and more distinctly gendered employment trajectories than in many Western industrial economies such as the U.S. (Brinton 1993).

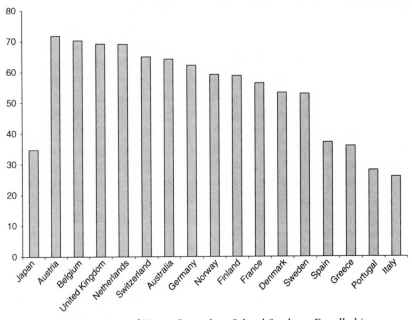

FIGURE 2.1. Proportion of Upper Secondary School Students Enrolled in
Vocational Tracks: OECD Countries.
Source: OECD 2003.

countries (on the far right-hand side of the chart), all of which have fewer
than 40 percent of upper secondary students enrolled in vocational education. Many of the countries with higher proportions of students in vocational tracks have apprenticeship or "modified apprenticeship" systems
where upper secondary students study for an occupation and schools
have partnerships with employers, who provide some job training to
students. These include Austria, Belgium, the Netherlands, Switzerland,
and Germany. In each of these countries, more than 60 percent of upper
secondary students receive vocational training (the United Kingdom and
Australia also have rates exceeding 60 percent).[4]

The proportion of a nation's students enrolled in vocational tracks is
an indicator of the degree to which students receive work-related education while they are in high school as opposed to focusing exclusively on

---

[4] The U.S. is not included in these statistics because very few American students are enrolled
exclusively in a vocational school or track. As of 2005 only about 250 of all American
high schools were solely vocational; the vast majority of American high school students
enrolled in vocational courses are in comprehensive high schools.

academic subjects that impart general knowledge and skills. In Japan, nearly three-quarters of high school students are in this latter group (enrolled nearly exclusively in academic subjects), developing their general human capital rather than occupation-specific human capital before they enter the workplace.

Although the American educational system served as the main foreign model for early postwar Japan's rationalization and streamlining of its complicated, highly tracked prewar educational system, the characteristic American "comprehensive high school" form was not adopted in Japan. Instead, students completing their last year of compulsory education (ninth grade) face an important fork in the road: whether to continue on to high school or not and, if so, whether to proceed to a general academic high school or a vocational high school. For students in general high schools, the job of the school system is to prepare them with general skills they need in order to enter a workplace where the employer will then take over and train them in the specific skills they need to be productive in that company. Hence the company itself is a crucial site or *ba* of young adults' human capital development. But even the 30 percent or so of Japanese junior high school graduates who go to vocational rather than academic (general) high schools receive an education that presumes that employers will pick up where schools leave off. In contrast to the occupationally specific vocational training and workplace experience involved in the "dual system" apprenticeship countries such as Germany, vocational education in Japan has a long history of being broader and, in that sense, shallower.[5]

The few available statistics on school-sponsored workplace experiences and apprenticeships in Japan are highly misleading. After hearing the term *intanship* (internship) mentioned by several teachers I enthusiastically made a note to explicitly ask about internships for students in my subsequent interviews at high schools. But when I did so the majority of high school teachers said that when apprenticeships or internships do occur, it is for a period of a few days or a week. This was quite stunning to me, representing as it does such a vast difference from the extended apprenticeships of secondary school students in dual-system countries. When I eventually located national statistics on internships from the National Educational Policy Research Institute in Japan, the numbers were quite impressive: The percentage of public high school students who had participated in an internship rose from 11 to 26

[5] For a brief overview see Murata and Stern (1993).

percent between 2001 and 2007. Among only those students in public vocational high schools, the figure rose from 29 to 60 percent during this time period. But the fine print was revealing in its match with the definition conveyed to me by high school teachers. To wit, the numbers were constructed from high school seniors who had had at least one "internship" experience during their three years of high school, and an experience met the definition even if it lasted for as short a period as a partial school day.

Japanese vocational high schools are of five main types: agricultural, fishery, home economics, commercial, and industrial. The latter two types are far and away the most popular choices; currently about 30 percent of vocational students attend industrial high schools and another 25 percent attend commercial high schools.[6] *Sōgō kagaku* (comprehensive technical or scientific) high schools are a recent development and comprise 18 percent of the current vocational high school student population. A number of Japanese prefectures are in the process of phasing out over several years some of their industrial high schools in favor of this new form of comprehensive school.[7]

The comparative figures on high schools' provision of vocational training show that the development of occupation- or industry-specific skills among Japanese students has not been a focus of public investment in comparison to educational systems in a number of European societies. These figures are highly consistent with the dominant wisdom concerning how skill development generally occurs in Japan: The educational system focuses principally on general human capital development, with occupation- and industry-specific skill development largely carried out by firms. Koike Kazuo has been the scholar most widely cited over the past few decades in regard to how Japanese firms invest in on-the-job training for both blue- and white-collar workers. Aoki Masahiko, Koike, and numerous Japanese and American economists have widely touted the degree to which human capital development in Japan involves employers' investment in workers' "firm-specific skills," skills that are not easily transferable across firms (i.e. in the external labor market) (Aoki 1988, Koike 1988).

The weakness of the external labor market in Japan – the labor market for workers with "portable skills" who move across companies – is also reflected in Japan's very low public expenditures for skill training,

[6] See Ministry of Education, Culture, Sports, Science and Technology (2009).
[7] For a discussion of the policy, see Ariga (2005).

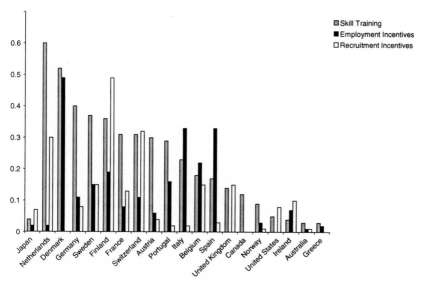

FIGURE 2.2. Government Investment in Skill Training, Employment Incentives, and Recruitment Incentives: OECD Countries.
Note: Government investment is measured as percentage of gross domestic product.
Source: OECD 2003.

employment incentives, and recruitment incentives. Figure 2.2 shows public expenditures in each of these areas as a percentage of a country's gross domestic product. The left-hand column for each country is the amount of public expenditure on skill training. Japan ranks very low among OECD countries. (Notably, the U.S. also ranks very low, indicating the American government's general inattention to the development of public training and retraining programs.) In contrast, the higher expenditures in the Netherlands, Denmark, Germany, and all other Northern and Western European countries indicate the greater level of government involvement in workforce training. Figure 2.2 also shows the scant amount of Japanese public funds devoted to employment incentives (column 2 for each country) and recruitment incentives (column 3) relative to Northern and Western European countries in particular.

In sum, the central actors in the development of Japanese workers' job skills have not been schools or the state, but rather, employers. Moving youth smoothly out of school and into the workplace is therefore a crucial component of overall labor policy.

THE ESTABLISHMENT OF SCHOOL-WORK INSTITUTIONS
IN POSTWAR JAPAN

Legal Foundations. In the post–World War II period Japan developed
distinctive institutions for effecting youths' school-work transition.[8]
Local public employment security offices (*shokugyō anteijo*, or *shokuan*
for short) were legally designated in the 1949 Japanese Employment
Security Law as information clearinghouses in the labor market – intermediaries between middle and high schools on the one hand and employers on the other.[9] This law explicitly acknowledged that schools could
serve an important purpose in job placement, as teachers' familiarity
with individual students' character and performance would naturally
exceed that of officials in the public employment security offices or prospective employers. The communication of teachers' knowledge about
graduating seniors was recognized as valuable, and the Employment
Security Law legitimated the important role that Japanese middle and
high schools could play in facilitating employers' recruitment of entry-
level workers:

> The public employment security office will cooperate with schools in providing to
> students information about labor demand and supply conditions, offering neces-
> sary assistance in job selection, and (through communication with other public
> employment security offices) making available as many job openings as possible
> and appropriate; it must endeavor to guide students into jobs appropriate to their
> abilities.
>   When the public employment security office finds it necessary to smooth out
> the employment introduction process, it can get permission from school princi-
> pals to share some of the work with the school.
>   At the discretion of the Labor Minister, schools can provide free introduction
> services to employers for their graduating students. (Translated from Kariya et al.
> 1997.)

The first provision originally applied to junior high schools, whereas
the second provision over time came to apply to high schools and the
third to institutions of higher education. These provisions are fascinating from the perspective of institutional design. They define the responsibilities of the public employment security offices but also indicate that

---

[8] See Brinton (2000), Honda (2004), and Kariya et al. (1997). For greater detail, see Kariya,
Sugayama, and Ishida, eds. (2000).
[9] The Japanese Employment Security Law was written in 1947 and revised in 1949 by the
newly established Ministry of Labor. In the late 1990s the government gave these offices
the more cheerful and colloquial-sounding name, "Hello Work."

these offices can shift some work to the schools if they decide to do so or if Ministry of Health, Labour and Welfare officials suggest it. The law forbids the involvement of private employment agencies as intermediaries between employers and graduating seniors – a clear reaction against the negative historical legacy of exploitative labor brokers in nineteenth-century Japan.[10]

The legal wording provides considerable leeway for how the Ministry can direct the public employment security offices' responsibilities and public employment security officials' interaction with teachers. It is consistent with standard principles of administrative guidance (*gyōsei shidō*) by the Japanese bureaucracy, granting wide scope for administrative action based on bureaucratic judgments of "necessity" and "appropriateness."[11]

In 1950 the Japan Employment Guidance Association – an association of teachers, bureaucrats in the Ministries of Labor and Education, and scholars – offered a further interpretation of why schools should be closely involved in the job placement of their graduates:

The secret for the success of employment guidance lies in understanding the candidate's background and carrying out the work with sincerity and enthusiasm. School personnel are the most appropriate to do this from the standpoint of knowing the candidate for several years and understanding the person and his or her record. If this responsibility is left with the public employment security office, we cannot expect that the student's record across several years will be fully taken into account. There is a danger that judgments will instead be based on just a short interview. Moreover, compared to school personnel, public employment security office personnel will have a more bureaucratic attitude towards students. As for employers, they prefer to receive a recommendation for a candidate from a school rather than from a public employment security office. This is because they historically have had a feeling of trust in the schools. Moreover, they know that the school personnel are sincere and enthusiastic. (Translated from Kariya, Sugayama, and Ishida, eds. 2000: 116.)

Further statements in the report refer to the "natural" role of schools in giving employment guidance to students who have "been under their [teachers'] tender care." Similarly, Labor Ministry documents from the

---

[10] See for example Garon (1990) and Tsurumi (1990). Ariga (2005) notes that beginning in 2003 the government relaxed the restrictions on private employment agencies entering the market for matching new high school graduates to full-time jobs, but that such agencies have not taken up this role.

[11] See Upham's cogent discussion of administrative guidance in Japan (Upham 1987).

mid-1950s include under schools' responsibilities not only the education of students but active participation in "watching over the future of graduates." (Translated from Kariya, Sugayama, and Ishida, eds. 2000: 116.)

Since the 1950s the Employment Security Law has strictly regulated employers' recruitment of graduating seniors from junior and senior high schools into full-time jobs, requiring employers to submit to the local public employment security office a nationally standardized form for each job opening. These job forms (*kyūjinhyō*) are very detailed, listing characteristics of the firm such as the total number of employees, the founding date, capitalization, address of the main office, and the branch that is recruiting. Job characteristics as well are recorded in considerable detail on the forms: job responsibilities, relevant skill and certification requirements (e.g. a driver's license), work hours, vacation days, and information on wages, bonus system, and benefits. In the lower left-hand corner of the elaborate job opening announcement is a space where employers can record the names of high schools to which they intend to deliver by hand or mail the job listing; most employers choose to fill in this section. After an employee at the public employment security office reviews the information and stamps the form, the listing employer is allowed to give the job opening announcement to high schools in order to inform their *shinro shidōbu* (guidance department) about the job opening and to solicit applications from graduating seniors.

Employers who are able to project their hiring needs for the official start of the employment year in April clearly benefit from this system, as they deliver their job opening announcements to high schools by early fall and can start interviewing applicants soon thereafter. As one high school teacher commented to me, "When you think about it, the Japanese system is really oriented toward big companies; they are the ones who can decide in July how many people to hire for the following April [the beginning of the work year]. Small companies just can't plan that far ahead."

The stable high school to work transition processes and dynamics have progressively unraveled in the past fifteen years with the increasing chaos of the youth labor market, which I will relate in the rest of the book. But the logic of having an intermediary between young people and employers is clearly deeply rooted, as illustrated by the quote from a high school teacher at the beginning of the chapter. This implicit logic is, in fact, so strong that descriptions of the 1949 Employment Security Law published in English typically state that the law "forbids" direct contact between students and employers (Naganawa 1999). I labored under this interpretation for some time before reading the original Japanese text and discussing the law with public employment security office personnel. It then became clear to me that a more appropriate translation into English is "discourage," not "forbid." In other words, the law can be read as making a strong normative suggestion as to appropriate and effective behavior, consistent once again with the flavor of administrative guidance in Japan.

The blurred line between legal rules and strong norms governing the school-work system came up in some of my interviews at public employment security offices and public high schools in Kanagawa prefecture during the mid to late 1990s. Officials at the Kawasaki-kita Public Employment Security Office echoed the logic of the 1950 Japan Employment Guidance Association report as to why these offices generally rely on schools to recommend students to employers: "They [the teachers] know individual students well, whereas we [civil servants] do not. This means that teachers can do a better job of guiding them into jobs." This logic was also reflected in my interviews with teachers in high schools' guidance departments. In early interviews I had rather naïvely asked teachers why the school was responsible for matching graduating seniors into jobs. The typical answer was "We don't know," followed by an explanation along the lines of "The public employment security office gives us the task of sorting through the job announcements our school receives, making contact with employers and recommending students to jobs. We don't know why we are supposed to do this. We just do it." It was clear that teachers made no practical distinction between whether this is legally required or whether it is simply a strong norm.

Theoretically, high school seniors can forego perusing the job opening announcements that arrive at their school and go instead to the local public employment security office, sort through the job opening listings for graduating seniors, and contact employers directly. This is not technically illegal. But until very recently it only rarely occurred, because it was nearly certain that a student who did this would fail to secure a promise of postgraduation employment from a firm. Employers seeking to hire graduating seniors into full-time jobs rely heavily on the recommendation that a school submits for each student. Students applying "cold" on their own, without their schools' recommendation, have stood little chance of being interviewed by an employer.

The expectation that there will be an intermediary between the high school senior and the employer to which he or she is applying was brought home to me by an interaction I happened to observe at a Kanagawa public employment security office in the late 1990s. As I was waiting to meet an official with whom I had made an appointment, my attention was drawn to a young man in conversation with a bureaucrat behind the counter. The bureaucrat was explaining to the young man that it would be much better if he called the employer than if the young man did so directly. The young man apparently accepted this logic and the bureaucrat proceeded to place the call and explain to the employer that there was someone there who would like to apply for the job. The bureaucrat eventually handed the phone to the young man, who spoke with the employer and arranged to meet. By the end of the interaction, it was clear that the bureaucrat had communicated to the young man that directly contacting the employer was not an effective strategy – it was better to go through the school's guidance department or at least to speak with an official at the public employment security office and have them make the initial contact with the employer.[12]

A human resource person I interviewed in a small men's clothing manufacturing company of about four hundred employees in Tokyo stated a common sentiment among employers: "It's best for the job application to come from the young person via the school, because students don't have much knowledge of society. So guidance from the school is necessary. However, as a company we can't make a decision based only on the school's recommendation. We need to figure out if the student is suitable for our company, and the student needs to figure this out, too. So we put a lot of weight on the job candidate's visit to our company and on the interview." In an interview on another occasion, a teacher at a low-ranked high school volunteered the following, indicating the extension of schools' intermediary role even into this later stage of the job-matching process: "Students visit the company after they are recommended by us for the job. If they decide they don't like the company or the work, we don't insist they take the job. In these instances, the main teacher in the guidance department calls the company and tells them." The teacher went on to say that if the school does this, then the fact that the student turned down the job does not necessarily have a negative effect on the school's relationship with the company.

[12] While there is some prefectural variation in the relative weight of the roles of high schools and public employment security offices, they both serve an intermediary role between high schools and employers. The job opening form for new high school graduates is also standardized across the country.

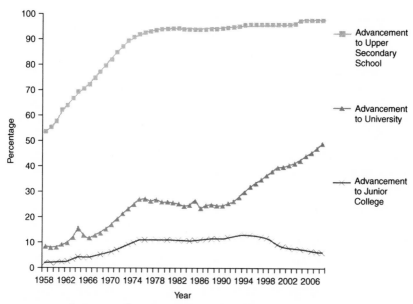

FIGURE 2.3. Japanese Advancement Rates to Upper Secondary and Tertiary Education.
Source: Japanese Ministry of Education, Culture, Sports, Science and Technology, *Gakkō kihon chōsa*, various years.

The assumption that high school students are naïve observers of society and of the world of work was frequently articulated by teachers in the guidance departments of the twenty high schools I visited in the course of my research. As I will go into later, this prevailing assumption is an ironic sidebar to teachers' own admission that the majority of students at Japan's middle- and low-performing high schools now work in part-time jobs while they are still in school.

The Evolution of Schools' Role in Job Placement. Greater attention in recent years by Japanese scholars to the distinctive school-work transition system in their country has demonstrated that particular conditions in the Japanese economy and in the reorganization of the workplace in the 1960s reinforced the important role of high schools in screening graduating seniors for employers. By 1965, only about one-quarter of junior high school graduates were entering the labor market directly upon leaving school; the remaining three-quarters were proceeding on to high school, even though it was (and remains) noncompulsory (Figure 2.3). With more than two-thirds of high school graduates choosing to enter the labor market rather than proceeding on to higher education, the legally established school-work transition process – designated by the Employment Security Law – applied to the majority of Japanese young people.

With double-digit growth rates in the 1960s, the Japanese economy faced a shortage of workers for manufacturing jobs. Honda describes how employers' "periodic blanket recruitment" (large-scale recruitment of new school-leavers to begin work on a specified date in the spring) extended from white-collar to blue-collar positions in the 1960s, becoming the standard hiring practice.[13] Firm-internal labor markets – with high job security, implicit guarantees for promotion, and heavy employer investment in workers' firm-specific skills – were already well developed for white-collar workers in large firms. Large employers reorganized their human resource practices in the 1960s to create internal labor markets for young blue-collar workers as well. Demographic conditions during this period were a fortuitous fit with employers' strong labor demand: Japan's still-high fertility rates had produced large cohorts of young people, not all of whom were needed in Japan's shrinking agricultural sector. By the 1960s nearly one-half of all new hires in Japan's labor force – from any level of education – were in the manufacturing sector. As more and more young people proceeded on to high school and increased their general human capital, new high school graduates were an appealing source of labor for Japan's manufacturing firms, replacing junior high school graduates as the proverbial *kin no tamago* (golden eggs) to be gathered up when they graduated.

The importance of the institutional connections between schools and firms in Japan, mediated through the public employment security offices, became widely recognized in the Western social science literature in the 1980s and 1990s. In particular, Japan was often cited as having one of the most efficient and fair systems of moving new high school graduates from school into work. The special role of Japanese schools in guiding students into jobs was contrasted with the U.S. in particular, where high school seniors generally do not get this type of support.[14]

A comparative study by the Japan Institute of Labour (now the Japan Institute of Labour Policy and Training) in the late 1980s found that approximately 60 percent of Japanese high school seniors went through their school to find their first full-time job, compared to only about 20

---

[13] Honda (2004), Kariya et al. (1997), Kariya, Sugayama, and Ishida, eds. (2000).

[14] Rosenbaum and Kariya (1989). Also see Blanchflower and Freeman (2000) and Rosenbaum (2001).

percent of American high school seniors (Japan Institute of Labour Policy and Training 1989). Studies of how American employers go about hiring noncollege graduates also show how infrequently employees are hired through school referrals. In research on American employers' recruitment of noncollege graduates in four major metropolitan areas, the labor economist Harry Holzer found that a scant 3 percent of the most recently recruited noncollege graduates had been hired through school referrals (Holzer 1996). Other studies are consistent in finding almost no institutionalized route through which American high school graduates move out of school and into work (Rosenbaum 2001; Rosenbaum et al. 1999). Instead, numerous studies in the U.S. have found that something other than schools is important in Americans' job search. Nearly always, that something is "social capital." This concept has now become so important in social scientists' research on how people find jobs in a range of economies that it bears scrutiny in the Japanese context. Given the historical-institutional context in which the school-work transition developed in Japan, does social capital matter in new graduates' job search?

FINDING A JOB: PERSONAL AND INSTITUTIONAL
SOCIAL CAPITAL

Social capital has been defined in a number of ways in the American social science literature. Common among all of the definitions is the idea that social capital is not a characteristic of individuals per se. Instead, it consists of the social connections and personal networks to which people have access.[15] These personal ties constitute resources that individuals can use to accomplish various goals, one of which is searching for a job. A person's social capital includes strong ties (family members and close friends) as well as weak ties or acquaintances, so-called "friends of friends."

The distinction between strong and weak ties entered sociologists' lexicon through a now-classic article by Mark Granovetter, cleverly titled "The Strength of Weak Ties" (Granovetter 1973). Granovetter studied how mid-career American men found new jobs when they had either quit or been fired from their prior job. Interestingly, he discovered that these men were more likely to find jobs through people that they saw

---

[15] For frequently cited definitions, see Coleman (1988), Portes (1998), Woolcock (1998).

infrequently (weak ties, or acquaintances) rather than through people they knew well. These men had either received information or been introduced to their job through a weak tie. What distinguished this research finding was that it contradicted the commonsense idea that strong ties such as family members or friends provide the most help in individuals' job searches, since they know the person well and are generally highly motivated to provide help.

Granovetter's original research finding spurred a huge body of research in American sociology and generated a large number of studies documenting Americans' use of weak ties in their job search activities. Some researchers examined the question in the Japanese context as well. Shin Watanabe modeled his study after Granovetter's in order to explicitly test Granovetter's hypotheses (Watanabe 1987). In contrast to the U.S. findings, Watanabe found that Japanese men who were making mid-career job changes were more likely to find their jobs through strong rather than weak ties. Contrary to Granovetter's assumption, men in Japan who used strong ties to find their new job reported getting more job information than other men. As a result they were more likely to increase their wages by changing jobs than were men who hadn't used strong ties.

Watanabe related the different roles played by strong and weak ties in Japan to the idea that establishing relationships requires a heavy "fixed cost." This is the time required to develop a trusting relationship with another person. To illustrate his point, Watanabe cited research by Thomas Lifson on the networks between Japanese business firms (Lifson 1979). Lifson showed that managers in one firm spend a considerable amount of time meeting with their counterparts in other firms in order to establish relationships with them. This large initial time cost is balanced by the relatively shorter time that needs to be spent in subsequent negotiations. In contrast, American managers tend to spend less time establishing the initial relationship and more time on each subsequent negotiation. Watanabe rephrased this finding in the context of interpersonal relationships as follows: "Strong ties are maintained through everyday interaction and activated in time of need in Japan. On the other hand, in the United States, interpersonal ties are explored and cultivated when a certain problem has to be solved" (Watanabe 1987: 395).

This points to a crucial difference in how social capital tends to be maintained and used by individuals in Japan and the U.S. – a difference that is intimately related to the difference in the human capital development systems in the two countries and to what I termed in Chapter 1 the structure of trust. In the U.S., it is important to have broad social networks and many weak ties in order to get information about more opportunities. This requires individuals to have the confidence and capacity to trust acquaintances and strangers at least at a minimal level, or to have the ability to quickly judge whether people can be trusted or not. Interestingly, Yamagishi has found in social-psychological laboratory research that high-trusters are significantly more skilled at forming accurate judgments of strangers' trustworthiness than low-trusters (Yamagishi 2003). He hypothesizes a virtuous circle between individuals' willingness to trust unknown others and their ability to read the signals of trustworthiness or nontrustworthiness of others. As he puts it: " … more socially perceptive people can afford to assume other people's trustworthiness in the absence of damning evidence and can leave the security of stable relations to pursue better opportunities outside that small circle because they can pull out of risky relations at the first sign of risk" (Yamagishi 2003: 290).

Consistent with this idea of the mutual reinforcement between an individual's ability to discern signs of trustworthiness and untrustworthiness in acquaintances or strangers and an individual's practice of using weak ties, in Japan levels of trust are quite low and it has been considered important to have reliable strong ties rather than many weak ties. The significance of this in relation to individuals' ability to adapt to social change will resurface as a theme in the final chapter of this book.

In research on the Japanese school-work transition, Kariya Takehiko and I further characterized strong ties into two types in order to capture the importance of the school as a type of strong tie that many Japanese young people use as they make the transition into the labor market. We coined the term "personal social capital" to refer to a young person's ties to family members, friends, or acquaintances as sources of information or introduction to a job, and "institutional social capital" to refer to the information and introductions that a young person can access through the main institution they belong to at that point in their lives – school (Brinton and Kariya 1998).

To see how Japanese young people's use of these different types of social capital has changed over time, we did a historical analysis of the job-search methods that had been used by successive birth cohorts as they

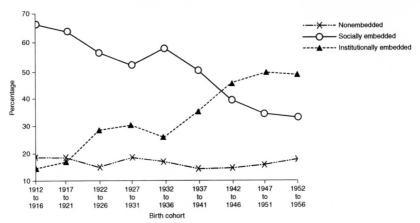

FIGURE 2.4. Japanese Men's Methods of Finding Their First Job: Changes Over Time (by Year of Birth).
Source: Reprinted from Brinton and Kariya 1998.

left school and entered their first full-time job. The oldest age group we looked at was men born between 1912 and 1916. This group entered the labor market in the late 1920s and early 1930s. The youngest men were born forty years later (1952–56), entering the labor market in the late 1960s and early 1970s.[16] We were particularly interested in seeing whether young men's reliance on their school to provide information and introductions to employers had increased over time, as the historical development of Japanese labor law would suggest. We categorized new graduates' job search methods into three types: personal social capital, institutional social capital, or nonembedded (methods that do not rely on the job-seeker's embeddedness or membership in personal networks or institutions, but instead, rely on newspaper advertisements or other "atomistic" methods of job search). Unfortunately, the quantitative survey data we used did not categorize personal social ties as strong or weak, so we had to consider the two together under the composite category "personal social capital."

Figure 2.4 shows that for nearly every cohort of men, the use of social capital – either institutional (school-firm connections) or personal (friends, family, acquaintances) – was much more common than the atomistic pattern of job search. In fact, the proportion of graduates who found their

---

[16] Consistent with the focus of this book, Kariya and I focused only on young male graduates in our analysis.

first job through neither social nor institutional ties was amazingly low and stable across time, ranging between 15 and 19 percent (the line with the x's in Figure 2.4, labeled "nonembedded"). This shows how consistently uncommon the use of atomistic job search patterns has been in twentieth-century Japan.

Young men's use of personal social capital (the line in Figure 2.4 demarcated with circles) has declined over time; personal social capital was the job search method used by 67 percent of men born early in the twentieth century and only 33 percent of men born in the 1950s. In contrast, young men's use of institutional social capital to find their first full-time job greatly increased over time – only about 15 percent of men in the earliest cohort were introduced into their first job by their school, and this figure rose to 49 percent for the most recent birth cohort. These data provide evidence that complements the interpretation one would garner from the development of Japanese labor law – that schools became more important over time in providing their graduating seniors with labor market information and introductions to employers.

Breaking these patterns down by men's educational level shows that the increasing use of institutional social capital (schools) in young men's job search occurred for graduates from every level of schooling (Table 2.1). We constructed larger age cohorts for ease of presentation in this table. The increasing reliance on school (institutional social capital, indicated by "I") was greatest for junior high and high school graduates. The upper left-hand corner of the table shows that only about 11 percent of junior high school graduates born in the period 1912–26 found their first job with the help of their school (institutional social capital). Reading down the first column, this quadrupled (to 42 percent) for men born between 1942 and 1956. The percentage of high school graduates who found their job through institutional social capital (column 4) also increased over this time period, from 35 to 52 percent. A similar but less dramatic change occurred for university graduates (column 7).

The institutional social capital used by high school graduates (and in an earlier period, junior high school graduates) is very different from the institutional social capital used by university graduates. Japanese university seniors, especially in elite universities, are able to benefit from their university's ties with certain firms but this involves substantially different mechanisms than those implicated in high schools' ties with

TABLE 2.1. *Japanese Men's Methods of Finding Their First Job: Changes Over Time (by Year of Birth) and by Level of Education*

	Level of Education								
	Junior High School			High School			University		
	I	S	NE	I	S	NE	I	S	NE
Men born 1912–26	10.5	71.5	18.0	35.3	52.0	12.7	42.7	33.7	23.6
Men born 1927–41	22.6	64.1	13.3	31.7	53.0	15.3	45.6	26.8	27.6
Men born 1942–56	42.1	46.8	11.1	51.9	33.1	15.0	47.4	31.4	21.2

Note: I=institutional social capital, S=social ties, NE=nonembedded job search method.
Source: Reprinted from Brinton and Kariya 1998.

employers.[17] Notably, seniors at elite universities depend more heavily on alumni networks and, depending on their major, the personal ties of their professors to certain industries or firms. So what is most distinctive about institutional social capital in Japan is the extent to which it has been available to less-educated, nonelite young people who graduate from junior or senior high school and who do not proceed on to university. The unusual degree of availability of this resource through the 1980s makes its subsequent decline, as later chapters will show, all the more disruptive.

Talking to employers can shed further light on the significant role of institutional social capital in young Japanese men's pathway into full-time employment prior to the economic downturn of the 1990s. To get at the meaning and value of school referrals for firms' human resource departments, I surveyed approximately 130 employers in the late 1990s in Kanagawa prefecture.[18] The survey included multiple-choice questions followed by space for the respondents to write in their reasoning for choosing a specific answer. These data, particularly the responses to the open-ended "why" questions, provide a rich resource for understanding the significance of institutional social capital (school introductions) for employers' recruitment of high school graduates.

[17] See Brinton and Kariya (1998). Also see Chiavacci (2005).
[18] I am grateful to **Hirata Shūichi** of the Japan Institute of Labour Policy and Training for helping me design the survey instrument.

JAPANESE EMPLOYERS' EVALUATION OF INSTITUTIONAL SOCIAL CAPITAL

The 128 employers I surveyed were drawn from the 850 employers who had submitted job opening announcements for graduating high school seniors to a local public employment security office in Kanagawa prefecture in the mid-1990s for approval before sending them on to local high schools. I am deeply indebted to a kind public employment security office official who bundled up and gave me all of the job announcements designated for high school seniors for an entire year. Some of the 850 employers had multiple job openings and thus filed more than one job announcement, resulting in more than 1,200 forms in total. These documents provide a window through which we can get a clear view of the job market for high school graduates at the midpoint of the 1990s, when the high school-work system was still operating but was beginning to falter. They inform the analysis in Chapter 4 and also provided a pool from which I could sample employers and do a more intensive survey on their attitudes and behaviors vis-à-vis hiring. The story of how I came upon the gold mine of detailed job opening announcements bears recounting, so I will take a short detour here to tell it.

When I went to the interview I had scheduled with an official at a particular public employment security office in Kawasaki, my intention was to get a sense of how the office handles the issue of being responsible for processing job opening forms and serving as the intermediary between employers and high schools. The older man I interviewed was glad to discuss his work with me, show me examples of numerous job announcements, and explain the mind-boggling minutiae entered on each job form sent by companies' human resource departments.

As we pored over the forms and my rapport with the official increased, I asked if it might be possible to xerox a few forms so that I could take them with me as reference material. I had been shown many job opening announcements by teachers in the guidance departments of the high schools I had visited, but had not had the temerity to ask if I could acquire some of them to study for my research. The official at first replied, "Sure, we can make copies of some of them for you – perhaps ten or so will be enough?" But as he got up from his chair and turned to the towering stacks of documents behind him, he had a second thought. "You know, we have all of the job announcements from last year ..., Shall I just give you all of them?" This suggestion was equivalent in my mind to being granted access to a gold mine. Trying to conceal my elation, I quietly but enthusiastically said that that would be wonderful. But already he was having second (and third) thoughts: There were so many job announcements that the volume of paper would be too heavy for me to carry, given that I needed to walk back to the train station and go home. I quickly responded that I was very *jōbu* (strong) and that it would be no problem at all. But by now he was mulling over his offer more thoroughly: Wasn't it inconsiderate to ask this small American woman to stagger out of the public employment security office with armfuls of legal-size documents? Furthermore, was it all right for him, a Japanese bureaucrat, to give them to me in the first place?

Seeing seeds of doubt sprouting before my eyes, I reminded the public employment security office bureaucrat that I would be using the data only for academic purposes and would be careful to protect the identity of the firms who had filed their job opening announcements with his office. I also briefly remarked how hard it is for researchers to get original data and that we are rather crazy to even want this type of information in the first place (adding once again, coincidentally, that I had very strong arms with which to carry the bags of documents). By the time we finished our conversation, I was somewhat chagrined to find myself being driven to the train station by a young, lower-status bureaucrat at the public employment security office so that I "wouldn't have to walk so far" carrying four large shopping bags of golden data.

After the extensive data entry and coding required to tabulate the characteristics of firms, I drew a sample from among them. I focused only on firms recruiting young men or recruiting both young men and young women, so as to target my questions to the male youth labor market.[19] I did this in order to assess how employers viewed their recruitment of new graduates into jobs that would potentially be long-term – a much more likely employer expectation for young men than women. Of the 1,208 job openings filed by the 850 firms, 60 percent were targeted only to men, 23 percent to men and women, and 17 percent only to women. I constructed my sample of firms so as to slightly over-represent small- and medium-sized firms because it became evident that some large firms listed as the contact person a human resource manager in the main office when in fact the recruitment was occurring at a branch. In cases such as this, the phone calls made by my research assistant or myself to the

---

[19] At this time it was still legal for Japanese employers to designate a job as only open to males, only open to females, or open to both sexes. In the late 1990s it became formally illegal to label job openings in this way.

TABLE 2.2. *Characteristics of Firms in the Employer Survey*

Firm size	30–10,773 employees (median=194)	
Establishment year	1870–1988	
Location of main office	Tokyo metropolitan area	69%
	Kanagawa prefecture (mainly Yokohama and Kawasaki)	31%
Industry	Manufacturing	25%
	Construction	24%
	Sales	20%
	Financial, educational, and other professional services	18%
	Personal services (e.g. auto repair, hotels, restaurants)	13%
Number of firms surveyed	128	

human resource department of the main office were sometimes met with the answer, "We don't know how recruitment at that branch is taking place, so we can't answer your questions."[20]

The largest firms among the total of 850 had more than 50,000 employees and the smallest had just two employees; the median company size was 150 employees. About 60 percent of the employers are in the Tokyo area and 40 percent in Kanagawa (mainly in Yokohama and Kawasaki). About one-third of the firms have more than one office or plant, and the median workplace size (what economists call "establishment size" as opposed to "firm size") is just 60 employees. I will have more to say about the industries and jobs in these firms in Chapter 5, when I return to the job opening data to analyze how specific local high schools were linked to these employers.

Table 2.2 shows the principal characteristics of the sample of firms in my survey (hereafter, the "Employer Survey"). In the questionnaire I asked employers about their strategies for hiring male high school graduates and about their views on how the high school-work system operates in Japan, such as the requirement that employers file job opening announcements with the local public employment security office

---

[20] I am indebted to Miyazaki Takeshi for his research assistance in conducting the employer survey.

before contacting high schools to ask them to recommend their best students. I inquired about the main characteristics employers look for in entry-level hires; whether they preferred to recruit repeatedly, year after year, from one high school or set of schools or whether they did not have such a preference (and why); how long they expected new hires to remain with the firm; and how they viewed the quality of high school graduates and whether they think it has changed over time.

One of the clearest things that emerged from this research on employers – the "demand side" of the labor market – was the value they attributed to institutional social capital. I asked employers to choose which of the following two methods for recruiting high school graduates they would ideally prefer: "hiring high school graduating seniors with the school as the intermediary, as is the current practice" or "making hiring decisions by dealing directly with the applicants, as is the current practice in the case of new university graduates" (where the main provisions of the Japanese Employment Security Law do not apply). Nearly 70 percent chose the current way of hiring high school seniors as the most desirable. This was true regardless of the type of industry the firm was in or other characteristics of the firm such as size. Among the minority of personnel officers who said that they do not like the system the way it is, the most common reason they expressed was that, after all, the interview with the applicant is the most important thing, so having the school as the intermediary is not a necessary step in the process.

Employers gave a number of reasons for favoring the system of having high schools serve as the intermediary between high school seniors and themselves. Their reasons can be categorized into three general types: 1) Reasons that reflect employers' perceived efficiency of the recruiting and job-matching process, 2) a feeling that since applicants are minors they require help from the school, and 3) reasons that reflect employers' feeling that if they can establish a relationship of trust with a small number of schools and recruit from those schools year after year, this helps strengthen and reproduce the particular culture inside their workplace (what I will refer to below as "culture-building"). In other words, many employers felt that the established system of having schools as the intermediary gave them a framework within which they could develop and nurture long-term relationships with specific schools – and in the process, hire workers whom they could train and expect to remain with the firm for a number of years. Employers expressed the view that close employer-school relationships heightened the likelihood that employees' relationships with one another in the workplace would be harmonious and productive.

Institutional Social Capital as "Efficient." Having teachers in high schools' career guidance departments prescreen applicants has been highly cost-effective for Japanese firms, especially in periods when they have had many job openings to fill. The *hitori isshasei* system (the "one person, one company" system where a school recommends only one student per job opening) was the strong norm until recently, and was a highly efficient and time-saving way for firms to hire graduating seniors. Because the school picked just one applicant to recommend to the employer for an interview, firms did not need to spend time interviewing multiple applicants from one school for the same job.[21]

Employers nurtured their ties with particular schools and these ties represented valuable institutional social capital for them as well as for job-seeking high school seniors. When I asked, "Does your company view it as desirable to recruit from the same high school(s) every year?", nearly two-thirds of the personnel officers in the survey answered affirmatively. This held across companies in different industries. Personnel officers in older, well-established companies were especially likely to feel that repeat recruitment from the same schools was a good thing. Among the minority (one-third) of firms with personnel officers who stated that recruitment from the same schools year after year is not a good thing, the principal reasons given were that "applicants themselves are more important than their schools" and "it makes the range of applications narrow."

Many personnel officers spoke of the importance of the trust relationship (*shinrai kankei*) between their firm and certain schools. The following comments were typical responses to the question of why repeat recruitment from the same school(s) is a good rule of thumb:

"The strong ties to the school(s) make it easier to hire someone if there is a boom in business."

> – Small pharmaceuticals manufacturing firm, established in 1931. The firm has 290 employees and sent job opening forms to two general high schools and one industrial high school.

"Because the schools understand our company."

> – Electronics appliance maker with 367 employees, established in 1968. The firm sent a job announcement to one general high school.

---

[21] For additional discussion of the details of high school-work processes, see Okano (1993).

"Repeat recruitment helps improve the implicit understanding and sense of trust between the school and the company. Hiring students recommended by the school can be done smoothly."

> – Apparel manufacturing firm with 392 employees, established in 1952. The firm sent a job opening form to one general high school.

"It is easy to recruit if there are already alumni from the school in the company. And the applicants from the same school also feel reassured (*anshin dekiru*)."

> – Sightseeing bus company with 217 employees, established in 1950. The company sent a job announcement to five general high schools and one commercial high school.

"Through the school's graduates we have hired in previous years, we are able to communicate an understanding of our company's environment to the students and to the teachers in charge of guidance counseling."

> – Electronics firm with 332 employees, established in 1961. The firm sent a job announcement to one industrial high school.

One of the most striking themes in employers' positive view of recruitment relationships with one school or a set of schools is the idea of being able to build on the shared connection of previous and current years' recruits to the high school from which they graduated. Although I distinguished three principal motivations for employers to favor the school-as-intermediary system – it makes the recruitment process more efficient, high school students are minors and need the assistance of their school in applying for jobs, and the system helps employers form trust relationships with certain schools – in point of fact, these motivations are often mixed together in employers' thinking and expressions. The comments above show that one of the reasons employers view continuous recruitment from the same school or set of schools as efficient is that they assume that employees will more readily socialize and train new recruits who are young alumni of the same school. Whether or not current employees personally knew these new recruits when they were in school, the implicit senior-junior (*senpai-kōhai*) relationship is a cultural idiom on which many employers draw. It is a template for human relationships that is well understood by all parties involved – employers, employees, high school students and their parents, and high school teachers.

Institutional Social Capital as Culture-Building. As many employers' comments evince, they do not think of efficiency only in terms of a reduction in the costs of screening and recruiting applicants. Many employers who prefer to recruit from the same high school(s) every year say that it facilitates new employees' adaptation to their jobs, which

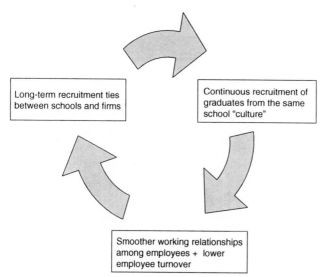

FIGURE 2.5. Japanese Employers' Use of Recruitment Ties to Build Strong Working Relationships among Employees.

ultimately reduces turnover. Employers attach importance to the building of social ties inside the workplace. They capitalize on existing social capital (over-time recruitment ties with certain schools) rather than starting from scratch and creating bonds among new employees who do not have a shared background. Employers can assume that if new employees come from the same *ba* (school) as older employees, they share a common culture and a common value system. One could say that employers use long-term recruitment ties with schools to actively convert the social capital from one *ba* (school) into social capital in another *ba* (company), as shown in Figure 2.5.

In response to the open-ended question in my survey asking employers to explain why they did or did not favor repeat recruitment from the same school or set of schools over the years, the *senpai-kōhai* idiom repeatedly appeared:

Recruitment from the same schools cultivates companionship in the work organization.

The senior employees tend to help the junior ones when necessary, if they come from the same school.

Senior employees will help junior employees from the same school to adapt to the work organization.

Having a trust relationship between our firm and the school(s) is helpful. If there are alumni from their school in the firm, the new graduates feel reassured.

Recruitment from the same schools tends to make the *senpai-kōhai* (senior-junior) relationships in the workplace good. And this makes our employee retention rate good.

This sense of security expresses well the conservatizing, stabilizing influence of employers' successive recruitment of new graduates from the same set of schools. It is a feeling of security – for both employers and high school graduates – that came to be the object of envy on the part of many other postindustrial societies by the end of the 1980s. But the other side of this security was that Japanese men's wages, promotional possibilities, and to some extent their identity rested on their attachment to a workplace *ba*. The importance of *ba* for economic and psychological well-being, together with the solid institutional pathway from the *ba* of school to the *ba* of workplace, constituted a rigid but reliable structure within which men's early work lives played out. The next chapter goes into this more deeply and shows how cracks began to develop in this structure by the early 1990s.

3

The Importance of *Ba*, the Erosion of *Ba*

"*Arubaito* [students' part-time jobs] are officially prohibited by our school. But even so, as teachers we know full well that students have jobs. We can't completely enforce the prohibition."

– Teacher in the guidance department of a low-ranking public general high school

Multiple contradictions emerged in the 1990s in the Japanese high school-work transition process. On the one hand, many employers continued to value what I called in Chapter 2 the institutional social capital of schools. They continued to rejuvenate their workplaces by hiring new graduates from the same schools they had traditionally turned to, drawing on the inherent predisposition for camaraderie that they presumed school alumni would feel for one another. Many employers continued to expect and hope that their new hires would stay in the firm for many years. In this way, they were stakeholders in their new employees' futures.

The institutional social capital students had access to via their attachment to school was translated by employers into institutional social capital and "social glue" among employees. Meanwhile, as I will say more about in this chapter, parents continued to rely on the school as a stakeholder in their adolescents' futures. Many parents whose adolescents were not proceeding on to higher education viewed high school as the principal institution that would actively guide their teenagers into the next phase of their lives and orient them to the world of work.

As the economic recession in Japan deepened and employment restructuring became more widespread across firms in the 1990s, large cracks emerged in this web of support for young men's journey out of high

school and into stable full-time jobs. The economic squeeze on employers became stronger. What came to be called the ice age of employment
froze ever more solidly. Fewer and fewer employers were able or willing
to follow the employment model for which Japan had become famous
in the 1960s–1980s, when firms had engaged in blanket recruitment of
young workers and had invested in them through on-the-job training and
implicit guarantees of long-term employment.

As employers cut back on the number of full-time positions they
offered to new graduates in the 1990s, many high schools found it harder
and harder to hold on to their stable recruitment ties with employers.
The number of full-time job openings shrank and the quality of jobs
available to high school graduates deteriorated. Employers' assurance to
high schools' guidance departments that they would hire new graduates
waivered.

With these developments, high school itself became a less important
ba for non-college-going students. While teachers in high schools' guidance departments continued to struggle to match high school seniors into
full-time jobs, more and more non-university-bound students began to
feel that their school couldn't be very helpful. Some young people began
to openly ask, "Why work hard in school, just to get your school's recommendation to a job you don't want?" A teacher at a low-ranking general
public high school expressed his frustration to me in the following way:

We have many students who want sales or office jobs ... but our school gets
almost no job opening announcements for these. So we sometimes say to students,
"How about switching to another type of service job or to a technical job?" But
their answer is usually something like, "No, forget it – I'll wait until I graduate
and then I'll look for a job." In that case, they don't need our [the school's] recommendation to an employer; they just need to show that they graduated from high
school. They don't need to show their grades or their attendance records."

An article in one of Japan's leading newspapers, the *Asahi Evening News*,
summed up the situation in stark terms: "With the number of jobs for
senior high school graduates continuing to plummet, teachers feel the
raison d'être of high schools is under challenge" (*Asahi Evening News*,
January 2000).

But it wasn't only high schools that became less central in young people's lives. It is ironic that attachment to a workplace became less relevant
as well. More and more employers offered part-time rather than full-time
jobs to new graduates. But just as important, employers stepped up their
hiring of high school students into part-time jobs (*arubaito*). In doing

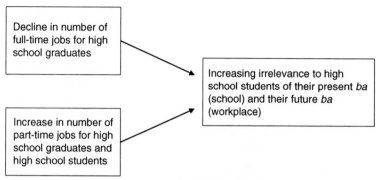

FIGURE 3.1. The Declining Importance of the *Ba* of School and Workplace for High School Students in the Lost Generation.

so, employers, in effect, thumbed their nose at what had been a long-standing credo of Japanese high schools that students should not hold jobs. Employers' willingness to hire students into part-time jobs further weakened the social control that nonelite high schools had exercised over their students. The significance to young people of being full-time, fully participating members of the *ba* of school and later, the *ba* of the workplace, began to get diluted. How could these affiliations be important anymore, if schools couldn't fulfill their promise of guiding their graduates into full-time jobs and if *arubaito* were there for the taking while one was still a student, with or without the blessing of one's school? Japan's renowned human capital development system just didn't work anymore for significant numbers of young men, especially the least educated among them. Figure 3.1 illustrates this chain of causality.

The loss of practical and psychological significance to young men of being a fully participating member of a high school and then of a workplace produced deleterious effects on young men by the early twenty-first century that rippled outward through Japanese society. To understand better why this is the case, the first part of this chapter explains the economic importance that work experience – especially long-term, full-time employment in one firm – held for Japanese men in the high-growth period preceding the last decade of the twentieth century. Using data from a national sample of Japanese men in the lost generation and in the two cohorts preceding that one, I show that an introduction through one's high school continues to be the most effective way for nonuniversity bound young men to move into employment in a large firm and to achieve a number of other desirable labor market outcomes – even as such introductions become scarcer and scarcer.

In the second part of the chapter, I relate how teachers endeavored to continue guiding nonuniversity bound seniors into jobs even as the centrality of high school as the launching pad into the labor market diminished in the 1990s. That decade saw the participation of more and more Japanese high school students in *arubaito* and the consequent bypassing of their high schools' guidance department. Many of these young people increasingly came to regard school and teachers as irrelevant to their lives. Later in the book I turn to the meaning of all of this for Japanese young people's identities and their relationship to society. The institutionalized school-work pathways were a piece of the scaffolding supporting the structure of trust in Japanese society. As that scaffolding has collapsed, the foundations of personal identity have become more unstable. This raises thorny issues for young people and for Japanese society writ large.

THE ECONOMIC IMPORTANCE OF *BA*: WAGES

Research has documented that work experience and attachment to a specific workplace are particularly important for an individual's earnings in Japan compared to other countries. Labor economists and sociologists have conducted many studies examining how individuals' wages are determined by their human capital, gender, and the industry and occupation in which they work. Human capital is typically measured as years of education and accumulated years of work experience, with work experience encompassing the number of years someone has been employed and, more specifically, the number of years he or she has worked for the same company (job tenure).[1]

Tachibanaki and his colleagues compared the determinants of men's wages across eight countries: Japan, the U.S., Canada, Korea, Australia, the UK, Germany, and France (Tachibanaki 1998). Not surprisingly, they found that in all of these countries upper white-collar workers such as managers and professionals tend to make higher earnings than lower-level service sector workers (workers in sales and services) or blue-collar workers such as those in construction and manufacturing. But Tachibanaki and his colleagues also found that the importance of a man's occupation in determining his wages differs across countries.

---

[1] Studies have documented that in Japan, gender is the most important individual characteristic affecting wages, trumping education, labor force experience, and job tenure. See Tachibanaki (1998).

TABLE 3.1. *Relative Effects of Social Background, Education, and Labor Force Experience on Individual Income: Japan, United States, and Britain*

	Japan	U.S.	Britain
Social background	39%	37%	44%
Education	19%	32%	38%
Labor force experience	42%	31%	18%
Total	100%	100%	100%

Source: Adapted from Table 4.2, Ishida (1993, p. 90). Percentages reflect the proportion of variance in income explained by each variable. The figures have been rounded by the present author.

Japan stands out as a country where occupation per se – the type of work a person does – is not very important in determining earnings. In other words, wage inequality across occupations is relatively low in Japan. As Tachibanaki points out, it is well established in the social science literature that education and occupation are highly correlated in country after country. So to find that occupation does not strongly determine wages in Japan also implies that education is not of great importance. This may strike readers as odd, given Japan's image as a "credential society." What then is especially important in determining Japanese men's earnings? Work experience.

Work Experience. Table 3.1 shows the proportion of variance in men's earnings that is attributable to social background (parents' education and occupation), education, and years of work experience in Japan, the U.S., and Britain. These data are for the mid-1970s, an appropriate time point because the so-called Japanese employment system, with its emphasis on on-the-job-training, seniority wages, and long-term employment, was in its prime in that period. We can therefore see what the "typical" pattern of wage determination was like under Japan's characteristic human capital development system.

The table shows that a man's social background has a large effect on his earnings in each country; it explains nearly 40 percent of men's earnings in Japan and the U.S. and even more than this in Britain. What is most striking about Japan is that the relative effects of education and labor force experience are the reverse of what they are in the U.S. and Britain. In other words, the effect of education on Japanese men's earnings pales in comparison to the effect of work experience. Years of education explain a little less than 20 percent of the variance in Japanese men's earnings, whereas work experience explains more than 40 percent.

In contrast, education and work experience have roughly equal weight in explaining the variance in American men's earnings, and education in Britain carries much greater importance than work experience in determining earnings.

These comparisons illustrate how important it is for Japanese men to accumulate work experience in order to reap high earnings. This should sound a warning bell when we consider the statistics on the numbers of young Japanese men who have accumulated little full-time work experience in postbubble Japan. The implications for their future earnings are sobering.

The relatively small effect of education on earnings in Japan is quite surprising. But it is consistent with the fact that Japan has had a relatively small wage gap between blue- and white-collar workers compared to many other countries.[2] It has often been noted that blue-collar workers in Japan tend to experience a pattern of wage increases as they age that is similar to that of their white-collar counterparts (Koike 1999). Blue-collar workers in most Western economies do not experience consistent wage increases as they age; Japanese blue-collar workers, especially those in large firms, do. This observation is reflected in Koike's now-classic phrase "the white-collarization of Japanese blue-collar workers" (Koike 1988).

The blanket recruitment of Japanese high school graduates into entry-level positions in firm-internal labor markets (job ladders within firms) that was explained in Chapter 2 has been partly responsible for the lesser importance of education and occupation for earnings in Japan than in many other countries. In other words, Japan has been a country where a young man could get a good blue-collar job by completing high school and getting a full-time job through his school's recommendation to an employer. But the importance of getting your foot in the door immediately after graduation – landing in either a full-time blue-collar or white-collar job in a good workplace *ba* – has been especially important in Japan for another reason too: Firm-specific experience contributes heavily to wages. As middle-aged Japanese males will attest, getting a good job and staying in a good job matter.

Firm-Specific Work Experience. Work experience has a double-barreled impact on Japanese men's earnings across their life cycle: Along with the sheer positive impact of continuous years of work experience, men get

---

[2] See Brown et al. (1997), Hashimoto and Raisian (1985), and Kalleberg and Lincoln (1988).

an additional earnings boost by accumulating long work experience in a specific firm. This effect is especially large for workers who have spent their careers in firms with more than 1,000 employees. Large-firm employment is important for Japanese workers' lifetime earnings because age-earnings profiles are steeper than in smaller firms and also because the risk of being laid off is lower than in smaller firms. In contrast, the difference in American men's earnings across firms of different sizes is lower (Hashimoto and Raisian 1985).

Given the economic benefits of full-time employment in a large firm, which men in Japan have been most able to take advantage of this system? From the beginning, Japan's lifetime employment model was premised on a dual labor market. In the core sector, men were hired straight out of school into large firms that trained them and paid successively higher wages over time on the premise that employer and employee were bound together in an implicit long-term contract. The majority of individuals, though, did not move into such jobs but instead into a more fluid secondary or noncore labor market characterized by individuals' movement in and out of smaller firms that were generally characterized by less financial stability. Self-employment or work in a family business was another destination for some graduates, although that option shrank markedly as the size of the agricultural sector declined with Japan's transition into a full-blown industrial economy.

THE PROCESS OF LABOR MARKET ENTRY:
CHANGE ACROSS SOCIAL GENERATIONS

Data from the 2005 Social Stratification and Mobility (SSM) Survey, a national survey conducted every ten years in Japan, allow us to see how education and the time period in which a man entered the labor market have affected the type of employment he entered after graduation, as well as the character of his employment experiences during his first five years out of school. These recent national data are especially valuable because they include members of the lost generation.

I separated the 2,600 men in the SSM sample with employment experience into three groups based on the time period when they finished their schooling: before 1978, 1978–91, or 1992–2000. I set the time periods in this way in order to represent social generations in the sense that Mannheim and Chauvel articulate (see Chapter 1); men who left school in each of these three time periods faced a very different labor market from that faced by the other two social generations. While alternative demarcations are certainly possible, I chose 1978 as a cutpoint because Japan's postwar era of high economic growth arguably ended by that point. After sustaining yearly rates of economic growth between 8 and 21 percent over a twenty-year period, Japan in the 1980s experienced economic growth rates in the range of 4 to 7 percent. The economic growth rate plummeted in 1991–2 and the economy has experienced only moderate and short-lived periods of recovery since then. I thus chose 1992 as the second cutpoint.

Table 3.2 shows the educational backgrounds, characteristics of first job, and early labor market experiences of Japanese men in these three social generations. Because my focus is on the similarity or divergence of the lost generation's experiences from prior cohorts, the table starts by displaying the figures for the lost generation in the first column on the left. Figures in the second column depict the early labor market experiences of men who finished school mainly during the decade of the 1980s (what we could call the economic bubble cohort), and figures in the third column represent the experiences of men who finished school earlier, during Japan's high-growth period.

The table shows the large increase over time in the proportion of men who graduated from university. Reading the table from right to left, fewer than 20 percent of men in the oldest cohort (who entered the labor market before 1980) were university graduates compared to nearly 45 percent in the lost generation. Conversely, 25 percent of older men had entered the labor market having only finished junior high school, whereas this was the case for fewer than 4 percent of men in the lost generation.[3] The proportion of men who completed their education with high school graduation fell from 50 to about 35 percent between the oldest and youngest cohorts. Conversely, attendance at two-year training schools (*senmon gakkō*) became a much more common phenomenon, with rates of attendance tripling across this time period.

While high school graduates are the principal focus of this book, most graduates from two-year training schools are also lost in the transition from school to work, albeit under different circumstances. Two-year training schools are not accredited by the Japanese government, and have not been subject to the well-oiled mechanisms of the school-work transition system. Rates of attendance at these schools, which are privately

---

[3] These figures on changes in educational attainment closely mirror national figures reported by the Ministry of Education, Culture, Sports, Science and Technology.

TABLE 3.2. *Education and Early Employment Experiences of Men in the Lost Generation, Economic Bubble Cohort, and High Economic-Growth Cohort*[1]

	Lost Generation (N=399)		Economic Bubble Cohort (N=723)		High Economic-Growth Cohort (N=1478)
Educational Attainment					
Junior high school	3.5		4.7	***	25.2
High school	34.7	***	45.0	*	50.2
Two-year training school[2]	18.6	*	13.4	***	5.8
University or higher	43.2	*	36.9	***	18.8
Employment Status in First Job					
Regular full-time employee	76.5	***	87.1	***	80.9
Temporary or part-time employee	16.0	***	7.2	*	5.0
Employee dispatched by agency or contract employee	3.4	***	.4		.6
Self-employed, freelance, or working in family business	4.1		5.3	***	13.6
For Employees Only:					
Regular full-time	79.8	***	91.9		93.6
Temporary, part-time, dispatched, or contract workers	20.2	***	8.1		6.4
Full-time employee in a large firm[3]	32.1	***	44.0		42.2
Entered workforce within one month of graduation	79.0	***	88.0		86.8
Route into first job					
School introduction	40.4		44.4		46.4
Social ties (family, friends, acquaintances)	18.3	*	24.6	***	32.1
Job advertisements	25.6	***	15.3	***	7.5
School alumni, public employment office, private employment agency, other	15.7		15.7		14.0
Held only one job during first five years since leaving school	57.1		62.6		65.5
Held at least one part-time job within first five years since leaving school	31.0	***	16.1		17.6

Notes:

[1] Asterisks in columns between each pair of cohorts indicate a statistically significant difference between the two cohorts on that variable. *p<.05, **p<.01, ***p<.001

[2] Junior college is also a two-year program, but it is almost exclusively a female track. Because the table represents only the experiences of men I do not include junior college here.

[3] Large firm is defined as a workplace with at least 750 employees.

Source: Author's calculations from SSM 2005 data.

run and specialize in a dizzying array of occupational preparation from the frivolous to the practical, grew dramatically in the 1970s-1990s. The employment outcomes for their graduates vary as widely as the tuition and fees charged for students at these schools (although there may well be a neutral or even a negative relationship between the costs of attending and the probability of securing a good job afterwards).

Along with the necessity of being experts on the workings of the labor market, high school teachers at middle- and low-ranking general and vocational high schools have had to become savvy as well with regard to judging the quality of the two-year training schools their students become interested in. With no accreditation or other official statistics to rely on, this is no easy task. While not the central focus of my research or interviews, teachers had a lot to say about two-year training schools, and their comments made it clear that they were expected to advise students and their parents on the pros and cons of proceeding to this next level of schooling. As one teacher put it, "Students can't get jobs just by saying they went to a two-year training school and studied. This works for maybe half the students who go. But really, if they don't gain some skills and qualifications, then graduating from a two-year training school is the equivalent of graduating from high school." He continued, describing how he and other high school teachers try to glean more information from two-year training schools in order to judge the quality of their curriculum: "We ask about the kinds of students they are looking for, what type of qualifications students can gain if they study hard, what the job outlook is like, and so forth. Then we can say to students, 'That two-year training school is pretty good' or 'How about such-and-such a school?' Right now we are doing this kind of thing."

This teacher continued:

The two-year training schools that have clear purposes are good. But it seems like the number of schools that don't do a good job is increasing; you know, they are not acting like high schools, where students study a certain number of hours at school ... . But some two-year training schools do send our graduates' grades to us, to show that they have a good educational environment. They know that if we think that such-and-such a two-year training school is not very good, we won't advise our students to go there. So they try to show us that the school is really giving something to its students, and in that way they are doing a kind of PR with us so that we will talk to our students about the possibility of going to that school.

Even though more men in the lost generation went to two-year training school or university than their predecessors, they are less likely than older men to have entered a regular full-time job when they finished school. Only three-quarters did so (column 1), compared to nearly 90 percent of the men who entered the labor market during the 1980s (column 2). Men who began working prior to the 1980s (column 3) had higher rates than later-born men of working in a family business or being self-employed (more than 13 percent); when these are added to the group who entered full-time regular employment, nearly 95 percent of men in the oldest cohort entered full-time work when they graduated. In contrast, the lost generation has by far the highest percentage of men (nearly 20 percent) entering temporary, part-time, or short-term contract jobs.[4] The likelihood of entry into this type of unstable work is more than twice as high for this generation than for each of the two preceding ones.

These figures are consistent with statistics on the increase in part-time, irregular work for young Japanese that I showed in Chapter 1. But the SSM data give additional insight into the ways men in the lost generation found their jobs and the characteristics of their early employment experiences compared to previous cohorts. Because the experience of becoming an employee is fundamentally different from the experience of entering a family business or becoming self-employed, I restrict the lower half of Table 3.2 to men who were employees in their first job (constituting the great majority of men in each cohort). That is, I delete self-employed and family enterprise workers in order to sharpen the focus on employees.

The distinctive experiences of men in the lost generation show up clearly: They are less likely to have entered the labor force as regular full-time employees (80 percent) than men in previous cohorts (92 and 94 percent respectively), less likely to have entered a large firm (32 percent versus 44 and 42 percent), and less likely to have started their job immediately after graduation (79 percent versus 88 and 87 percent). It is notable that the difference in these experiences between the lost generation and the generation that entered the labor market in the 1980s is much greater than between the latter generation and the older one. This distinction is indicated by asterisks, which show whether the difference across adjacent cohorts is statistically significant or not.

Consistent with the discussion in Chapter 2, for all three cohorts of men a school introduction was the most prevalent way of finding their first job. At least 40 percent of men secured their first job through this route, and the differences across cohorts are not statistically significant. The proportion of men using social ties (either strong or weak) has

[4] Contract workers are typically dispatched to companies from a private employment agency where they have registered their availability for work.

declined markedly from the oldest to the youngest cohort. The use of job advertisements has likewise increased significantly. One-quarter of men in the lost generation report that this is the way they found their first job, compared to just 15 percent of men who entered the labor market in the 1980s and less than 8 percent of men who entered before 1980. The proportions of men entering employment through any other path (introductions from school alumni, consultation with the public employment office, or referral from a private employment agency) are trivial, amounting to only about 15 percent of men in any of the cohorts.

The last two rows in the table summarize men's first five years of work experience after school graduation. Statistically equivalent proportions (about 60 percent) of men in each cohort worked in only one job across the first five years of their careers. But men in the lost generation are nearly twice as likely (31 percent) as men in the previous cohort (16 percent) to have experienced part-time work at some point, whereas the probability of experiencing part-time work did not change between the oldest and the middle cohort.

In sum, the biggest differences in early work experiences show up as those between the lost generation and the cohort immediately preceding it. This highlights the recency of the change in work circumstances in Japan. A second conclusion from the table is the continued prevalence of school introductions as a way into the labor market, with the use of job advertisements greatly gaining in importance and the use of social ties declining markedly over time.

These experiences reflect men at all levels of education. To see more precisely the experiences of the male educational nonelite – high school graduates – who became employees after finishing school, I constructed Table 3.3. As in the previous table, the biggest differences in early employment experiences are between men in the lost generation and men in the cohort that entered the labor market in the 1980s.

I also did a further comparison (not shown here) between high school graduates and university graduates in each cohort to see if level of education matters more for the lost generation than it did for men in prior cohorts. The results show that lost generation high school graduates do not fare worse relative to their university-educated counterparts than was the case for older cohorts when it comes to the timing of entering the labor market after leaving school, the probability of staying in the same job during the first five years after leaving school, or the probability of having a part-time job at some point during those early years of employment. In all cohorts, university graduates tend to hold a more privileged

TABLE 3.3. *Early Employment Experiences of Male High School Graduates in the Lost Generation, Economic Bubble Cohort, and High Economic-Growth Cohort*[1]

	Lost Generation (N=191)		Economic Bubble Cohort (N=384)		High Economic-Growth Cohort (N=527)
Employees in First Job					
Regular full-time	73.4	***	92.0	*	95.0
Temporary, part-time, dispatched, or contract	26.6	***	8.0	*	5.0
Full-time employee in large firm	27.3	***	40.0	*	46.7
Route into first job					
School introduction	46.1		49.9		53.4
Social ties (family, friends, acquaintances)	18.8	*	26.5		27.2
Job advertisements	21.1	*	10.3	**	6.7
School alumni, public employment office, private employment agency, other	14.0		13.3		12.7
Entered workforce within one month of graduation	75.8	**	88.7		87.3
Held only one job during first five years since leaving school	44.5		57.3		63.0
Job was a regular full-time job in a large firm[2]	27.3	*	40.2	*	53.0
Held at least one part-time job within first five years since leaving school	39.8	***	18.5		16.4

Notes:
[1] Asterisks in columns between each pair of cohorts indicate a statistically significant difference between the two cohorts on that variable. *p<.05, **p<.01, ***p<.001.
[2] Large firm is defined as a workplace with at least 750 employees.
Source: Author's calculations from SSM 2005 data.

position in the labor market in terms of employment during the first five years out of school. But it is in the lost cohort where the quality of the first job differs the most between high school and university graduates: Whereas more than 90 percent of both groups of employed men in

the economic bubble cohort and the older cohort were full-time employees in their first job, this was true for only about three-quarters of high
school graduates in the lost generation. These men thus fell way behind
prior cohorts of high school graduates, in addition to faring worse than
their same-age counterparts who are university educated. They clearly
stand out as a social generation that has experienced a different environment than the prior two groups of men.

The Value of School Introductions. It is interesting that even though
high school graduate males in the lost generation were as likely as their
predecessors to secure their first full-time job through a school introduction, a much higher proportion of them entered part-time work instead.
Did the high school introduction system thereby serve men in the lost
generation less well than it had their predecessors? Actually, quite the
opposite is true. My statistical analyses show that 100 percent of lost
generation men who secured their first job through a school introduction started the job within one month of graduation, compared to about
half as many (55 percent) who had not secured their first job through an
introduction from their school. Among men in the "economic bubble"
cohort, almost as many (97 percent) of those who had used a school
introduction entered their first job within one month of leaving school,
but so did 80 percent of those who did not go through the school introduction process. The figures are similar for men in the older generation.
In other words, the probability of a young man starting a job soon after
leaving school if he used his school's institutional social capital rather
than another job-finding route is significantly higher in the lost generation than in the prior two cohorts.

Figure 3.2 shows how likely it was that a school introduction was
related to a young man securing a job as a full-time employee in a large
firm, having just one job over the first five years since graduating, and
experiencing part-time employment at any point during those first five
years. If a school introduction was no more or less associated than other
job-finding routes with each of these employment outcomes, then the
number is 1.0. Numbers higher than 1.0 mean that the likelihood of each
employment outcome was greater with a school introduction than with
other job-finding routes; numbers below 1.0 indicate that the likelihood
is lower.

For all cohorts of male high school graduates, those who had been
introduced to their first postgraduation job through their school were
significantly more likely to be in what has traditionally been considered a
good job – full-time employment in a large firm – than their counterparts

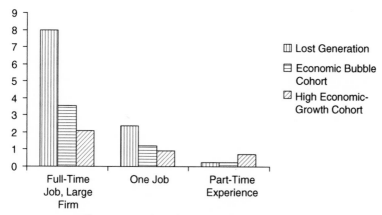

FIGURE 3.2. Effectiveness of a School Introduction for Men's Early Employment Outcomes.
Source: Author's calculations from SSM 2005 data.

who had landed their jobs through social ties or job advertisements. Men in the lost generation benefitted from a school introduction more than men in the other two cohorts; the young men who used a school recommendation were nearly eight times as likely to get such a job as others in their cohort who used other routes to find a job. Men in the older two cohorts who had a school recommendation were about two to three times as likely to get such a job compared to the rest of their cohort who had used other job search methods.

Men in the lost generation who used a school introduction to enter the labor market also benefitted more than men in the other two cohorts in terms of securing stable employment (one continuous job) across the first five years after they left school. The probability of experiencing part-time employment was lower for men in the lost generation and the economic bubble cohort who had a school introduction (shown by values less than 1.0 in the set of columns on the far right-hand side of Figure 3.2) but not for men in the oldest cohort.[5]

---

[5] These statistics cannot tell us whether the school recommendation itself made all the difference in young men getting these jobs or, on the other hand, whether the young men who got a school recommendation were the ones who were more qualified to begin with. If it is the latter – that the more qualified men increasingly selected themselves into the school recommendation process over time – then this could explain why a school recommendation seems to be the most advantageous for the youngest cohort. This type of selectivity in relation to the changing "quality" of high school graduates is also discussed by Ariga (2005).

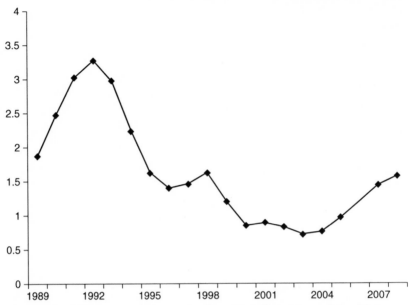

FIGURE 3.3. Change Over Time in Number of Job Openings per New High
School Graduate.
Note: This figure shows the job opening/job seeker ratio as of the end of
September of each year.

Overall, these results suggest that a school introduction has become
more – not less – valuable for male high school seniors' entrance to the
labor market. However, the number of full-time job openings shrank dramatically during the years that men in the lost generation were graduating from school. That is, even though getting a school introduction to an
employer continued to be advantageous, it became less possible as time
wore on.

Since Japanese employers specify the educational level they require for
job applicants, the government keeps statistics on the number of entry-
level jobs for new high school graduates. Figure 3.3 shows the change
over time in the *kyūjin bairitsu* (number of job openings for each job
seeker) for graduating high school seniors since 1989, when the Japanese
economy was still in its bubble period. This figure is based on statistics collected by public employment security offices throughout Japan
at the end of September each year, soon after companies announce their
job openings and well after high school seniors have told their schools
whether they will be seeking postgraduation employment. As an example,

September 16, 2007 was the official date on which firms were allowed to begin recruitment of high school seniors into full-time entry-level jobs that would begin in April 2008.

The job-opening-to-applicant ratio soared to 3.27 by 1992, which means that for every graduating high school senior there were more than three job openings. The figure fell to 2.97 in the next year and then continued to fall precipitously, reaching a dismal .72 in 2004. Since that year it has been increasing once again, but it has not yet recovered to the pre-bubble level.

These figures show the dramatic decline in the number of full-time jobs for which Japanese employers have sought new high school graduates over the past decade and a half. And it is important to recognize that even when there is more than one job opening on average per high school graduate, the labor market does not necessarily "clear," in economists' terms. That is, there may or may not be a match for every job seeker. It could be that the available jobs are in a different region than the job seeker, or that they are designated by the employer for one sex rather than the other, or simply that job applicants are a poor match for the types of jobs available. As an officer at one public employment security office remarked to me, "Even if the job-opening-to-applicant ratio suggests that on paper, each person can get a job, that is not the case. In my experience, there need to be about three times as many jobs as people in order for individuals' job wishes to be satisfied at all."

The job-opening-to-applicant ratios and youth unemployment rates vary significantly across Japan, with urban areas generally having more jobs than rural areas. This brought me to the Yokohama-Kawasaki area southwest of Tokyo as a field site for more intensive research. Here, there were still manufacturing plants in the mid-1990s ready to absorb high school graduates, the proverbial *kin no tamago* or "golden eggs" that employers wanted to gather up. A dense network of railway lines connects the area to metropolitan Tokyo with its numerous small manufacturing districts, thriving construction sector, and a service sector thirsty to absorb entry-level workers as drivers and delivery men, servers and cooks in restaurants, attendants at gas stations, and cashiers in convenience stores. I reasoned that if the school-work process was continuing to function anywhere in Japan in the 1990s, it should have been in urban areas such as Yokohama and Kawasaki.

But Chapters 4 and 5 will show that, in fact, Japan's acclaimed school-to-work transition process unraveled to a large extent even here, where in many ways it had the greatest chance of surviving.

THE VIEW FROM TEACHERS: STRUGGLING TO
PLACE GRADUATES

I have already sprinkled quotes and examples from my interviews with
high school teachers throughout the pages of the book so far. These interviews with high school teachers took place at sixteen public high schools
in Yokohama and Kawasaki (Kanagawa prefecture) and four in Sendai
(in Miyagi prefecture). I added Sendai to verify that the information and
opinions given to me by Kanagawa prefecture high school teachers were
not somehow idiosyncratic. I sampled high schools from the lower half
of the academic hierarchy in their respective school districts, as these are
the schools that send relatively fewer graduates to university and more
into the labor market. In Yokohama and Kawasaki I chose twelve general
academic high schools (throughout, I refer to these simply as "general"
high schools) and four vocational high schools, and in Sendai I chose two
general high schools and two vocational high schools to visit. Because
my focus is primarily on young men, the vocational high schools I chose
are ones that specialize in industrial preparation such as the basics of
mechanical and electrical engineering. Although industrial high schools
do not prohibit female junior high school students from applying, the student population at most industrial high schools is overwhelmingly male.
The other principal type of vocational high school is commercial, and
these are more often chosen by young women who want to prepare for
jobs in office work.

Japanese high schools' ranking in the local academic hierarchy is
easily ascertained by the minimum score achieved by the previous
year's entrants on the prefectural entrance exam for high school and by
the proportion of the school's graduates who proceed on to four-year
universities after graduation. Kanagawa turned out to be a very strategic research site for a reason I had not anticipated: The high school
guidebooks published by private companies for the benefit of the parents and teachers of middle school students contain a wealth of information about each school. (As it turns out, the guidebooks for Miyagi
prefecture, where Sendai is located, do not include individual high
schools' entrance exam scores or the postgraduation educational destinations of graduates. This makes it more difficult to ascertain schools'
relative rankings.) After buying one of the high school guidebooks for
Kanagawa prefecture, I showed it to a Japanese friend (whom I will
call Hayashi-san) who teaches high school in Yokohama. Even though
the statistics in such guidebooks are not produced by the Ministry of

Education, Culture, Sports, Science and Technology, my friend was surprised by the level of accuracy in the statistics. She was not aware of how the private publishing companies access the information, but suggested that "someone in each school must be supplying the information" (an idea I was never able to verify). As Hayashi-san commented, "These guidebooks are widely used by junior high school teachers when they are advising students about which high school to go to. The teachers' reputations depend on how well they counsel students about which high school to try for, so it is very important for them to have accurate information."

Based on advice from Hayashi-san and from officials at the Japan Institute of Labour Policy and Training, I did not focus exclusively on high schools at the very bottom of the academic hierarchy. There were two reasons. First, they wisely convinced me that my research would be less generalizable were I to sample only the "worst" high schools. Instead, they suggested that it would be best to sample public high schools from those in the bottom half of the hierarchy in a school district. The second reason not to choose the lowest-performing high schools was based specifically on Hayashi-san's own experience as a teacher in Yokohama. It was not so much the nongeneralizability of the sample that concerned her. Instead, she expressed the following concern:

The problem is that there is almost no guidance in those schools, but guidance is what you want to study, right? The teachers in schools like that have to spend all of their time just trying to keep things under control.

Unfortunately, Hayashi-san spoke from experience. She had recently been transferred from a higher-ranking school to the lower-ranking school where she currently worked. In Kanagawa, teachers at general public high schools typically put in three years at one school and then are transferred. Because Hayashi-san thought it would be wrong to refuse the placement she was given, she went along with it. But she was amazed and discouraged by what she had experienced in the first five months of teaching at her current school. As she put it, "I spend all of my time saying, 'Don't talk to your friends in class'; 'Turn off that music and take off those headphones'; 'Stop eating your lunch in the middle of class'; and so on. It's unbelievable! The students, even some of the boys, wear multiple earrings and sometimes even a lip ring. They bleach their hair blond. The girls cut inches off the skirts of their school uniforms, turning them from mid-calf length skirts into miniskirts."

When I asked Hayashi-san how long she would be at the school, she
grimaced. "The minimum [in Kanagawa prefecture] is three years. So I'm
counting .... I have two years and several months more. And then if other
teachers who are asked to transfer here refuse the request, who knows?
I may have to stay here even longer. Some of the teachers at this school
and others like it end up having to stay for seven or eight years. If no one
will rotate into the school, that's what happens. Teachers are not supposed to refuse a school placement but some do. There's no punishment.
But personally, I thought I had to accept the transfer."

My final Kanagawa sample included twelve high schools from the
lower half of the school quality distribution in four of the eight school
districts in Yokohama and Kawasaki, together with four of the nine vocational high schools in the Yokohama and Kawasaki area that have an
industrial curriculum. Students who apply to industrial high schools are
free to go outside their local school district, as not every district has an
industrial high school. Because of this, industrial high schools compete
with one another for students who are serious about having reasonable
employment prospects when they graduate. Increasingly, the top industrial high schools also send graduates to local universities.

As a teacher at one of the industrial high schools in Kanagawa proudly
told me, "Students come to this school from throughout the prefecture."
In response, I commented that newly established schools must have a hard
time getting their students into jobs. The teacher agreed, saying "*aruite
imasu*" (literally, they "walk around," meaning that they have to go out
and make the rounds of companies.) According to him, his school is lucky
because at this point in time they are on their third generation of people
who attended the school. As he commented, "A father might say to his
son, 'I went to xxx Industrial High School. Why don't you go there too?'
Also there are quite a few alumni of the school in responsible positions in
local firms – even presidents of firms – so this helps the school quite a lot
because it provides natural connections with these firms." In the context
of discussing the number of job opening announcements received by his
school for consideration by graduating seniors, a teacher at another, even
older industrial high school proudly said to me, "*Dentō ga atte*" (We have
a history), indicating that they have a long track record of placing their
graduates into companies.

Table 3.4 shows the public high school hierarchy in one of the eight
school districts in Yokohama and Kawasaki. The table shows the highly
stratified nature of the nine high schools in the district. To enter the
top high school, a student would have had to score sixty-four on the

TABLE 3.4. *High School Characteristics in a Representative School District, Yokohama-Kawasaki Area (2000)*

School	Required Entrance Exam Score	Proportion of Graduates Proceeding Directly to University
1	64	50
2	56	49
3	53	36
4	50	34
5	45	20
6	43	16
7	38	9
8	35	2
9	31	5

prefectural high school entrance examination; this contrasts to a score of just thirty-one for the lowest-ranked high school in the district. I chose four schools from this particular district for my interviews: Schools Five, Six, Seven, and Eight. The school where Hayashi-san taught is in a different district, and is similar in academic quality to School Nine in this district. Even though the discipline problems were indeed severe at her school, her personal introduction to the guidance department teachers in that school ensured that they gave me ample time to ask my questions and engage them in discussion. In fact, at her school and a number of the other low-ranking ones in my sample, teachers seemed genuinely appreciative that someone from "outside" (in my case, outside the school and outside the country as well) came into the school to ask them about their work and – in doing so – provided them a distraction to the daily frustrations they encountered in their jobs.

Similar to the gap in exam scores, there is typically a substantial gap between the percentage of graduates in the top high school and the lowest-ranked high school in a district that go directly to university. In the district shown in Table 3.4, High School One sent 50 percent of its graduates directly to university and Schools Seven, Eight, and Nine each sent fewer than 10 percent of their graduates directly to university. This gap is even wider if we add in an estimate (as I will demonstrate in Chapter 5) of the large proportion of graduates from the top-ranked high school who are *rōnin* (literally "masterless samurai") studying for an extra year or even two years to retake and pass the entrance examination to the university of their choice. Once we add these students into the mix, the percentage of university-bound graduates from the top school in this district is closer to 66 percent, fully 61 percentage points higher than its lowest-ranked counterpart in the same district. This span between high-performing and low-performing schools within the same school district is typical throughout districts in Kanagawa prefecture and, according to specialists at the Japan Institute of Labour Policy and Training, in districts throughout Japan as well.

The four industrial high schools in my sample are similar in academic quality to the general high schools I chose; entrance exam scores were not always available, but the percentage of graduates proceeding to university was generally under 5 percent.

When I initially visited each school, I interviewed teachers in the career guidance section for at least one hour and often closer to three or four hours. As the teachers became more comfortable talking with me, I was able to ask many questions about the details of how the school-work system operates from their point of view. I have continued to visit several of the Yokohama and Kawasaki schools in my sample over the years, to have further conversations with teachers in the guidance department and to hear how the job-hunting process for high school seniors has been changing over time.

Teachers fully appreciate the importance of getting students placed into a postgraduation job; they are highly cognizant of the fact that it can mean the difference between a senior starting a full-time job on April 1 or floundering in the labor market for months or even years. While of course not using the academic language of "social capital," teachers talked extensively about the value of recruitment ties between schools and firms, and about the effort both they and employers have made to maintain these ties. In describing the system as it functioned prior to the mid-1990s, teachers articulated how schools and employers cooperated with each other. One of the ways I elicited detail from teachers was to ask them to describe what happens in various situations. Through listening to their descriptions of specific circumstances that might unfold, I was able to get a better sense of how schools and employers deal with each other and how each takes responsibility, especially in situations that do not work out as planned.

As an example, I asked teachers: Who takes responsibility if a high school senior is recommended to an employer by the school, passes the job interview and receives a hiring promise (*naitei*) from the firm, starts working there on April 1, the first day of the new work year, and later

quits? Teachers typically replied in the following way: If the new graduate quits within the first three months or so, they (the teachers) feel that
it is their responsibility and that it reflects badly on the school. In such a
situation they might call the employer or go to the workplace, apologize,
and say that they will make every effort not to have this happen in the
future. At this time they may also try to get more information about the
circumstances that seem to have led the young person to quit. They want
to see what the problem was and to determine if there are problems in
the particular workplace of which they should be aware in the future.
(They would like to make sure that this is a reliable employer to whom
they feel confident recommending other students in the future.) In cases
where the graduate had particularly close ties with one or more teachers at the school, he or she might spontaneously visit the school and
talk about what happened. In this way, too, teachers learn more about
the particular circumstances surrounding their graduates' employment in
that firm. Through these means, knowledge of the specific school culture
and the specific culture of individual firms is shared between teachers and
employers.

Teachers' role as intermediary between students and firms is multifac-
eted in terms of its functions. As I have alluded to in previous chapters,
the legitimacy granted to schools in the placement process gives teachers
considerable responsibility and authority. For better or worse, having
teachers serve as intermediaries means that students are in a dependent
position and their own individual initiative does not serve as the ticket to
success. For example, a teacher at a general high school explained: "If a
student fails the company's exam and really wants to enter another company that has sent a job opening announcement to the school, then the
guidance department teacher will call the company and ask if they still
need someone. We are always the *madoguchi*" (literally, "the window,"
meaning the intermediary between the student and the employer).

Teachers' management of the job-matching process was articulated at
length by a teacher at a low-ranking general high school in Kawasaki:

We often go to the local public employment security office and there we can see
what the whole employment situation looks like in Tokyo; the officials talk to
us about it. Once a job opening announcement is approved by the local public
employment security office, the company might send the announcement only to
our school. That is, they don't try to recruit from other schools for that position. So it is like a tacit understanding between the company and our school.
They may say something like, 'Well, if we can only get two graduates from you

instead of four, we will supplement those by getting two from another school.'
The company's implicit understanding with us includes what the company
wants, such as students with okay grades, good attendance, or other things.
These things get communicated by the company's personnel officer to the head
teacher in the school guidance department. The personnel officer might say
something like, 'We want a student who hasn't been absent more than ten days
in high school so far.' To the extent that they tell us concrete things like this,
it makes it easier for us to choose an appropriate student for the job they are
offering.

Despite (or perhaps because of) teachers' keen recognition of the
importance of their work in the guidance section (they typically rotate
through this section of the school, spending perhaps three years there),
the job search process is exhausting for them as well as for students.
Teachers at many of the schools I visited sorted through the job opening
announcements the school received and separated out those that they
considered "bad" or "inappropriate." As one teacher commented, "In the
mid-1990s, companies still sent our school quite a lot of job openings.
But frankly speaking, I couldn't really recommend many of these jobs –
they just weren't very good ones." Similarly, as another teacher wearily
stated, "Many pamphlets from two-year training schools flow into the
school. These days, we get more of those than we get job openings from
companies. We do our best to sort through these brochures and figure out
which schools are worth talking to students about."

Schools with the lowest academic standards typically have a number
of students with whom teachers must spend a great deal of time in order
to make them presentable for job interviews. At one of the general high
schools I visited, a teacher ruefully admitted, "I figure that we are doing
well if we can get Satō-san to take the earring out of his ear. The employer
will see that he has a hole in his ear, that's for sure. But at least he will
think well of the student because he had the sense to take the earring out
before he came to the interview!"

I asked teachers at each school, "What counts as a 'success' when you
are helping students in the job-hunting process?" From an ethnocentric
American viewpoint, I half-expected them to say something like, "A success is when we help students find a job that really suits them – a job that
is what they think they want to do." But this was a naïve expectation, as
evidenced by the fact that it was an answer I never heard from a Japanese
high school teacher. Instead, over and over again the reply was, "A success is when we find a company for the student."

As described at the beginning of Chapter 1, the typical reason teachers gave when I asked why they had this definition of success was

simply: "*Anshin dakara*" (because it is safe – it gives peace of mind.) Their definition of success was that they had completed the job of placing the graduating senior into a company. They had guided them into a good *ba*. Logically, teachers are not going to recommend students for jobs they desire but have only a slim chance of getting. It is hard on students if they fail the job interview and it is hard on teachers as well, as they have to do additional advising and guide the student to apply to another job.

Anshin or peace of mind was frequently mentioned by teachers as the thing that students' parents seek to maximize as well. Parents constitute the third leg of what is colloquially known as the "three-legged stool" in the job search process, the other two legs being the student and his or her homeroom teacher. A manager in a small electronics sales firm on the edge of what is considered one of Tokyo's more upscale business districts eloquently recounted to me how his company recruits new workers from other prefectures:

High school teachers come from other prefectures to do *kaisha kengaku* (visits to companies) to see what kinds of companies may be interested in recruiting their graduates in the following year. These teachers generally visit three or four companies a day. About twelve teachers come each year on *kaisha kengaku* to our company. When they are coming from other prefectures they are usually people who someone in the company knows or has been introduced to. We meet them in the workplace and we go out drinking with them. The teachers can get to know the company and they can have *anshin* in recommending it to students. They can also provide more accurate information to students about the company once they have visited and talked with us.

He continued:

Also, if the teacher says to the student, 'You should go to this company; I visited it and met the president, and he is also from xxx [the prefecture where the school is located], so he will look after you,' then the students and their parents will accept the teacher's recommendation – *anshin dakara*. The guarantee of *anshin* becomes a PR point in the company's favor, in relation to parents. And in my opinion, rural students are more likely to believe their teachers because, well, they are generally more naïve and less worldly than urban kids.

Teachers' definition of success for job seekers makes sense in a context where, as I showed earlier in this chapter, Japanese men's earnings build over time with stable attachment to one workplace or *ba*, more or less irrespective of the specific occupation they are in. But in his review of school-work institutions across a range of advanced industrial economies, the economist Paul Ryan noted perceptively that the Japanese system "matches jobs and school-leavers across two essentially unidimensional rankings – one of school quality and pupil achievement, the other of company job rewards and reputation. The [Japanese] government has criticized it [the school-work system] as insensitive to the increasing aspirations of young people – associated with higher incomes, and possibly with changed attitudes to work – for a more bespoke tailoring of jobs and careers. At its worst, it simply bangs square pegs into round holes. Japan's need for more search and matching in the youth market appears to be making its mark, as youth turnover rises" (Ryan 2001: 59–60). These comments highlight the strong focus of the Japanese system on matching individuals to companies rather than to jobs per se. The latter would necessitate a more complete consideration of the type of work the individual desires and is good at, something that has been a weak point of Japan's job-matching system.

If the job-hunting process for graduating seniors is not fundamentally based on what they want to do in their lives but instead centers on which *ba* they will enter, what happens if there are fewer and fewer employers who recruit them into full-time jobs, as full-fledged members of the workplace (*ba*)? What happens if employers instead recruit more and more high school students into *arubaito* – part-time jobs for which students do not need their school's introduction? This is equivalent to schools' social capital becoming more and more irrelevant. It also signals the weakened role of teachers and employers in young people's human capital development and early adulthood. This is what happened beginning in the 1990s.

HIGH SCHOOLS' INCREASING IRRELEVANCE

In high school after high school that I visited from the late 1990s onward, teachers told me in countless ways that school was losing its importance as the central *ba* in adolescents' lives. Employment restructuring – the conversion of more and more full-time entry-level jobs with a training component into low-paid, dead-end part-time jobs – certainly may have been a rational response on the part of many Japanese employers to the severe economic pressures they felt in the 1990s. But an unintended consequence is that it accelerated a disease that afflicts other postindustrial societies where rates of university attendance have also increased: The students who are left behind, with neither the parental financial resources nor the necessary grades to enter a good university, find school to be less and less relevant to their lives. The Japanese high school teachers I have interviewed are struggling mightily with this.

As the number of full-time jobs offered to new high school graduates shrunk more and more as the 1990s wore on, low-level general high schools in particular increasingly lost control over their students. Ironically, the very success of the design of Japan's postwar school-work system – matching work-bound students into companies – spelled trouble once companies downsized and shifted to hiring more and more part-time and *arubaito* workers. As companies destroyed more opportunities for fresh high school graduates to enter stable full-time jobs, they simultaneously created more opportunities for high school students to work in part-time jobs during the period of their lives when, according to social norms, they were supposed to be full-time students and to have the school performing its role as a stakeholder in their future. The outlines of the orderly life course began to blur for substantial numbers of young people. Students responded to employers' demand for cheap, part-time, temporary labor. And most of those who responded were students at low-quality general high schools who did not have any hope of getting into a good university.

One of the sadder manifestations of students' move into part-time jobs and their increasing disengagement with school at many of the high schools I visited was the notable absence of the lively, extracurricular clubs that used to characterize many mid-ranked Japanese high schools. As one teacher commented:

Rather than tiring themselves out and getting sweaty and dirty in demanding sports activities after school, many of our students prefer to wear clean clothes or a uniform and work [e.g. as a cashier] and make a little spending money so that they can buy things they want … . As far as their future is concerned, it would be better if they were active in school clubs or sports. If they continue in a club for all three years in high school, employers look positively on it. Why? Because it proves that even if things get difficult or [in the case of sports] challenging and exhausting, they don't easily quit. This conveys something positive about their personality to employers.

This teacher's point is well taken: Almost all of the teachers I interviewed across various high schools said that they advise students not to list part-time jobs on their resumé, as employers will likely view these jobs in a negative rather than a positive light.

The Pervasiveness of High School Students' Disengagement from School. Changes in high school policies regarding students' part-time jobs show how Japan's low-level high schools began losing control over their students: Almost all of the high schools in my research had either given up their longstanding prohibition against students doing part-time jobs by the mid-1990s or had maintained this rule on paper but were simply ignoring the fact that the majority of their students were working. As one teacher commented with a deep sigh, "If their parents don't keep them from doing part-time jobs, we aren't able to either." A teacher at another school made a similar comment: "We don't forbid part-time jobs or even require students to fill out a permission form anymore. It's just uncontrollable. Almost all of our students work." A teacher at another school told the following humorous story: "Sometimes funny things happen, such as a student saying directly to a teacher, 'Tomorrow there is going to be a sale at the store where I work.' Sure enough, if the teacher shows up at the sale, the student is there. But in such a situation, the teacher will generally just pretend not to see the student. There are also cases where students come up to their teachers at school and say things like, 'Yesterday I missed class because I had to work.' You see, it isn't just that they are working on weekends. Many of them work on weekdays, too."

One teacher at a low-ranking general high school sardonically remarked that because most of the students in his school are from low-income households (and his school also has a wildly disproportionate number of single-parent households relative to the total population of households), some students actually make more money in their part-time jobs than their parents make in their own jobs. Even so, the vast majority of students who work while they are still in high school are doing so to earn pocket money rather than to provide needed support to their household.

To learn more about the school experiences and early labor market experiences of the lost generation, two Japanese colleagues and I conducted an interview survey of nearly five hundred young men who had attended high school in the Yokohama-Kawasaki area or in Sendai. Satō Yoshimichi (Tohoku University), Hirata Shūichi (Japan Institute of Labour Policy and Training), and I designed and implemented the survey in 2005.[6] Hereafter I refer to this simply as the "Youth Survey." Our target group was young men between the ages of twenty-five and thirty, so that we could tap into the labor market experiences of men who had finished high school in the depths of the Japanese economic recession in the late 1990s. About 75 percent of our sample had attended general

---

[6] We were ably assisted by Miwa Satoshi (then at Tokyo University) and Yoshimura Harumasa (Aomori University).

TABLE 3.5. *High School Attendance Record of Men in the Lost Generation*

	Students at High-Ranking High Schools	Students at Low-Ranking High Schools	Students at Low-Ranking High Schools	
			General	Vocational
Proportion with no absences	21%	14%	14%	15%
Proportion with some absences	72%	68%	64%	74%
Proportion with many absences	7%	18%	22%	11%
	100%	100%	100%	100%

Source: Based on author's calculations from Youth Survey data.

high schools and the other 25 percent had attended vocational high schools.

Data from the survey demonstrate the alienation from school experienced by many young Japanese men at low-ranking high schools. Students' regular attendance at school was positively correlated with the rank of their high school. Table 3.5 shows that among young men in high schools that send at least half of their graduates to university or junior colleges, more than 20 percent reported near-perfect attendance records during high school. This compares to just 14 percent of the young men in high schools that send fewer than half of their graduates to university or junior college. Conversely, less than ten percent of young men in high-ranking high schools reported that they had "some" or "many" absences during their three years at high school. The figure for young men at low-ranking high schools is more than twice as high. At the right-hand side of the table I consider only students who went to low-ranking high schools and compare school attendance for students at general and vocational schools. What shows up clearly is that male students in general high schools were twice as likely to have poor attendance (22 percent reported some or many absences) than male students in vocational high schools (11 percent).

These figures hint at the disparate incentives felt by students at different high schools to attend school regularly. The greater propensity of students at low-ranking general high schools to skip school compared to their counterparts at vocational schools is especially interesting.

Further analysis shows that about 45 percent of young men at low-ranking high schools had part-time jobs during high school, compared to only 26 percent of men in high-ranking schools.[7] Within the population of young men at low-ranking schools, those in vocational high schools held part-time jobs at a slightly lower rate than those in general high schools.

An overwhelming proportion (85 percent) of the young men in the survey who did part-time work during high school say that their primary reason was to earn spending money. The importance of this motivation did not differ between students at high-ranking and low-ranking high schools. A much smaller percentage (only 5 percent) said that they had worked part-time because they felt that "working is interesting." What kinds of gains, if any, do students report from having worked at a young age? Here again, the data speak very clearly: The greatest gain these young men report is "the accumulation of life experience." Nearly 80 percent of young men report this, irrespective of whether they were students at high- or low-ranking high schools. As far as having acquired useful skills, young men are fairly equally divided between those who feel that they did gain such skills and those who feel that they did not. Few young men report that being able to save money was a benefit of working, and most young men did not seem to have gained much knowledge from their work experience about the types of jobs that do or don't suit them.

While school attendance and part-time work provide ways of judging young men's degree of engagement with school, another way of thinking about attachment and reliance on school is whether individuals who did not plan to go directly on to higher education used the resources in their school's guidance department (e.g. employers' brochures, job opening announcements, teachers' advice) during their job search. Table 3.6 shows some surprising results from the Youth Survey.

A higher proportion (more than 30 percent) of young men who went to low-ranked rather than high-ranked high schools used their school's guidance department for help in job hunting. Less than 10 percent of young men at high-ranking schools did so. This makes sense because nearly all students in high-performing high schools are focused on advancing to higher education rather than job hunting. But it is quite surprising that

---

[7] We asked about part-time jobs held during the school year, not during school vacations, as we were interested in jobs that potentially interfered with schoolwork and that weakened students' attachment to school.

TABLE 3.6. *Proportions of Young Men Who Consulted with School Guidance Department in the Job-Hunting Process*

	Students at High-Ranking High Schools	Students at Low-Ranking High Schools	Students at Low-Ranking High Schools	
			General	Vocational
Proportion who consulted with school guidance department in the job-hunting process	8%	31%	19%	53%
Proportion who did not consult with school guidance department in the job-hunting process	92%	69%	81%	47%
	100%	100%	100%	100%

Source: Based on author's calculations from Youth Survey data.

nearly 70 percent of the young men in our survey who went to low-ranking high schools say that they did not rely on their school's guidance department for job-hunting assistance. The far-right column of the table shows that this behavior is especially concentrated among young men who went to general high schools: About 80 percent of them did not consult with the guidance department, compared to just 47 percent of industrial high school students who did not.

The tendency not to use the school guidance department turns out to be particularly pronounced among young men who reported a high number of school absences. Among the high school seniors at low-ranked high schools who did not intend to pursue further education after high school, only 23 percent of those who reported "I was often absent" or "I had quite a few absences" used the school guidance department for job-hunting guidance. In contrast, the guidance department was used by more than twice as many (47 percent) of their counterparts who only sometimes missed school and by 64 percent of students who rarely or never missed school.[8]

---

[8] These differences were all statistically significant.

Moreover, the students at low-ranking high schools who are the least likely to avail themselves of their school's guidance department are those who report having ranked low in academic performance during their senior year. But the strength of the statistical relationship between school absences and not consulting with the guidance department about job search is larger than the relationship between poor academic performance and not using the guidance department. In other words, students who missed many days from school were the ones most likely to brush off the guidance department.

Altogether, these statistics show the lack of attachment and dependence on the *ba* of school for a sizable segment of young men who attended low-ranking high schools. Within this group, general high school graduates reported more school absences, had a slightly higher propensity to do part-time work while they were students, and had a lower propensity to consult with their school's guidance department than industrial high school graduates. Overall, low-ranking general high schools do not seem as central to their students' lives as industrial high schools do.

Low-Ranking High Schools' Struggle to Remain an Important Ba. Although school was becoming a more and more irrelevant *ba* for students in the lower reaches of the high school hierarchy by the late 1990s, many teachers were still struggling to maintain its relevance. They were putting tremendous effort into trying to maintain their school's faltering recruitment ties with local employers. With the world of part-time jobs enticing their students into the workplace and the world of stable postgraduation full-time jobs for high school graduates disintegrating, I found in my school interviews that many teachers were at a loss as to how to fulfill their deep commitment to prepare adolescents for their entry into the adult world.

One particularly articulate young teacher expressed his conflicting feelings about whether his school should fail students if their academic performance fell below acceptable standards: "It still stigmatizes someone in Japanese society if they fail high school, so we don't want to let them do that." He continued thoughtfully, "I also think it is important not to let these kids loose in society. So I end up feeling like we are keeping them in a holding pen, trying to keep them from causing trouble to society." These statements eloquently expressed this teacher's desperate wish to make school relevant enough that students would study. At the same time, his statements revealed his steadfast view of school as its own *ba* or social location separate from society.

*At the Other End: High-Performing High Schools' Struggle to Remain
an Important* Ba. Are high-performing Japanese high schools also losing
their significance as the central *ba* in students' lives, or is it only low-
ranking high schools that are suffering from this? Ironically, by the early
twenty-first century Japanese teachers at both ends of the high school
quality hierarchy were struggling to uphold high school's relevance to
students.

Hayashi-san is a case in point. She was elated to be transferred to the
top-performing high school in the district after spending three years at
the rather chaotic school where she had been teaching when I first conducted teacher interviews. But when I met her for coffee several months
after her three-year stint at the low-performing high school had ended
and her transfer to the high-ranking school had occurred, her comments
were deeply ironic. She reported that virtually all of the students at the
top high school spent long hours every week at *juku* (after-school exam-
preparation schools, privately funded by parents). As a result, they were
almost as sleepy and unresponsive at school as the students she had taught
at the prior school, who had habitually come to class tired and irritable
after having worked the prior evening at their part-time jobs. My friend
had been delighted to be transferred to teach at a high-ranking school,
eagerly anticipating the opportunity to teach academically ambitious students. She did find them to be ambitious. That wasn't the problem. They
were so ambitious that some of them said to her, "We don't need you."
Why? Because they felt that the private after-school cram schools they
attended were teaching them what they needed to know to pass the university entrance exams.[9]

Another teacher with a similar spectrum of experience at very low-
performing as well as high-performing high schools summed up his
feelings in the form of an overall critique of the Japanese educational
hierarchy:

My thinking is that in Japan, students that in the U.S. would be dropouts are
cocooned in schools like this one. In other words, when Japanese students move
from junior high school to high school they become perfectly segregated by their

[9] Similar issues are raised by Fukuzawa in her study of Japanese middle schools. In her
ethnographic research in three Tokyo middle schools, Fukuzawa found that many teachers expressed frustration that *juku* undermined their classroom authority and led to dis-
ruption in the classroom from students who were bored because the school curriculum
lagged behind the curriculum in the "express" *juku* they attended. Express *juku* advertise
themselves as providing instruction that will help students succeed on entrance exams for
elite universities. See Fukuzawa (1994).

exam scores. So while from the outside it may not look like the crisis that it is
in the U.S., isn't the problem really just about the same? It's just more hidden in
Japan. The hierarchy of schools is very clear. Almost all the students at the top
local high school go to university but the students that would be dropouts in the
U.S. are sequestered in schools like this one.

He continued with a view that had clearly been shaped by his experience
teaching across a range of low- and high-performing high schools, as
well as his prior experience as a graduate student at Tokyo University:

I've taught at this school for seven years now. The school where I taught before
was the second from the top in its district. After another two or three years I will
move again. When I was a university student and a graduate student I taught university exam entrance preparation courses for students at xxx [a top high school in
Tokyo]. So I've seen the students that have been separated into the various levels of
high school. At my current school, it is clear that we are training students for simple
labor in industry. At xxx and the other top high schools where I taught, the big
thing was how many students got into Tokyo University. At xxx, maybe thirty students every year get into Tokyo University. For high schools in local areas, it is sort
of like one person every three years gets into Tokyo University. But at this school,
it's how many students out of the whole school get into *any* university.

What I feel is that at this school we are supplying manual labor and in this
way sort of supporting the subcontractors in the economy. But what I felt at xxx
was that we were developing and supplying high-ability, high-quality 'parts' to
the government and to companies. You know, the Japanese university entrance
exam system is criticized from many different angles in Japanese society as being
bad for high school students. This is strictly my own opinion, but the university
exam system seems amazingly well tailored to Japanese companies. It is not that
universities purposely select students with this in mind, but ultimately this is the
role they end up playing.

EMPLOYERS' ROLE

I showed in Chapter 2 that postwar Japanese labor law put great importance on high schools as a crucial intermediary between students and
employers. Individual Japanese employers developed a strong interest in
participating in the school-work system because it provided them with
reliable information about possible entry-level hires into full-time blue-
collar and low-level white-collar jobs. The majority of employers in the
Employer Survey stated that they had a desire for their new male high
school graduate-recruits to stay in the firm for ten years or more. This
means that they needed to choose these recruits carefully in order to
forestall mutual dissatisfaction and high turnover. Hiring them through
the route of institutional social capital (recommendations from schools)

rather than simply hiring them in the "open market" helped employers get more and deeper information about individual applicants. Knowing the culture of individual schools also helped employers judge whether these recruits would adjust well to the interpersonal relationships in the firm.

Employers capitalized on existing institutional social capital to build new personal social capital (strong interpersonal ties and work relationships) among workers in their firm, presumably leading to greater productivity overall. But employers' emphasis on new workers' common background and shared understandings was predicated on the template of a workplace where employees have long-term ties with one another and with their employer. This template was rapidly shifting by the mid-1990s ice age of employment. Once employers cut the number of full-time jobs available to new graduates, a major structural transformation was underway: More and more young people entered the contingent labor force, holding less stable jobs. The importance of the trust relationships between schools and employers and of strong bonds between more experienced workers and new recruits, so eloquently articulated by employers in the Employer Survey, began to decline.

As I argued in Chapter 1, membership in some type of stable *ba* has been very important in the lives of the great majority of individuals in Japan – for students this is school, for men it is the workplace, for women it has been the family in particular. This has diminished for the current generation. By the early twenty-first century an increasing number of young Japanese experienced the irrelevance of school and the workplace as sources of identity. Although not the subject of this book, an increasing number also experienced the irrelevance of forming a family. This is evidenced by rising rates of singlehood, rising age at marriage (among those who marry at all), and a birth rate so low as to place Japan in the dubious category of what demographers have dubbed the "lowest-low" fertility societies.

If Japanese students at low-performing high schools increasingly "blow off" the teachers in their schools' guidance department who are trying to help guide them into a full-time job they could start after graduating, do they have anyone to blame but themselves? After all, no one forced them to take part-time jobs in high school. Few of them did so in order to contribute financially to their household. And it is very unlikely that teachers actively discouraged them from availing themselves of the full-time job listings and counseling sessions offered in their school's guidance department.

But what were schools able to offer? More pointedly, has Japan's renowned high school-work system been abandoned by young people, or has it abandoned them? The next two chapters tell this story.

4

Unraveling School-Employer Relationships

> "Ultimately, our graduates' job search relies entirely on the school's relationship with employers."
>
> — Guidance counselor at a general high school in Yokohama

Looking only at the behavior of Japan's young nonelite youth – those who are in low-ranking high schools – it can be easy to label them as rebellious and lacking in seriousness about their future. The attachment to school, club activities, and sports that used to bind many Japanese adolescents to their schools has declined. In its place is a preoccupation with part-time jobs – jobs that until recently were uniformly discouraged or even prohibited by school authorities. But are nonelite youth rejecting a system that is functioning as well as it used to? How well has the high school-work system weathered the economic conditions of the past decade and a half?

Japan's high school-work system was rooted in the macro-level conditions of the high-economic growth period. These conditions unraveled to a large extent in the 1990s. Together with this unraveling, the effectiveness of the system has seriously declined. This, in turn, has made the transition from high school into full-time work harder for the lost generation. While institutional social capital and the school-work system have not collapsed completely, this chapter will suggest that the system seems to remain healthy only for certain types of high schools and employers. The majority of Japanese adolescents are in high schools that no longer maintain many recruitment ties with employers. Because of this, these adolescents have lost access to the time-honored direct route into full-time jobs that their parents had.

The breakdown of school-employer ties poses a serious problem in a society where institutional social capital – not personal social capital, especially "weak ties" – has been so important in helping young people launch their work lives. Concurrent with weakening ties between high schools and firms, employers have expanded the opportunities for high school students to get part-time jobs in the service sector that tend to lead nowhere. Students work evening shifts in convenience stores and restaurants and doze through their high school classes during the day. Are the ensuing problems attributable to students' own "bad" choices to circumvent their schools' guidance department? Before reaching such a conclusion, it is important to see how and why Japan's traditional school-work system has crumbled under the weight of macro-level changes that Japanese young people played little role in creating.

FROM INSTITUTIONAL EQUILIBRIUM TO DISEQUILIBRIUM IN JAPAN'S LOST DECADE

During the three decades leading up to the 1990s Japan experienced a fortuitous institutional equilibrium between the structure of the secondary school system, the conditions of labor demand and supply, and the long-term employment system. Japanese high schools' motivations and employers' motivations complemented each other well. As large Japanese firms extended greater employment security to blue-collar as well as white-collar workers during the high-growth 1960s, employers who wished to recruit new high school graduates into entry-level jobs were highly motivated to obtain as much information as possible about job applicants. This helped them make the best decisions about who to hire and subsequently who to invest in, in terms of on-the-job training.

Employers' hiring decisions were made easier by the way the secondary educational system was organized and by schools' legally designated role in graduates' job placement. The fact that Japanese middle school students compete for admission into specific high schools means that the academic quality of students in each high school is quite homogeneous. Moreover, the requisite decision in ninth grade to proceed to a general high school or a vocational one means that students sort themselves into academic or vocational tracks at that point in time. The high school that a student attends constitutes a strong "signal" to Japanese employers about the quality of a job applicant's general skills, and also tells employers whether students are acquiring any specific vocational training. As a result, it is relatively easy for employers to judge which high schools are appropriate targets for their labor recruitment efforts. This is a strong contrast with the American comprehensive high school model, where a high school is meant to offer something to all students.[1]

Japanese employers benefited from the government's designation of the school as an important intermediary institution between adolescents and employers. As high schools' involvement in introducing job applicants to employers became institutionalized during the mid-twentieth century, schools competed with one another to form implicit recruitment relationships with local employers. These long-term relationships served the interests of both schools and employers when labor demand remained high in the 1970s and into the 1980s. Secondary schools could attract better students if they could offer assurance that they would be introduced into jobs as they graduated, and employers could greatly lower their recruitment costs if some schools tacitly agreed to send them high-quality graduates year after year.[2]

One of the first empirical studies of ties between Japanese high schools and employers was carried out by the educational sociologists James Rosenbaum and Takehiko Kariya (Rosenbaum and Kariya 1989). Using data from a sample of Japanese high schools in the 1980s to examine the prevalence of schools' long-term or "contract" employers (employers who repeatedly recruited from the same schools), they concluded: " ... contract employers dominate the labor market for each high school's graduates, and each high school relies heavily on a few contract employers to place its graduates into jobs" (Rosenbaum and Kariya 1989: 1341). While they found that only 11 percent of the employers who recruited from specific high schools did so on a repeat basis, these firms hired an average of 50 percent of all the work-bound students from each school. (Many so-called contract employers had multiple job openings and hired several graduating seniors from each of the high schools with whom they had ties.) Contract employers tended to be larger firms and generally offered the most desirable jobs in terms of job security and training.

But the final decade of the twentieth century saw the conditions for Japan's high school-work system and strong institutional social capital begin to unravel. As I have already mentioned, some commentators compared the economic conditions in Japan in the early part of the

---

[1] This makes it harder for an American employer to use the name of a high school as a signal for where to recruit new employees.
[2] As noted in Chapter 2, the operation of the system is described in Kariya (1991), Kariya, Sugayama, and Ishida, eds. (2000), Okano (1993), and Rosenbaum and Kariya (1989).

twenty-first century to the oil shock of the early 1970s. To be sure, the number of job openings for high school graduates fell very steeply in the recession following the 1970s oil shock, dropping to a ratio of 1.7 openings per job-seeker by 1979. But this pales in comparison to how the bottom fell out of the labor market for high school graduates by the early twenty-first century, with the job opening-to-applicant ratio dropping to its lowest-ever recorded level – less than half that of 1979. Most of the key elements that had cemented the stability of the school-work system in prior decades were disintegrating. The structure of the educational system had not changed, but the conditions of labor demand and supply had. So too had the employment system.

Labor Demand and Supply. The meager number of job openings for recent high school graduates reflects in part the increased global competition for manufacturing jobs. Similar to the U.S. in the heyday of its manufacturing economy in the 1960s to early 1980s, manufacturing jobs were one of the principal destinations for Japanese male high school graduates through the early 1990s. But as Japanese manufacturing firms have increasingly turned to China and other locations for new plants because of the opportunity for dramatically lower labor costs, the manufacturing sector has suffered by far the greatest job loss of any industrial sector in Japan over the past decade. In contrast, the service sector has experienced the greatest growth. With fewer and fewer manufacturing jobs for high school graduates to move into, a problematic situation developed: In competing for jobs in the service sector, high school graduates generally lose out to university graduates for high-end jobs such as those in finance, insurance, and information technology. Instead, they are relegated to jobs in the lower reaches of the service sector. As one high school teacher told me in the late 1990s: "This year a bunch of department stores along with banks and other firms in the finance industry told us in May or June that this year is tough so they can't hire. Their personnel director came to the school and said that when economic conditions improve, they will hire from our school again. Sometimes we try to talk to companies some more and say 'please hire some of our graduates' but if they are not recruiting in general, then we have to resign ourselves to it."

A teacher at another school offered a similar commentary:

Two years ago we received job opening announcements from about 1,200 companies; then last year it halved and this year it has gone down some more. For example, companies that make passenger cars are not hiring many people. But companies like Isuzu that make buses and trucks and are shipping them to other parts of Asia are still not too bad. Still, they are only hiring about 70 percent of the number of high school graduates they were hiring before. You can see the same trend in electronics and *tekkō* [the iron and steel industries]. I think this trend will continue. Even if the domestic economy gets better, manufacturing is moving to Asia and this is not going to change. Labor costs are high in Japan, so a lot of medium-sized companies are moving to Southeast Asia and making products there. Japan re-imports them. As for large firms, well ... they are restructuring and it is pretty much the same thing. They are tending to go outside of Japan and build factories in other parts of Asia.

Another teacher commented on the state of service-sector jobs as well: "Jobs for high school graduates in department stores declined in the 1990s. So jobs in supermarkets have become really popular with our graduates, and the competition for those jobs is really intense, like one job opening for every twenty seniors who want the job. So stores like Daiei [a large grocery store chain] have said they'll hire just one person each year from our school from now on ... if they hire at all."

Instead of the jobs they consider desirable, general high school graduates often must take jobs in the lower-paid parts of the service sector, working as cashiers in small stores, as delivery people for small businesses, or as kitchen help in restaurants. Few of these jobs offer the opportunity for stable employment; these are not the ones that large Japanese firms converted to long-term employment in the 1960s. They were not stable, well-paying jobs then – nor are they now.

While a similarity to the situation of high school graduates in the U.S. could be claimed, Japanese high school graduates were hit by a perfect storm in the 1990s: Not only did Japan complete its definitive transition to a mature postindustrial economy characterized by a smaller manufacturing sector overshadowed by a burgeoning service sector, but there was a large change in the composition of the labor supply from which employers could draw. To wit, rates of advancement to university climbed more than 15 percent in Japan from the early 1990s to the early years of the twenty-first century, increasing the pool of young college graduates from which employers could hire (this was shown in Figure 2.3 in Chapter 2). This rate of increase had not been seen since the change between the mid-1960s and the mid-1970s, when the rate of university matriculation rose from a low rate of 15 percent to a figure nearly double that. Solga has argued that as educational expansion proceeds in a society and the size of the least-educated group declines, members of this group increasingly become stigmatized as "incapable" (Solga 2002). This occurs whether or not the quality of the less-educated labor pool has objectively declined. Even in the employer survey I conducted in the late 1990s (discussed in

Chapter 3), about 40 percent of employers who had been recruiting high school graduates said that if they could hire a university graduate instead, they would do so. The main reason they gave is that they perceive university graduates to have more social skills and greater potential ability.

The stigmatization of high school graduates as well as an actual decline in their academic preparation both appear to be occurring in Japan. Prominent Japanese social scientists such as Kariya have argued persuasively that recent educational reforms that dilute the curriculum and lower the requirements for high school graduation have had a negative effect on the human capital of noncollege bound graduates.[3] Moreover, this worries Kariya and others in terms of the implications it holds for an increased tendency for social class reproduction. Why? Because in a society where the university entrance gates have been opened more widely but parents generally are responsible for paying the bill, those who are left behind – noncollege-bound high school graduates and dropouts – increasingly tend to be concentrated in families that cannot afford to provide their offspring with the requisite educational preparation to succeed in the educational competition.[4] In Japan, this translates into the financial inability to pay for the supplementary after-school cram schools which so many upper middle-class adolescents attend.

Obtaining systematic information about students' social class background from the teachers I interviewed at low-performing high schools was impossible due to privacy concerns. Instead, I had to glean impressions of students' social class backgrounds from the schools' milieu, from comments made by teachers and principals in the course of my interviews, and from the Youth Survey. In that survey, the correlation was high (and statistically significant) between young men's assessment of their households' relative economic status when they were teenagers and their estimate of the proportion of graduates from their high school who went on to higher education. Moreover, there is a statistically significant difference in the survey sample between young men from high- and low-ranking high schools in terms of whether their father was present in the household during their adolescence. Ninety-three percent of young men who had attended high-ranking high schools reported living with their father and mother together in the same household during adolescence,

---

[3] While I cannot assess the validity of this argument here, I find it very plausible. See Kariya and Rosenbaum (2003).

[4] For theoretical statements of this general problem across postindustrial societies, see Raftery and Hout (1993) and Lucas (2001).

but this was true for only 85 percent of young men who had attended low-ranking high schools. The apparent relationship between students' household circumstances and the quality of the high schools they attend is consistent with heightened anxiety in postbubble Japan that social class reproduction is increasing.

Employment Restructuring across Industries. As Japanese firms struggled to keep from laying off middle-aged male employees, they fundamentally altered the assumption that the new young men they hired would be implicitly guaranteed the long-term employment their fathers had experienced. The proportion of part-time entry-level jobs swelled (see Genda 2000, 2001; Iwata 2004). The percentage of all employees that are part-time increased two-fold in manufacturing between 1980 and 2000 but closer to three-fold in the sales sector (wholesale and retail trade) and in other parts of the service sector. As a result, while almost 90 percent of workers in Japanese manufacturing are full-time, only about 65 percent of service-sector workers are in full-time positions. The manufacturing industry remains one of the few isolated pockets of the Japanese economy where the high school-work transition system has had a chance of continuing to function, and evidence for this supposition will be shown later in this chapter and the next. But it is a sector that is not nearly as sizable or important in the Japanese economy as it was before the 1990s. This has important ramifications for Japan's young educational nonelite.

THE DECLINE OF SCHOOL-EMPLOYER TIES

Japanese media and popular reports over the past several years have suggested that ties between high schools and firms have weakened or even disappeared. But what is the evidence that this has happened? It turns out to be quite difficult to systematically analyze the stability or decline of these ties. In fact, their presence to begin with is hard to measure. Two recent studies made such an attempt. Ishida compared new data with what Rosenbaum and Kariya had shown with 1980s data. He found a large decline in the number of firms that guidance counselors at general high schools reported as having strong recruitment ties with their school (Ishida 2000). But Ishida found few signs of decline in the number of such employers for vocational high school graduates. Honda also used recent data to examine the prevalence of recruitment ties between schools and firms, and likewise found almost no ties for general high schools (Honda 1999).

Which types of firms continued to maintain ties with high schools once Japan entered the ice age of employment? And which types of high schools were able to maintain ties with employers despite the overall decline in full-time entry-level jobs? Prior studies have not answered these questions. With cooperation from teachers at one of the vocational high schools and two of the general high schools I studied in Yokohama and Kawasaki, I was able to obtain yearly data for all graduates' job placements from the late 1970s to the late 1990s. This was lucky: The data cover the 1980s when the Japanese economy was still quite stable and the 1990s when the economic growth rate and labor demand tumbled. Data for the vocational high school cover the longest period (1976–2001), and data for the two general high schools cover 1988–2000 and 1981–96 respectively.

I drew the school-level data from each school's student and parent handbook (known as *shinro no tebiki*, literally "handbook for future paths"), a pamphlet that outlines the different postgraduate options for graduates and explains how to prepare for them. Invaluable for my research purposes is the section at the end of such handbooks that lists each year the names of universities the high school's graduates entered, the numbers of students who went to junior college and to *senmon gakkō* (two-year training schools), and, for graduates who entered the labor market, the names of all the firms where they got jobs. Typically, the handbook is an internal document to the school and is not given to outsiders, whether Japanese or foreign. Indeed, as I conducted repeat visits over several years to many of the high schools I originally visited in the mid-1990s, a few eventually declined my request for their handbooks – something that had not happened to me in the mid-1990s. The teachers whom I had originally interviewed had by then been transferred to other schools, leaving me to start over again in building rapport.[5] Probably even more important were two other phenomena: a greatly increased public concern in Japan with privacy resulting from a number of highly publicized scams, eventuating in a new privacy law that went into effect in spring 2005; and the worsened placement situation at many low-ranking general high schools. The former made it exceedingly difficult to get student information even in the form of highly aggregated numbers

[5] The exception was industrial high schools, where teacher rotation across schools tends to be much less frequent because of teachers' particular expertise in subject areas taught only in industrial high schools; these high schools are much smaller in number than general high schools.

and the latter further lowered schools' incentives for giving out graduate placement numbers, as most schools had little to brag about.

In the end I counted myself very lucky to have been able to get a good run of placement data from three schools in the first place. Using the across-time placement information from schools that I had been able to collect before these restrictions went into effect, I constructed a year-by-year data set with the names of the employers that hired from each school. I appended firms' characteristics by consulting a listing of Japanese companies.[6] Comparison of firms' recruitment patterns from the three schools provides a bird's-eye view of how recruitment relationships with employers changed over the past few decades for a vocational high school, a general high school of equivalent quality, and a general high school of lower quality. While these schools of course cannot be presumed to represent Japanese high schools at large, detailed graduate placement data spanning many years is nevertheless an unusual and valuable data source.

The school I will refer to with the pseudonym "Nishi Takase" is one of the best vocational high schools in its particular area of Kanagawa prefecture. It is a rather unusual school because it has both industrial and commercial curriculum tracks. The school I will call "Funezawa" is a general high school of equivalent academic quality to Nishi Takase, and "Tōkai" is a lower-ranked general high school. All three schools are coeducational. Data that I coded separately for Kanagawa prefecture's more than 180 public high schools shows that the three schools are quite representative of the high schools in Kanagawa that produce many work-bound graduates.

Table 4.1 shows the characteristics of the three schools. I use 1994 data in the table because this was after the Japanese recession had begun and is the midpoint of the time span in which I am looking at the decline of school-employer ties.

Ninth graders needed a score of at least forty-one on the prefectural entrance exam for high school in order to enter Nishi Takase. It is an old, well-established school with many ties to local employers. As Table 4.1 shows, nearly 68 percent of Nishi Takase seniors in the

---

[6] I used the *Japan Company Handbook, 2007* to try to find the size and industry of every firm a graduate entered. The *Handbook* includes all companies listed on the first or second section of the Tokyo, Osaka, and Nagoya Stock Exchanges. These naturally tend to be large firms, whereas many of the firms that hire high school graduates are small- or medium-sized firms. Consequently, only about one-half of the firms that recruit from these three high schools are listed in the *Handbook*.

TABLE 4.1. *Characteristics of Nishi Takase, Funezawa, and Tōkai High Schools*

	Nishi Takase (Vocational)	Funezawa (General)	Tōkai (General)
Minimum required entrance exam score	41	39	34
Founding year	1921	1927	1979
Percent of graduates going directly into:			
Full-time jobs	68.0	7.5	29.6
University	3.1	12.5	6.3
Junior college	6.8	14.9	7.7
Two-year training school	17.8	27.0	30.0
Uncertain destinations	4.3	38.1	26.4
Total number of graduating seniors	227	275	216

mid-1990s had full-time jobs lined up by the time they graduated. A trivial proportion of seniors (3 percent) proceeded directly to university. Nishi Takase has a commercial as well as an industrial track and sends about 25 percent of its graduates to junior colleges and two-year training schools.

Nishi Takase and Funezawa were both founded in the 1920s and Tōkai was founded a half-century later.[7] Funezawa and Tōkai have lower minimum required entrance exam scores than the average (forty-five) for general high schools in Kanagawa prefecture. Very few of their graduates go to university. Their graduates' destinations reflect the diversity of outcomes for students who graduate from general high schools that are in the lower half of the educational quality distribution in each school district. Even so, they are not among the bottom quintile of high schools in Kanagawa prefecture in the early-mid 1990s, which had required entrance exam scores below thirty-four. So these two schools are an appropriate comparison with the vocational school.

The three schools produced very different proportions of graduates who immediately entered jobs after graduating: Compared to 68 percent from Nishi Takase, just 30 percent of Tōkai graduates and only 8 percent from Funezawa did so. Some of this difference is explained by the higher

---

[7] I mention the establishment date because some school officials and employers suggested in interviews that older schools are more likely to have established and maintained strong ties with employers.

rates of matriculation to institutions of higher education, including two-year training schools, from the two general high schools.

Table 4.1 also shows that many more general high school seniors than vocational seniors have "uncertain" destinations when they graduate (26 percent and 38 percent for the two general high schools and only 4 percent for the vocational high school). Graduates in this "uncertain" category are idle, neither proceeding directly on to higher education nor into a postgraduation job. This is important, because in the next chapter I will show that only a small proportion of the idle graduates from low- and mid-ranked general high schools can reasonably be assumed to be *rōnin* – graduates who sit out for one or more years to engage in extra preparation for university entrance exams. A much larger proportion neither have plans for higher education nor are gainfully employed – they are essentially NEET (not in education, employment, or training). The high rate of graduates' idleness for the general high schools shows that many seniors had not been matched with employers by the time they graduated. Does this reflect the fact that their schools had few ties with employers?

Measurement of School-Employer Ties. I used the same method to measure recruitment ties between schools and firms as used by Kariya in his original research on the high school-work transition in Japan (see Kariya 1988). A tie is defined as existing between a firm and a school if the firm has hired one or more students from the school for at least five consecutive years.[8] In Table 4.2 I show the total number of firms that recruited from each school across the time period for which data are available, and the proportion of those that were tied firms.

Nishi Takase is by far the most "popular" school among employers, with more than 1,000 employers flocking to it over the 1980s and 1990s. In contrast, fewer than 250 employers showed up at Funezawa's gates, and around 600 hired Tōkai's graduates. It is also abundantly clear that Nishi Takase, the vocational high school, has more tied firms than the other schools: an average of about 9 percent of all the employers that hired its graduates each year (row 1 in the table). This contrasts

---

[8] A five-year period is long enough to eliminate most "random error." It does not count situations where firms generally hire in the "open" market but happen to hire from the same school across a few consecutive years. And it is long enough to indicate genuine commitment to a school (i.e. it counts firms that strategically hire from the same school over an extended period of time but may not do so in an occasional year). I consider a firm to be a "tied firm" with a school in year *t* if it hired from the school in that year and each of the previous four years.

TABLE 4.2. *Schools' Ties with Employers*

	Nishi Takase		Funezawa		Tōkai	
	Tied Firms	Non-Tied Firms	Tied Firms	Non-Tied Firms	Tied Firms	Non-Tied Firms
Number of firms	109	1,152	8	227	30	598
Percent of all employers	9.1	90.9	3.4	96.6	4.8	95.2
Percent of work-bound students hired by each employer type	45.0	55.0	13.1	86.9	27.2	72.8
Average number of graduates hired per year	20.2	2.5	7.3	1.7	13.0	1.7

with just a little more than 3 percent of the employers that hired from Funezawa and a little less than 5 percent of the employers that hired from Tōkai.[9] Rows 2 and 3 of the table show how important it is for a school to have ties with employers. Even though only 9 percent of the employers who hired from Nishi Takase were tied firms, these employers hired nearly half (45 percent) of the school's work-bound graduates. For the other schools too, the percentage of graduates hired by tied firms is much higher than the percent of tied firms itself, indicating that many tied firms hire more than one graduate from the school. The third row of the table shows that, indeed, for each school the average tied firm took in many more graduates per year than the average non-tied firm. Nishi Takase's tied firms particularly stand out, hiring an average of twenty graduates per year.

These contrasts across the schools are striking, especially given the fact that the schools produce similar numbers of graduates from one another (Table 4.1). In fact, the school with the lowest number of recruiting

[9] A skeptic might argue that Nishi Takase only appears to have more tied employers because there is a longer run of data for this school. To address this, I selected out the nine-year period 1988–96 for which all three schools have available data and recalculated the placement statistics. Even when "controlling" for the same nine-year period, a higher proportion of the employers who hired from Nishi Takase were tied employers than was true for the other two schools. This reinforces the interpretation that vocational high schools are more attractive to employers and are more able to establish relationships with employers than mid-ranked or low-ranked general high schools.

TABLE 4.3. *Characteristics of Tied Firms and Non-Tied Firms*

	Nishi Takase		Tōkai	
	Characteristics of Tied Firms	Characteristics of Non-Tied Firms	Characteristics of Tied Firms	Characteristics of Non-Tied Firms
Average firm size (number of employees)	8,694	3,025	4,833	3,882
Industry (%)				
Construction	6.0	9.6	4.6	7.3
Manufacturing	53.7	34.3	36.4	23.3
Sales	10.3	22.7	31.8	39.7
Prof. services	18.0	18.2	9.0	12.3
Other services	12.0	15.2	18.2	17.3
Total	100.0	100.0	100.0	100.0

employers and by far the lowest proportion of tied employers (Funezawa) has more graduating seniors than the other two schools.

Table 4.3 shows the two most important characteristics of tied firms: They tend to be larger than non-tied firms, especially in the case of the vocational school, and more of them are in manufacturing than in any other sector. (Because Funezawa had only thirty tied firms, it is not meaningful to look at their distribution by industry so Funezawa is not included in this table.) Manufacturing companies are especially numerous among the tied firms of the vocational school, constituting more than one-half of such firms. But they also make up more than one-third of Tōkai's tied firms.

In sum, three things stand out clearly: 1) The vocational high school has more tied firms than the general high schools, 2) manufacturing firms are especially likely to maintain recruitment ties with schools, and 3) manufacturing firms' general propensity to maintain ties appears to give the vocational school an advantage in helping its graduates find jobs. Firms in the manufacturing and sales sectors make up the largest share of firms that recruit these high schools' graduates into full-time jobs. But the table demonstrates that it is manufacturing firms more than any other type of firm that tend to maintain stable recruitment ties with schools – and these firms flock to the vocational high school.

The employer survey I conducted in the late 1990s (described in Chapter 2) offers interesting substantiation of these recruitment data. In the survey, I asked employers of male high school graduates whether they had a preference for a particular type of high school and, if so, which type. The great majority (84 percent) of the surveyed employers stated that they did indeed have a preference; only 16 percent said that they would recruit from any type of high school. Among those who stated a preference, a majority said that the main reason is because the jobs they offer require special skills. This was particularly apparent among employers who favored recruiting only from industrial high schools, which was the choice of nearly 60 percent of all the employers who expressed any preference at all about high school type. About 10 percent of employers instead expressed a preference, respectively, for recruiting from both industrial and general high schools, from commercial and general high schools, or from industrial and commercial high schools. Firms that stated a preference to recruit only from a general high school or only from a commercial high school each represented an additional 5 percent of the total number of firms.

Nearly 80 percent of all employers in the survey reported being satisfied with the high school graduates they had hired during the past three years – a figure that remained the same when I considered only employers who recruited solely from industrial high schools. The rate of satisfaction was strikingly lower among the small number of employers who say that they only recruit from general high schools – only 40 percent of them said that they were satisfied with the quality of the high school graduates they had hired. As a human resource manager at one small firm commented, "The quality of students at general high schools is generally lower than the students at vocational high schools. We don't recruit from general high schools because we *want* to – we recruit from them because we *have* to [because the company is small and therefore not as popular with potential recruits as larger companies]."

Declining Ties? What do the data from these three Kanagawa high schools indicate vis-à-vis a decline over time in school-employer ties? Evidence offered by Japanese researchers has been based mainly on teachers' own reports of a decline. But the yearly data for Nishi Takase, Funezawa, and Tōkai make it possible to calculate a measure of the yearly probability that an employer is engaged in a five-year hiring streak from each school. Figure 4.1 shows a graph of these probabilities for the time span of data I have for each of the schools.[10]

---

[10] The lines in this and subsequent figures are five-year moving averages. Because the measure of implicit contracts is based on at least one five-year hiring streak, the numbers calculated at both ends of the time span of available data for the schools are less reliable than those in the middle of the time span. This applies to subsequent analyses as well.

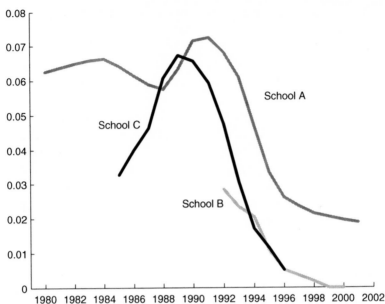

FIGURE 4.1. Changes in the Probability that Employers Engage in Five-Year Hiring Streaks.
Note: School A is Nishi Takase, School B is Funezawa, and School C is Tōkai.

The story in the 1980s is somewhat mixed. Although there were slight ups and downs, the probability in a given year that an employer of graduates from the vocational school Nishi Takase (School A) was a firm that continuously hired from the school was relatively stable, at around .06. In other words, of every 100 firms hiring from the school in a given year, six were likely to be tied employers. (But as mentioned previously these firms often each hired several graduates each year from the school.) For Tōkai (School C), this probability increased continuously from .03 in 1985 to almost .07 in 1989 – one of the peak years of the bubble economy. For Funezawa (School B) the data series begins only in 1992, and the probability that the firms hiring from this school are tied firms shoots downward from that year on.

The story in the 1990s is straightforward for all three schools: There was a definitive decline in the probability that any firm hiring their graduates was doing so year after year. The probability for employers of Nishi Takase (School A) to be tied employers dropped from more than .07 in 1991 to .02 in 2001 and also declined dramatically for the two general high schools. By the late 1990s, the general high schools basically had no employer ties anymore.

Why the Decline? The steep decline in the number of tied employers is a fact, but it is not clear why this happened. It is therefore hard to predict whether school-employer ties will resuscitate in the future if the Japanese economy is able to grow at a higher rate than it experienced in the doldrum years since the early 1990s. Could it be that employers still would prefer to have ties with schools but they simply have not been able to in recent years because they have not been hiring as many new employees as they used to? If so, then we might expect school-employer ties to revive as the Japanese economy recovers and labor demand increases again. But an altogether different scenario would be predicted if employers' preference for having long-term recruitment ties with schools has weakened. This would signify the deeper effect of employment restructuring in the Japanese economy; employers might regard it as less important now to screen high school graduates because they are placing so few of them into career-track jobs anyway. It is important to distinguish between these two possibilities in order to judge whether the declining number of tied firms is based on fluctuations in the economy or whether it represents instead a more fundamental and permanent change in employers' behavior. While it is hard to establish a definitive answer to this question, my former student Zun Tang and I devised a way to try to distinguish between these two distinct scenarios for the future.

Tang and I created something called "counterfactual probabilities" – the probabilities that firms would maintain ties with schools if labor demand were sufficiently high.[11] Figure 4.2 compares the actual (observed) proportion of employers hiring from each school who were tied firms to the counterfactual proportion (the proportion of tied employers that would be predicted only on the basis of labor demand). The dotted lines bracketing the counterfactual lines indicate that if the line for the observed proportion falls outside of that range, we can be fairly certain that the proportion of tied employers cannot be predicted simply by the volume of labor demand.

From the figure it is clear that the behavior of employers hiring from the vocational high school could not have been predicted only by labor demand, especially through the mid-1990s. This suggests that this school had some employers who were committed to hiring from it

[11] The methodology is explained in greater detail in Brinton and Tang (2010).

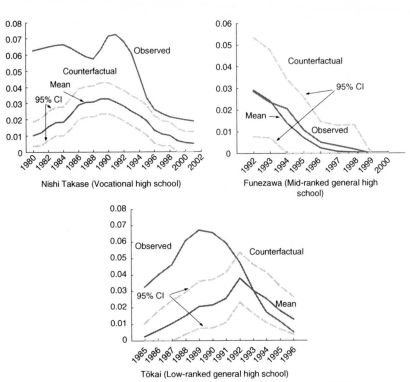

FIGURE 4.2. Changes in the Observed and Counterfactual Probabilities of Employers Engaging in Five-Year Hiring Streaks.

year after year despite fluctuations in labor demand. The figure shows that employers with this commitment certainly became much rarer by 1996, but the proportion of tied employers was still higher than the proportion that would have been predicted solely by the level of labor demand.

The two general high schools suffered much more in terms of losing their tied employers in the 1990s recession. In fact, employers of Funezawa's graduates have consistently behaved as if their decision to hire a Funezawa graduate in any given year has been independent of their decisions in prior years. In other words, Funezawa has consistently had only a trivial number of tied employers. The probability that an employer has had a stable recruitment relationship with Funezawa is not statistically distinguishable from what we would predict solely on the basis of knowing employers' overall demand for high school graduates from year to year. Tōkai, the low-ranked general high school, had a volume of tied employers up until 1992 that was well above what labor demand alone would have predicted. But with the onset of the economic recession, Tōkai's proportion of tied employers also became statistically indistinguishable from what labor demand alone would have predicted.

These data analyses clearly point to changes in the celebrated high school-work transition process in Japan. When we compare the actual proportion of employers that had recruitment ties to high schools to the proportion that would be predicted on the basis of overall labor demand for new high school graduates, two of the three schools for which I have detailed data had a proportion that indicated significant recruitment ties in the 1980s. These were the vocational school and the low-ranked general high school. The mid-ranked general high school appears to have had so few tied employers that the number did not differ from what we would have expected solely on the basis of labor demand.

But the 1990s saw a dramatic decline in the yearly probability that firms would engage in hiring streaks from any of the schools. Only Nishi Takase, the vocational school, had a hiring distribution that remained statistically distinguishable throughout the 1990s from the counterfactual hiring distribution. And even for that school, the proportion of tied firms declined sharply from the early 1990s on, reaching a level that appeared relatively stable by the early years of the twenty-first century. Meanwhile, the two general high schools lost virtually all of their tied firms once the economic recession was under way.

The analyses shown in Table 4.3 indicated that manufacturing firms have been the most likely to engage in repeat recruitment from the same high schools. Among the high schools in my data, the vocational school has been the main beneficiary of this proclivity. This is highly consistent with the idea that there are still some "good" career-entry jobs in Japan's manufacturing sector for which high school graduates qualify, especially if they have gone to a vocational high school. In contrast, fewer firms in the sales and service sectors have implicit recruitment contracts with high schools anymore. This reflects the rapid increase in low-paid, part-time jobs in fast-food restaurants, convenience stores, and other retail outlets over the past decade and a half. These are jobs for which employers do not provide extensive training and for which they have little need to rely on a school's strong recommendation for a particular applicant. This obviates their need to maintain a trust relationship with schools over time.

RESUSCITATING SCHOOL-EMPLOYER TIES?

If the economic situation in Japan gradually improves, will employers
return to the practice of recruiting year after year from the same high
schools, engaging in the kind of trust relationships described by teachers
and employers in Chapter 2? This is an important question for Japan's
least-educated youth, who have relied on their schools' connections to
smoothe their way into the labor market. What kinds of information
can be marshaled to predict employers' future behavior if and when economic growth recommences?

The data in this chapter suggest the greater prevalence of school-
employer ties in the manufacturing sector, which is consistent with the
flourishing of the high school-work system during the 1960s–1970s
expansion of Japan's manufacturing industry. But new job creation in
Japan, as in other postindustrial economies, is now heavily concentrated
in the sales and service sectors, where school-employer connections have
been weaker. Especially with the increased supply of university graduates, there seems little reason for employers in these industries to revive
recruitment ties with high schools. University graduates are simply too
plentiful.

A teacher in a general high school in Kawasaki spoke to the dearth
of white-collar jobs for high school graduates by the late 1990s: "As for
office jobs, I'd say there was only about .5 of a job opening for every
senior who wanted one. For sales, there was perhaps one opening for
every graduate who wanted that type of job. There were more jobs in
manufacturing." These sentiments were echoed in one of my interviews
at another high school:

Relatively speaking, there are still quite a few jobs in the computer- and
information-related areas of manufacturing. And of course there are jobs in the
service industry, such as working as a gas station attendant. But students do that
kind of thing as a part-time job in high school and are not really interested in
doing that in the future.

Mirroring trends in other postindustrial societies, employment in
Japan's service sector in recent years has become more and more polarized
between high-paying full-time jobs in finance, insurance, real estate, and
other information-related businesses and low-paying, repetitive, dead-
end jobs in retail sales or service establishments such as restaurants. The
former category is increasingly reserved for university graduates. Jobs
in the latter category have become a mishmash of full-time jobs for new

high school or two-year training school graduates, part-time jobs for high school students, part-time jobs for housewives returning to the workforce, and full- and part-time jobs for a growing number of young people who have not found stable employment in other sectors of the economy. Given these trends, it seems very unlikely that high school-employer ties in the sales and service sectors will rebound in the future.

Employers' sentiments as expressed in the Employer Survey are consistent with the quantitative behavioral data on school-employer ties in this chapter. An overwhelming proportion (84 percent) of surveyed employers expressed a preference for recruiting only from certain types of high schools. Just as the vocational high school, Nishi Takase, had the greatest concentration of school-employer ties among the three schools examined in this chapter, the employers in my survey who had recruitment preferences were the most enthusiastic about recruiting only from industrial high schools. While more than half expressed this preference, fewer than five percent expressed instead a preference to recruit only from general high schools. The rest preferred to recruit from some combination of industrial, commercial, and general high schools.

Employers in my survey who recruit only from industrial high schools were also very likely to say that they expect male high school graduates to stay with the firm for at least ten years – nearly nine out of ten feel this way. This is consistent with the idea that such employers "invest" in long-term recruitment relationships with a set of schools whom they trust to send their best graduates, and they likewise expect to invest in these young workers and gain their commitment to their firms. The same employers estimated that in fact nearly half of the male high school graduates they hire do stay in the firm for at least ten years. In stark contrast, among the handful of employers who stated a preference to recruit only from general high schools, none said that they expect workers to remain with the firm for ten or more years. And in point of fact, they reported that no workers do stay with the firm that long. Not surprisingly, firms in the sales sector and in the low-level service sector reported the highest rates of turnover for the high school graduates they hired compared to firms in other industries. Employers in the sales industry were considerably more likely than other firms to say that they were not satisfied with the high school graduates they had hired over the prior three years. And employers in this industry were more likely than employers in any other industry to say that if they were able to, they would hire only university graduates and skip the high school graduate labor market entirely.

None of this bodes well for graduates of nonelite general high schools who do not go on for higher education. If they want to go directly into the labor market, they are less likely than industrial high school graduates to enter Japan's remaining jobs in manufacturing, skilled construction, or other skilled blue-collar areas, and the most likely instead to go into low-level service sector or sales jobs. Compared to vocational high school graduates, general high school graduates have few vocational skills to offer employers and have little access to introductions to employers through their schools. Compared to higher education graduates, they have little general human capital. What will become of them in the future? In the next chapter I dig deeper into this question.

5

Networks of Advantage and Disadvantage for New Graduates

"Firms vary in the types of employees they want. There are some that want to hire cheerful and energetic young workers and others that are mainly interested in young people who earned good grades in school. We can judge what the firms want when we meet directly with them – I wouldn't say that this is difficult, but it certainly is time-consuming. In a sense, the firms are doing their PR and we are doing ours."

– Teacher in the guidance department of a vocational high school

Japanese high schools' stable ties with employers thrived during the 1960s-1980s when Japan experienced economic growth rates that were the envy of other industrial nations, a period when the manufacturing sector and the demand for high school graduates were booming. Then the economy slipped, and Japanese employers embarked on the most significant employment restructuring they had undertaken in half a century. Most employers anxiously tried to preserve employment stability for the corps of middle-aged men to whom they had implicitly guaranteed permanent employment two to three decades ago. Meanwhile, rates of unemployment and part-time employment shot up for Japanese youth. Of even greater concern to the Japanese government, the rate of youth idleness increased. By the middle of the present decade, nearly one-fifth of all fifteen- to nineteen-year-old Japanese were idle – neither employed, in school, nor unemployed (officially defined as actively searching for a job).

The high rates of unemployment, part-time employment, and idleness (not searching for work) among young men show that a large number of them failed to embark on a stable work trajectory in the 1990s and in the first part of the present decade. The magnitude of their numbers sent shock waves through Japanese policy circles, with vigorous debate over whether the labor demand side (economic recession and employment restructuring) was primarily responsible or whether the labor supply side was to blame (young people's "fickleness" regarding the type of work they want, or their lack of a strong work ethic).[1]

In the course of the debate over who is to blame for the current generation's employment instability, an important element of Japan's hitherto efficient high school-work system has been largely ignored: the structural inequality inherent in the system itself.

In this chapter I argue that one of the keys to understanding the problem of idleness among high school graduates lies in the highly uneven distribution of job opportunities across schools – a skewed distribution of opportunities that was built into the school-work system itself. The recession of the 1990s clearly exposed this underlying segmentation. I use two original data sets I constructed. The first is comprised of data on Kanagawa prefecture's public high schools, and the second is comprised of detailed data on the labor market recruitment of graduating seniors from all high schools in one district in the Yokohama-Kawasaki area. This district serves as a case study for how employers distribute their employee recruitment efforts across high schools of different types (general and vocational) and different quality. I use network analysis techniques to explore the uneven distribution of entry-level job openings sent to high schools in the mid-1990s after the economic recession was underway. This analysis shows just how few jobs were available to general high school graduates and how many more job openings were funneled to graduates of vocational schools. By drawing a connection between the uneven distribution of job openings across high schools and the patterns of youth idleness these high schools produced, we can see in greater detail which young people have been the most "at risk" for falling into idleness.

The methods used in this chapter are quite different from those used by Japanese social scientists in their attempts to better understand which youth become NEET (not in education, employment, or training) or *furītā* (young people who voluntarily change jobs frequently and who also sometimes "stop out" of the labor force). These populations have been very hard for social scientists to systematically study. Labor force data collected by the government make it possible to estimate the overall number of young people who are not in school

---

[1] See the discussion in Genda (2001).

or in the labor force. But finding them in order to interview them in person in a systematic way is very difficult. This has made it difficult to understand much about the educational backgrounds and experiences of young people who fall into idleness after graduating. By using high schools as the unit of analysis, this chapter offers a clearer view of which types of high schools may in a sense be "producing" idle youth. Young people's pathway into idleness, I argue, is often related to the dearth of employment opportunities their particular high school is able to provide under Japan's highly regulated school-work transition system.

PATTERNS OF IDLENESS AND THE
HIGH SCHOOL-WORK TRANSITION

Rates of idleness among Japanese fifteen- to nineteen-year-olds increased from 11 percent in the early 1990s to almost 20 percent by 2004 (a rise of nearly 80 percentage points) and from 5 to 12 percent for twenty- to twenty-four-year-olds. In every region of Japan, idleness rates were the highest among late adolescents, a group that includes many high school graduates and some dropouts. The Kanto region – including the Tokyo metropolitan area as well as Kanagawa, Saitama, Chiba, Ibaraki, Gunma, and Tochigi prefectures – has had a lower rate of NEET than other regions of Japan such as Hokkaido, Tohoku, and Kyushu.

A comparison of these high rates of NEET with Japanese government statistics on the "rate of promised employment" (*naitei*) for new high school graduates yields a puzzling picture.[2] Figure 5.1 shows government figures on the percentage of job-seeking high school seniors who had found a postgraduation job by March of the year they were graduating, signifying that they would start their new job on April 1 along with the rest of that year's new hires. In Chapter 3 I showed that the job-opening-to-applicant ratio for these students as measured in September of each year increased to more than 3.0 during the years of the bubble economy and then tumbled to slightly over 1.0 in the present decade. But Figure 5.1 shows that the rate of promised employment hardly varied across these years, remaining well above 90 percent in nearly every year.

---

[2] This rate is called the *naiteiritsu*, and measures the percentage of all job-hunting high school seniors who succeeded in getting a postgraduation placement into a full-time job that will begin on April 1 – the traditional date at which new graduates begin work.

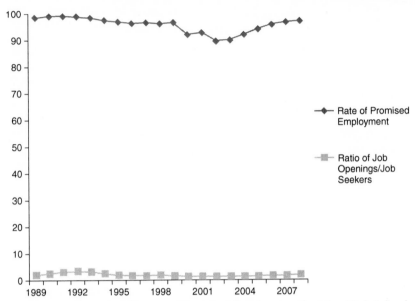

FIGURE 5.1. Change in the Rate of Promised Employment for New High School Graduates: March of Each Year.
Source: Ministry of Health, Labour and Welfare, *Heisei 19 nendo kōkō-chūgaku shinsotsusha no shūshoku naitei jōkyō nado ni tsuite.*

Based on that statistic, things do not seem to be as bad as suggested either by the increase in the number of idle young people or the decline in the number of job openings. How can the rate of promised employment have remained so stable and so high throughout these troubled years of low labor demand?

Government statistics, as well as my interviews with high school teachers, indicate that the rate of job-changing among youth is quite high. Could this explain the seeming contradiction between the high rate of initial job placement after graduation and the high rate of idleness? In other words, young people who quit or are dismissed from their jobs and neither go on for further education, enter another job, or register as unemployed workers will naturally fall into the category of "idle." Can we therefore explain away the problem of youths' idleness by their pickiness about the type of work they do, as indicated by the rates at which they simply leave their jobs and the workforce altogether?

This explanation doesn't work very well. When I visited high schools in Kanagawa in the mid-1990s, early 2000s, and 2005, teachers narrated a more complicated reality to me. When I began doing interviews with them in the mid-1990s they recounted the extreme difficulties their students were facing in the job market and told me about the increasing numbers of seniors who could not find jobs by the time they graduated. These narratives were highly discrepant with statistics published by the Ministry of Health, Labour and Welfare showing that about 90 percent of graduating seniors had a job in hand when they graduated. (This official rate is also the statistic that has been consistently reported in the English-language social science literature on the Japanese school-work system to indicate that even in the depths of the economic recession, the system was performing very well.) This was puzzling.

I learned the reason for this discrepancy through my discussions with teachers in schools' guidance departments. Once I established rapport with teachers, they were very frank and honest about the difficulties they faced in trying to place their students into full-time jobs they could start on April 1, the conventional start of the work year. Each month, every high school is required to send to the local public employment security office the statistics for how well the school has done in terms of securing promises of employment from companies for job-hunting seniors. The public employment security offices across Japan aggregate these statistics to produce the overall rate of promised employment for high school graduates in the prefecture. But as the fall months tick by, some job-hunting students who get an interview with an employer after being recommended by their school do not pass the interview. Up until the past few years, students have been restricted to applying to only one job at a time (called the *hitori isshasei*, or "one person, one company" rule). They must get the school's recommendation for a job, wait to see if they get an interview, and then hope that the interview results in a job offer. If they go through this process and fail, they must consult once more with the guidance department teachers and get the school's recommendation for another job, then try once again to get an interview and a hiring promise from the next company. Once a student fails in this process two or three times, he or she may simply give up and drop out of the process altogether. Instead, the student might change plans and think about going to a two-year training school or trying another way of looking for a job after graduation, such as answering ads in job-hunting magazines.

Because many two-year training schools have low entrance requirements (sometimes matched, unfortunately, by very high tuition fees), this is the most likely educational alternative for students who have failed in successive job interviews. If students decide to follow this route, their case is shifted to the column in the school's statistics that tabulates the number of students proceeding on for higher education. Their case is removed from the column that lists job-hunters. Likewise, if students find a job through a relative or through another method, they are counted as successful job hunters even though they did not use an introduction (institutional capital) from the school. Finally, if they drop out of the placement process altogether and are unsure about what they are going to do after graduation, they are entered into the "uncertain" category (along with *rōnin*, students who failed to gain entrance into the university of their choice and who plan to sit out for one year and retake the entrance exam the following year). So ultimately, the denominator (the number of job-seekers) that is used in calculating the rate of promised employment becomes smaller and smaller. This artificially increases the rate of "successful" job-seeking, because the number only includes those students who kept looking for a job rather than becoming discouraged and dropping out of the job-hunting process.

Returning to the published government statistics on the job-hunting success of high school graduates, I also noticed a large difference in the rates depending upon the month in which the data were collected. Figure 5.1, the one conventionally used in English-language research praising the Japanese high school-work system, is based on statistics from the end of March, after the school year has ended and just before the new employment year commences (April 1). By this time, most high school seniors who had intended to get a postgraduation job but failed to do so had dropped out of the process altogether and were therefore no longer counted as job-hunters. No wonder, then, that rates of "successful job-hunting" are so high and hardly vary from year to year!

My further investigation into statistics from the Ministry of Health, Labour and Welfare yielded Figure 5.2. This figure shows how the rate of high school graduates' job-hunting success changes from September through March of each year. Rates are below 50 percent just after the start of the job-hunting season, and increase significantly by November and then again by January.

Over this four-month period two processes are unfolding, according to the high school teachers I interviewed. On the one hand, many students succeed in receiving a postgraduation employment promise. On the other hand, another group of students becomes discouraged by their

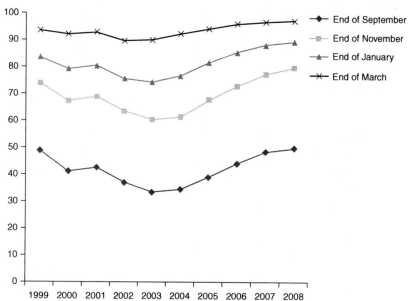

FIGURE 5.2. Rate of Promised Employment for New High School Graduates: Change in Figures for September–March of Each Year.
Source: Ministry of Health, Labour and Welfare, *Heisei 19 nendo kōkō-chūgaku shinsotsusha no shūshoku naitei jōkyō nado ni tsuite.*

failure to find a job. They switch gears and take themselves out of the process. According to teachers, very few students receive job offers after December – by that time, the job matches that are likely to occur at all have taken place. Small companies that were unable to predict their labor needs in the early part of the recruitment season (in the fall) may come up with a job or two in December, January, or even February but this only slightly affects the overall job placement rate, especially because teachers have a hard time convincing students to take jobs in such small companies. It is highly likely that most of the reported increase in job placement rates between January and March (as much as a 16-percentage point increase in 2003 and 2005, as shown in Figure 5.2) is due to discouraged students dropping out of the process and thereby dropping out of the denominator.[3]

---

[3] After completing this manuscript I realized that Kosugi Reiko also discusses these processes in *Furītā to iu ikikata* (2003), published in English as *Escape from Work* (2008).

This story illustrates the importance of digging deep to find out how official statistics are created. Once I realized how schools calculate their statistics, I became more interested in looking in depth at their statistics reporting the postgraduate destinations of students. Surely these could provide a window into the processes through which patterns of successful job search and its counterpart – idleness – are produced. To pursue this, I used two strategies: 1) I compiled the postgraduate destination statistics reported by all public high schools in Kanagawa, and 2) I constructed a database of all of the job listings for high school seniors in one district of Kawasaki, which I had obtained through the generosity of an official at a local public employment security office. (This story was recounted in Chapter 3.) In the rest of the chapter I show what these data reveal about where Japan's "idle" graduates come from and why.

WHERE DO NEW HIGH SCHOOL GRADUATES GO?

Table 5.1 shows the destinations of new high school graduates in Kanagawa prefecture between 1997 and 2004, averaged over all public high schools in the prefecture.[4] Consistent with the overall increase in university entrance rates in Japan, the rate of matriculation to university rose steeply in Kanagawa over this period. Rates of matriculation to junior college declined, which is also consistent with national trends. Rates of entrance to two-year training schools increased during the 1990s and reached a fairly stable level (about 22 percent of all high school graduates) by the end of the decade. The proportion of high school graduates who entered a job at the time of graduation fell to 8 percent in 2003 and then rose to 11 percent in 2004. But again, it is important to remember that this is the rate of successful job-hunting. It does not include high school seniors who became discouraged while using their high school's guidance department resources and dropped out of the job-hunting

---

[4] For some prefectures such as Kanagawa, statistics are available on the postgraduation destinations of students in each high school from *juken annai* (literally "test-taking yearbooks"), yearly publications put out by private publishing companies to help ninth graders and their families decide which high school they should apply to. I used one of these, the *Kanagawa-ken Juken Annai*, to tabulate statistics for all high schools in the prefecture. The yearbook shows a pie chart for each high school in Kanagawa-ken, with percentages attached to the pieces of the pie to represent the proportion of graduates from that school who proceeded on to each of five possible destinations: university, junior college, two-year training school, a job, or an "unknown" destination.

TABLE 5.1. *Immediate Postgraduation Destinations of High School Graduates in Kanagawa Prefecture, 1997–2004*

	1997	1999	2001	2002	2003	2004
University	19.8	20.2	27.3	31.5	33.5	34.2
Junior college	14.4	15.0	13.4	11.9	11.1	8.9
Two-year training schools	23.3	23.2	21.9	22.4	22.5	22.1
Job	11.7	10.8	9.3	8.7	8.4	10.7
Uncertain	30.8	30.8	29.1	27.7	26.6	24.8

Notes:

1) Unfortunately, I was not able to obtain data for 1998, so that year is not included in the table.

2) Statistics were calculated by the author from data available in the *Kanagawa-ken juken annai*, for various years.

process – or perhaps even dropped out of high school – before receiving a job offer. Such students are included in the "uncertain" category, which surprisingly comprises nearly 30 percent of Kanagawa public high schools' graduating seniors.

The "uncertain" category is very heterogeneous. It includes high school seniors who decided to be *rōnin* as well as seniors who had no immediate postgraduation plans. The latter group is equivalent to the "idle" population of eighteen-year-olds. The category of "uncertain" mixes these youth together with *rōnin*, when in fact the two populations are quite different in terms of their ultimate destinations in the labor market or in higher education. In order to estimate the "true" rate of idleness, we need to separate out *rōnin* from those youth who are truly idle – who are not in school, not working, and not preparing for the university entrance competition.

If a high school is a top-performing one with many graduating seniors who successfully pass the university entrance examination, it is likely that a large proportion of the seniors who fail to pass the examination become *rōnin*. That is, the strong sorting of students into high schools at the end of middle school by ability and aspirations means that in high schools with a large percentage of seniors immediately matriculating to universities, a high proportion of the students with "undetermined" destinations at the point of graduation will sit out a year and retake the entrance exam. If this is the case, we can estimate the "true" percentage of idle graduates by subtracting the percent of *rōnin* from the total percent uncertain.

TABLE 5.2. *Postgraduation Destinations of High School Graduates in Kanagawa Prefecture, 1997–2004, Including "True" Rates of University Matriculation and Idleness*

	1997	1999	2001	2002	2003	2004
Reported university matriculation rate	19.8	20.2	27.3	31.5	33.5	34.2
"True" university matriculation rate	30.2	30.9	38.8	43.6	45.3	46.6
Reported rate of idleness	30.8	30.8	29.1	27.7	26.6	24.8
"True" rate of idleness	20.5	20.3	17.2	15.1	14.0	12.4
Highest proportion of "true" idle graduates from any high school	48.1	48.1	46.0	46.3	44.1	40.6

I estimated the percentage of *rōnin* as the product of the percentage of graduates who proceeded directly to university and the overall percentage uncertain. That is,

$$P_i = P_u - P_c P_u$$

where P_i is the "true" idleness rate, P_u is the percent uncertain and P_c is the percent directly entering university.[5] This estimate results in a downward revision of the percent idle because we have essentially subtracted out the percentage of graduates who are probably *rōnin* from the overall percentage of idle graduates. We can then add the estimated percentage of *rōnin* ($P_c P_u$) to the observed percentage of graduates who go directly to university, to obtain an estimate of the "true" percent who go to university (either immediately after graduation or a year or two later).

This procedure can be used to estimate the true rate of matriculation to university and the true rate of idleness for each high school in Kanagawa prefecture. Table 5.2 compares the reported rates (from Table 5.1) to the "true" rates.

As shown in the table, once the rate of university matriculation has been adjusted to include the estimated percentage of graduates from each high school who become *rōnin*, the overall rate of university matriculation increases to 47 percent for 2004. This figure is very close to the

---

[5] I am indebted to my former student Hiroshi Ono for suggesting this estimation procedure.

TABLE 5.3. *Relationship between High School Quality and the Destinations of Graduates, Kanagawa Prefecture*

	1997	1999	2001	2002	2003	2004
University	.92*	.95*	.93*	.93*	.93*	.93*
Junior college	−.34*	−.45*	−.05	−.12	−.16	−.17
Two–year training school	−.81*	−.86*	−.73*	−.75*	−.70*	−.68*
Job	−.80*	−.73*	−.83*	−.82*	−.81*	−.81*
Uncertain	.52*	.59*	.03	−.02	−.04	−.05
"True" university	.92*	.96*	.95*	.95*	.95*	.95*
"True" uncertain	−.66*	−.74*	−.82*	−.84*	−.84*	−.86*

Notes:
1) *p<.05.
2) Figures are correlations calculated by the author.

actual figure (49 percent) reported by the Ministry of Education, Culture, Sports, Science and Technology for Kanagawa prefecture in the same year, which testifies nicely to the accuracy of the estimation procedure. The estimation procedure reduces the percentage of idle graduates from each school by about one-third to one-half.

There is tremendous variation in all of these rates across high schools. For instance, in 2004 the top high school in Kanagawa prefecture had a minimum entrance exam score of 68 and sent 78 percent of its graduates directly to university. The lowest-ranked high school, with a minimum entrance exam score of only 30, sent just 4 percent of its graduates directly to university. The bottom of Table 5.2 shows that the highest rate of "truly" idle graduates for any high school in Kanagawa-ken in 2004 was an astounding 41 percent.

Which high schools tend to produce the most young people with no certain destination at the time they graduate? And is there a strong statistical relationship between a high school's quality (as measured by the minimum entrance exam score required for admission) and the proportion of its graduates that are in the true idle category? Table 5.3 shows these figures, as well as the statistical relationship between a school's required entrance exam score and the percentage of its graduates going to all other destinations besides into idleness.

As one would expect, there is an extremely strong positive statistical relationship between a high school's minimum entrance exam score and the proportion of its graduates who go directly to university. Row 1 shows that this correlation is consistently higher than .90. There is generally only a weak and nonstatistically significant relationship between a school's entrance exam score and the proportion of its graduates who go to junior college (row 2), and a negative relationship between exam score and the proportion of graduates who go directly to two-year training schools or into the labor market (rows 3 and 4). Naturally, very few graduates of top-ranked high schools go directly into the job market; most go instead to university.

Once the statistical adjustment is made for *rōnin* and they are included in the "true" number of university matriculants, the relationship between high school quality and the university matriculation rate is even stronger (row 5). But it is the relationship between a school's quality and the proportion of its graduates with "uncertain" (idle) destinations at the time of graduation that is the most interesting of all. Notably, although there was a positive and statistically significant relationship between these two phenomena in the late 1990s, by the early 2000s the relationship had changed considerably and was no longer statistically significant. What does this indicate? It is probably closely related to the fact that it has become easier to enter university in recent years in Japan, given the very small size of recent cohorts of eighteen-year-olds. Second- and third-ranked universities have gone begging for students. So it is likely that among students reporting uncertain destinations after high school, the proportion who are *rōnin* has substantially declined over time, leaving in the uncertain category only those young people who truly are idle and jobless. This is reflected in row 5, which shows that a high school's quality is no longer closely related to the proportion of idle graduates it produces.

Finally, the statistical relationship between a school's minimum required entrance exam score and the percentage of its graduates who are truly idle (row 6) is opposite to the relationship between the exam score and rates of university matriculation from the school. In other words, the high schools in Kanagawa prefecture that rank lowest in academic quality produce the highest percentages of idle graduates. Moreover, the size of the coefficient in the bottom row of the table shows that this tendency has increased over time. This is an important clue to where idle young people are increasingly coming from: not from elite high schools but from the lowest-ranking ones.

Should we conclude that students in the lowest-ranking high schools are the least motivated to go on to higher education or work? In other words, are they the ones whose preferences have changed the most, and in the least agreeable direction in terms of the standard value system in Japan? Before reaching this conclusion, let us look concretely at the limited opportunities faced by students in some of the prefecture's "worst" high schools.

NETWORKS OF DISADVANTAGE

How is employers' recruitment interest spread across high schools of different types and different quality? The Yokohama-Kawasaki job opening announcements in the mid-1990s to which I gained access (described in Chapter 2) include all the job openings[6] distributed to the twelve high schools in the local administrative district under that public employment security office's jurisdiction during the previous year.[7] The 1,208 job opening forms were filed by 849 firms that intended to recruit seniors graduating in 1995 from at least one of the twelve high schools in the district. The vast majority (88 percent) of these 849 employers specified on their job announcement forms the school or schools they were targeting for recruitment. This makes the documents an invaluable source of data that allows us to link the characteristics of employers and their job openings on the one hand to the characteristics of the local high schools from which they wanted to recruit graduating seniors on the other.[8]

The beauty of the job announcement data is that they give a "snapshot" of the labor market faced by high school seniors in a particular local area. I do not want to claim that this area can be considered representative of all areas in Japan. As mentioned earlier, rates of youth idleness vary across regions of Japan, and Kanagawa prefecture has one of the lower rates; the job market has remained fairly good relative to a number of more remote regions. But having access to these fine-grained job opening data offers the chance to look closely at the opportunity structure facing graduates from

---

[6] Job openings are different from actual job placements. A firm sends its job announcements to a school to express an interest in inviting students from the school to interview for positions within the firm. But the school may not necessarily recommend its students to interview with the firm, and likewise, the firm may not necessarily decide to hire students recommended by the school.

[7] In total there were fourteen administrative districts in Kanagawa in the mid-1990s. The district analyzed here is highly representative of the prefecture as a whole, especially the most urban districts, in terms of the percent of high school graduates who go on to further education versus entering the labor market. Standardized test scores of students in this district are also very close to the average for the prefecture.

[8] Firms that chose to recruit from schools in this district could also recruit from schools outside the district. Because firms provide a complete listing of the local schools in which they are interested but do not necessarily give a complete listing of the nonlocal schools (outside of the local public employment security office's jurisdiction) to which they send their forms, the analysis here is restricted to the local area.

high schools of different quality (as measured by their required entrance exam score) and different types (general and vocational).

The data consist of a total of 969 job opening announcements sent by the 749 firms that specified at least one school as a recruiting target in the public employment security office's administrative district. My colleague Zun Tang and I formatted the data into a firm-by-school matrix, and then converted the network affiliation data into a one-mode school-by-school network dataset. This facilitates an analysis that shows which schools are competing with one another for the attention of the same employers.[9]

Table 5.4 shows the characteristics of the twelve high schools in the administrative district of the public employment security office. I designate this as "District 1." To protect the identity of the high schools, I have given each one a pseudonym.

Nine of the twelve high schools are general and three are vocational. Of the three vocational schools, two are industrial and one is a combined commercial and industrial school. The latter (Nishi Takase) was one of the schools from which I received the most cooperation in my research, and it figured prominently in Chapter 4 as a school with a history of strong ties with employers. After listing the vocational high schools, the table lists the general high schools starting with the one that has the highest minimum required entrance exam score and the highest percentage of students going directly to university after graduation.

The three vocational high schools send large percentages (between 46 and 62 percent) of their graduates directly into the labor market. This is shown in the "job" column in Table 5.4. For the general high schools, this percentage ranges from 0 (Hayashi) to 42 percent (Seibi).

The academic quality hierarchy in this school district is starkly apparent, as is true for most school districts throughout Japan. Hayashi (fourth in the list) is a "feeder" school to a specific university, which explains why such a large number of its graduates (93 percent) proceed directly to university.[10] The percentage of university-bound graduates falls as one moves down the table, reaching a dismal 1.5 percent for Seibi. This is mirrored in the distribution of the minimum required entrance exam score across the twelve schools, which ranges from a high of sixty-one (Hayashi) to a low of thirty-two (Yamakawa), with missing information for Seibi.

---

[9] The technical procedures for producing the network structures are described in Brinton and Tang (2010).

[10] A very small percentage of Japanese high schools are feeder schools, meaning that entrance into them privileges graduates for entrance into an associated university.

TABLE 5.4. *Characteristics of District 1 High Schools*

School	Type	Minimum Required Entrance Exam Score	Students' Destinations				
			Higher Education			Job	Uncertain
			University	Junior College	Two-Year Training School		
A. Kibane	Industrial	44	9.0	5.5	24.2	46.5	14.8
B. Matsui	Industrial	NA	1.7	0.9	18.9	61.8	16.7
C. Nishi Takase	Industrial/Commercial	40	3.9	7.1	22.1	58.8	8.1
D. Hayashi	General	61	93.0	0.2	0.1	0.0	6.7
E. Chūkai	General	50	38.4	10.4	11.4	1.0	38.8
F. Yamanishi	General	43	17.7	24.6	16.1	7.3	34.3
G. Funezawa	General	39	12.5	14.9	27.0	7.5	38.1
H. Kuruhashi	General	36	4.4	9.1	29.9	29.9	26.7
I. Nitta	General	34	NA	NA	NA	NA	NA
J. Shinano	General	33	NA	NA	22.6	38.7	33.9
K. Yamakawa	General	32	3.2	9.4	31.3	23.0	33.1
L. Seibi	General	NA	1.5	1.3	24.6	42.0	30.6

What types of firms aim to recruit graduating seniors from these high schools into full-time jobs? The job opening announcement data show that the firms range in size from tiny ones with just two employees to extremely large ones with many thousands of employees. The average firm size is about 1,300 employees but the median size is around 150 employees. Nearly three-quarters of the firms have fewer than 500 employees; the majority of firms in this geographical area that hire high school graduates are mid-sized or small firms. Some firms were established as late as 1994 and others more than a hundred years ago.[11] The average age of firms is about forty years.

Table 5.5 shows the industrial distribution of the firms and the occupational categories into which their job openings fall. About half of the firms are in the construction or manufacturing industries. Overall, jobs are relatively evenly distributed across occupations, with the fewest firms advertising for operators or laborers.[12] Many more firms designate jobs as being for males (59 percent) than for females (11 percent) or for either sex (30 percent). I do not show this in the table, but the jobs advertised for females are very heavily concentrated (85 percent) in clerical, sales, and service occupations, whereas the job openings for men are much more broadly distributed across occupational categories. Slightly less than 70 percent of the firms are in the immediate geographical area or in the nearby Tokyo metropolitan area.

There are a number of interesting features of these firms. Consistent with the conception of new young employees as minors who are entering a significant and encompassing new *ba* in their lives, nearly two-thirds of the firms provide company-owned housing. The job opening form even includes the question, "Will someone in the firm bring the new worker to the workplace?" This is presumably a holdover from earlier times when many fresh graduates were recruited into manufacturing firms in the Kawasaki-Yokohama area from rural prefectures and literally had little

[11] All but two firms were younger than 125 years old. The two exceptions (one established in 1544 and the other in 1699) are mid-sized seafood processing companies located in Tokyo; one has 380 employees and the other has 785 employees.

[12] Unskilled blue-collar jobs became very unpopular even with high school graduates during the "bubble economy" of the late 1980s, when labor demand was high and graduates could afford to snub these jobs in favor of skilled blue-collar and, especially, service and sales jobs. During this period, unskilled manual labor came to be regarded as "3K" jobs, with the k's indicating *kitanai, kiken,* and *kitsui* (dirty, dangerous, and difficult). Employers increasingly turned to foreign laborers and to Japanese middle school graduates to fill these jobs, and this trend (along with high school graduates' disdain for such jobs) has continued.

TABLE 5.5. *Characteristics of Recruiting Firms*

Variables	Percentage
Industry	
Construction	27.9
Manufacturing	22.6
Commercial services	22.6
Wholesale and retail sales	17.1
Personal services	9.9
Occupation	
Production	24.4
Technical, professional	22.4
Clerical	21.1
Sales, service	17.8
Operators, laborers	14.5
Gender of job (as specified by recruiting firm)	
Male	58.9
Female	11.1
Either	30.0
Location of firm	
In the local district or in Tokyo	68.7
Other area	31.3
Number of firms	749

Notes:
1) Among the firms that sent out multiple job announcements, 130 firms offered jobs that are in different occupations. So the distribution of occupation is calculated not by firm but by position (N=969).
2) Percentages were calculated by the author from job announcement data.

knowledge of where they were going when they took a job. Only a trivial proportion (6 percent) of the employers in the present study stated on the job opening announcement that someone would be available to accompany the new graduate to the workplace. Still, for more than one-fifth of the listed jobs, employers stated that they would pay the new worker's moving expenses.

An extended interview with a manager at one of the companies that sent its job opening announcement to schools in the district as well as to schools in other regions of Japan illuminates how and why some companies adopt what might be called a nurturing attitude (or more negatively put, a paternalistic attitude) toward new recruits. The personnel officer at this particular company told me that the firm recruits about half of its new hires from Tokyo and surrounding areas such as Saitama and

Kanagawa and the other half from more distant prefectures. The company has a dormitory and pays travel expenses for high school seniors' interviews, too. As the personnel officer put it, "This helps a lot – otherwise, we would not be successful in recruiting from *chihō* [more remote areas]." In our discussion he stressed the importance of these policies in terms of reassuring parents of the students who were being hired from other prefectures.

Virtually all of the jobs listed in the job opening announcements carry health insurance, accident insurance, and unemployment insurance. This bears on one of the many concerns that high school teachers often expressed to me about the part-time jobs their students hold during the school year – jobs that students sometimes contemplate continuing after graduation in lieu of searching for a full-time job with the school's help. As one teacher put it, "The main problem I see with part-time jobs for high school students is that they rarely include accidence insurance. So if the student gets injured on the job, what happens?"

In addition to providing insurance, virtually all of the firms recruiting seniors into full-time postgraduation jobs have a bonus system. In the large majority of cases, the bonus is given on a semi-annual bonus. The bonus amounts listed on the job opening announcements range from two to three and a half times the monthly salary, amounting to a substantial supplement to the base pay. Here again, part-time jobs for high school students pale in comparison.

All told, the nearly one thousand full-time jobs advertised to graduating seniors in the district are hardly "bad" jobs. The median number of workers being recruited by each of the firms in the mid-1990s was five, and the average job offered a monthly salary of 165,000 yen (in 1994) and a yearly salary of 2.7 million yen including bonus. These figures translated into about $1,650 per month and $27,000 per year in 1994 dollars.

But these job opening announcements are not distributed by employers evenly across high schools. Which high schools do employers tend to favor? Are there observable patterns, and is it possible to form generalizations from these patterns?

Firm-School Networks. Figure 5.3 is a visual representation of which firms sent job opening announcements to which schools. The dark-colored circles demarcated by letters indicate schools and the light-shaded circles represent individual firms.

It is immediately clear that Schools A (Kibane) and B (Matsui), the two industrial high schools in the district, are in an altogether different

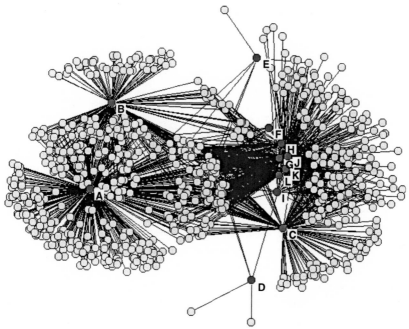

FIGURE 5.3. The Firm-School Network of Job Announcement–Sending Relations. *Note*: Dark-colored circles represent schools and light-colored circles represent firms. Lines connecting the circles represent the job announcement–sending relations.

league than the other schools. One cluster of firms sent their job opening announcements only to School A, another cluster sent them only to School B, and a considerable number of firms sent their announcements to both schools. Alternatively, the firms in the lower right side of the figure contacted only School C (Nishi Takase, the sole high school in the district with both a commercial and an industrial track). The firms in the middle and upper right side of the figure contacted some combination of schools F through L (in Table 5.4, Yamanishi through Seibi high schools). In the middle of the figure are employers that sent their announcements both to Schools A and B on the left and to School C and some schools in the large cluster of general high schools on the right.

Schools D and E, Hayashi and Chūkai, are definite outliers; they receive very few announcements of job openings. This is understandable because they are the top two general high schools in the district. With most of their students aspiring to go to universities and colleges and very

TABLE 5.6. *Firms' Recruiting Strategies*

Target Schools	Type of School	Number of Recruiting Firms	Percent of All Firms
A (Kibane)	Industrial	205	27.4
A+B (Kibane, Matsui)	Industrial	128	17.1
B (Matsui)	Industrial	52	6.9
C (Nishi Takase)	Industrial/commercial	48	6.3
A+C, B+C, or A+B+C	Industrial + industrial/commercial	14	1.9
Mix	Vocational + general	202	27.0
Only general high schools	General	100	13.4

Note: Calculations are based on network analysis of job announcements sent to schools.

few entering the labor market right after graduation, it is natural that they are at the periphery of the network linking firms and schools. Any employers who sent job opening announcements to these schools would likely find few if any takers. The other seven schools, F through L, are in a cluster that represents the middle and lower end of the quality hierarchy of general high schools in District 1.

Employers' Recruitment Strategies. To analyze the structure of the network, we calculated what is called the Euclidean distance between firms. This produces groupings of firms based on the strategy they followed in sending job opening announcements to high schools (Table 5.6). Not surprisingly, firm groupings are very consistent with the network structure shown in Figure 5.3. Firms' strategies number 125 in total (far fewer than the theoretically maximum number of possible strategies), but the majority of firms follow one of just a handful of recruiting strategies. In fact, a little more than 50 percent of firms follow one of three strategies: They recruit only from School A (Kibane), only from School B (Matsui), or from both of these schools. Another 6 percent of firms send their job opening announcements only to the industrial-commercial high school in the district (School C, Nishi Takase), and 2 percent of firms choose a combination of the commercial and industrial high schools.

Adding together the firms that recruit only from industrial high schools, only from the industrial-commercial high school, or from both types of schools shows that about 60 percent of firms only contact vocational high schools – they do not send notices of job openings to any general high schools in the district. Among the remaining firms, 27 percent contact a mix of vocational and general high schools, and about 13 percent contact only general high schools. From this analysis, it is abundantly clear that the majority of employers focus their attention only on vocational schools – especially the two industrial ones – in their recruitment of new high school graduates.

What leads firms to adopt a specific recruiting strategy? In particular, what leads employers to recruit from vocational compared to general high schools? This was explored using multinomial logistic regression. Neither firm size nor the age of a firm appears to reliably predict the recruitment strategy employers use, but larger firms are somewhat more likely to contact only vocational high schools. If large firms have multiple positions for which they are recruiting, they are more apt to contact both vocational and general high schools rather than solely focusing on one or the other. Firms with higher-paying jobs are the least likely to target only general high schools to the exclusion of vocational schools. This is further evidence that vocational high schools have a somewhat privileged position in the recruitment process. This is consistent with the analyses in Chapter 4 and with the views expressed in the Employer Survey.

While gender is not my focus here, it is very noticeable how much employers' labeling of jobs as "male," "female," or suitable for either sex affects their recruitment strategy. Compared to firms that state no particular gender preference for the job for which they are recruiting, employers who only want to recruit men are more likely to send their job announcements to industrial high schools. This makes sense in light of the fact that industrial high schools are predominantly male. Construction and manufacturing firms tend to favor the industrial high schools, and firms in the sales and service industries tend to avoid focusing their recruitment efforts on these schools alone. This also makes sense given industrial high schools' particular emphasis on preparing students for jobs in the construction (or engineering) and manufacturing sectors. Firms in the sales and personal service industries are more likely to rely on the industrial-commercial high school or on the general high schools for job candidates.

Overall, it appears that employers' recruiting strategies are heavily driven by the content of the work and the number of job openings they have, whether they want to hire males or females into the job, and the firm's industry. Firms appear to be very strategic in choosing to recruit students from schools who will fit well into the job openings they have. As a result, recruitment is highly patterned across the twelve schools in

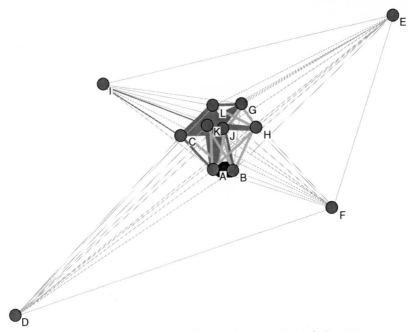

FIGURE 5.4. Competition among High Schools to Receive Job Opening
Announcements for New Graduates.

the district, with some schools receiving a large amount of attention from
prospective employers of their graduates and others receiving very little
attention.

School Competition. So far I have talked about the network structure
from the perspective of firms. But we can also think of the network structure from the perspective of schools. Figure 5.4 is a visual picture of the
structure of competition among the twelve high schools in the district.
This shows several interesting things about the competition among high
schools – especially general high schools – to attract employers' recruitment attention to their graduating seniors.

The analysis of employers' recruiting strategies has already shown
that the two best general high schools in the district (Schools D and E,
Hayashi and Chūkai) attract very little recruitment attention from firms.
Figure 5.3 confirms this. It also shows that Schools F (Yamanishi) and
I (Nitta) are not in the cluster of schools competing with one another
for employers' attention. Yamanishi is the third best general high school
in the district and its exclusion from the network core is understandable because a significant proportion of its graduates aspire to higher

education. Nitta is the only all-female school in the district, and it does not compete very much with the schools that are the most "popular" among employers.

Schools A and B (Kibane and Matsui, both industrial high schools) compete mainly with each other and School C (Nishi Takase, industrial-commercial) competes mainly with the lowest-ranking general high schools. The advantageous position of Nishi Takase High School vis-à-vis general high schools is nicely summed up by its teachers, some of whom I have interviewed on multiple occasions over the past ten years. Nishi Takase was founded in 1921 and its long-standing reputation of offering good training to students and working hard to maintain ties with employers has clearly helped the school through very difficult times. As one teacher comments with pride in regard to the school: "We have a long history and a good track record." Even in the mid-1990s, Nishi Takase High School was very successful in placing its graduates. In my interview at the school at that time, one of the teachers reported the following:

The rate of promised employment for students at our school who start out saying that they want to search for a job is 100 percent. Only about 5 percent of students say from the start that they want to take a part-time job or be a *furītā* after they graduate. In Yokohama in 1996 the average job opening-to-applicant ratio for female high school graduates was just 0.5, and for boys it was 1.7. This school is better. Ninety girls searched for postgraduation jobs that year and all of them got jobs. There are firms that hire not just one but two or three students from us.

Another teacher at Nishi Takase made the following comment when I visited the school again in 2002: "When the number of office jobs is much lower than the number of high school seniors who want that type of work after they graduate, many companies decide to send their job opening to only one sure place. That's us. But last year [2001] there was a case where a small company came to us in February and said they'd like to hire two graduating seniors. We only had one person left who did not have a job promise. So we called xx general high school and said 'What do you think? Do you have a student who might want this job? If so, we'll give it to you.' Then we called the company and said, 'How about trying xx High School?'"

The most interesting phenomenon evident in Figure 5.4 that was not so apparent from the other diagrams is that the three schools at the bottom of the academic hierarchy – Shinano, Yamakawa, and Seibi (J, K, and L) – receive more attention from employers than the schools in the

TABLE 5.7. *Job Openings per Graduating
Senior at Each High School*

School	Ratio
A. Kibane	2.97
B. Matsui	1.73
C. Nishi Takase	1.30
D. Hayashi	0.01
E. Chūkai	0.09
F. Yamanishi	0.15
G. Funezawa	0.76
H. Kuruhashi	0.47
I. Nitta	0.17
J. Shinano	1.42
K. Yamakawa	1.52
L. Seibi	1.15

middle of the hierarchy – Yamanishi, Funezawa, Kuruhashi, and Nitta. This also shows up in another statistic I calculated: The number of job openings each school received relative to its total number of graduating seniors.[13] Table 5.7 shows this.

The three vocational schools (Kibane, Matsui, and Nishi Takase, at the top of the table) and the three general schools at the bottom of the academic hierarchy (Shinano, Yamakawa, and Seibi) have the largest ratios of job openings to graduating seniors. Seniors in these schools have an average of more than one job opening to which they can apply. On the contrary, schools at the top and middle of the academic hierarchy (D through I, Hayashi through Nitta) have a ratio smaller than one, indicating that there are not enough job interview opportunities in these firms for all of their students. Since schools tend to avoid direct competition

[13] A cautionary note: In using the number of graduating seniors as the denominator, I underestimate for high-ranking schools the number of job openings available to those students in the school who are not higher-education bound. Alternatively, I could have used as the denominator the number of seniors not proceeding on to higher education, which might arguably be a more accurate estimate of the number of job-seekers. I chose not to do this because of the endogeneity problems involved; that is, many high school teachers report that students who initially look for postgraduation jobs during their senior year but fail successive job interviews decide to take themselves out of the running entirely, and are no longer job-seekers. Some of these students decide to go to two-year training schools or other educational institutions and some neither attend school nor enter jobs. This makes it impossible to construct an appropriate denominator for Table 5.7 other than the total number of graduating seniors.

among their own students by recommending only one student for each job interview, many of the students in general high schools D through I (Hayashi through Nitta) would not be recommended for a job interview in any of these firms. For students at the top general high schools, Hayashi and Chūkai, this is irrelevant because they do not intend to go directly into the labor market anyway. But for students in the schools below these in ranking but not at the very bottom of the list, this is very relevant – they are essentially left out of the job matching process with these employers.

At first I was somewhat surprised by these results showing that employers tend to ignore students in the middle-ranked general high schools. But when I thought about it more, it began to make sense. Employers in the youth labor market are very strategic in targeting specific schools to recruit labor. Responses to the Employer Survey I conducted in the late 1990s (discussed in previous chapters) did not indicate that employers are centrally concerned with the specific job preparation of students, so this is not necessarily why they gravitate to industrial high schools. Rather, they know that most students who enter industrial and commercial high schools do so because they plan to enter the job market after graduating. This in itself is a valuable piece of information for employers to have.

If we apply a similar logic to how employers target general high schools, it makes sense that they focus a little more on the bottom of the school hierarchy rather than the middle. Just as they know that students in the elite general high schools aspire to go to university and are not interested in finding a job, employers know that students in the lowest-ranked general high schools have little hope of passing the college entrance examination and that many of them would like to find a job and earn a living. However, it is hard for employers to predict how many and which students in the middle-ranked high schools want to go on to higher education or go into the labor market. Some of these students may dream about college, others may find working an attractive option, and still others simply have no idea of what to do after graduation. Employers may find it more straightforward to target their hiring efforts on schools with students who have a clearer and less heterogeneous mix of aspirations. Since many American high schools are, by contrast, more similar to these middle-ranked Japanese high schools with a range of student aspirations, this is an important point to return to in the comparison of the Japanese and American contexts in the closing chapter of the book.

As Table 5.4 showed, Yamanishi and Funezawa (Schools F and G) and possibly Nitta (School I, for which almost no information is available)

have especially high heterogeneity in terms of graduates' destinations –
between 12 and 27 percent of graduates go to university, junior college, and two-year training schools respectively. This probably makes
it difficult for employers to evaluate how seriously the seniors in these
middle-level general high schools think about job-hunting. It is also
possible that employers perceive that graduates from these schools may
easily become dissatisfied with low-level service sector jobs and quit,
thus creating a high-turnover situation. This is an outcome employers
try to avoid.

The stratification among vocational and middle- and low-ranking general high schools is further illuminated by looking at school-specific rates
of graduates' idleness.

Firm-School Networks and the "Production" of Idleness. Combining
the school-level data and the school-employer network data helps elucidate the mechanisms producing large numbers of unemployed, part-time
employed, and idle Japanese high school graduates. As I showed earlier, the meaning of the residual "uncertain" category in individual high
schools' graduate statistics is highly heterogeneous across school ranks.
"Good" high schools produce large numbers of *rōnin* and "not-so-good"
high schools produce few *rōnin* and many NEET. In my view, this latter
group includes students for whom the highly structured school-work system has failed. They are the "true" idle who have no immediate destination at the time of graduation.

The far-right column in Table 5.8 shows the estimated "true" percent
idle for each school in the urban district analyzed in this chapter. If a
figure is in boldface this indicates that it is higher than the average for
Kanagawa high schools. This is the case for every general high school
in the district except Hayashi, the top-ranked school – all of the other
general high schools have a true idleness rate higher than 20 percent. In
fact, the idleness rate at three of the general high schools is more than 30
percent.[14] By contrast, all three vocational schools (Kibane, Matsui, and
Nishi Takase) have rates of idleness far below the average for Kanagawa
high schools. This pattern of idleness rates for graduates from different

[14] Given the reported percent "uncertain," Shinano would have a high true idleness rate
were we able to calculate it. (I am not able to do so because the percent of graduates
going to university was not reported by this school.) I do not have any information at all
on student destinations after graduation for Nitta and cannot estimate its true idleness
rate. But this school's required minimum entrance examination score is thirty-four, one
of the lowest in the district. The true idleness rate of its graduates is therefore probably
quite high.

TABLE 5.8. *"True" Percent of Idle Graduates from Each High School*

School	Minimum Required Entrance Exam Score	Job	University	Uncertain (Idle)	"True" Idle
A. Kibane	44	46.5	9.0	14.8	13.5
B. Matsui	NA	61.8	1.7	16.7	16.4
C. Nishi Takase	40	58.8	3.9	8.1	7.8
D. Hayashi	61	0.0	93.0	6.7	0.5
E. Chūkai	50	1.0	38.4	38.8	23.9
F. Yamanishi	43	7.3	17.7	34.3	28.2
G. Funezawa	39	7.5	12.5	38.1	33.3
H. Kuruhashi	36	29.9	4.4	26.7	25.5
I. Nitta	34	NA	NA	NA	NA
J. Shinano	33	38.7	NA	33.9	NA
K. Yamakawa	32	23.0	3.2	33.1	32.0
L. Seibi	NA	42.0	1.5	30.6	30.1

schools mirrors the very uneven distribution of job opening announcements across schools.

Falling Through the Cracks: Students at Low-Performing General High Schools. When full-time entry-level jobs for high school graduates were plentiful in the 1960s–1980s, even low-ranking high schools received job opening announcements for their graduates and were able to achieve high placement rates. In that case, the inequalities inherent in having schools rather than individuals receive job opening information were not particularly evident. In the language of Chapter 2, institutional social capital worked quite well for just about everyone. Jobs were abundant and employers needed to dip low into the quality hierarchy of high schools to meet their recruitment needs for new workers, especially as manufacturing plants expanded and thrived in Japan's export-led economy. But ever since this period ended, the hidden inequities of the highly orchestrated school-work system have become starkly apparent.

These inequities – the highly uneven distribution of information about full-time postgraduation jobs across different types and levels of high schools – are closely related to some of the severe problems in Japan's current youth labor market. In focusing on the troubling increase in youths' disengagement from school and from work, Japan's policymakers and media have largely missed a critical feature of this disengagement: The stratification of schools and the fact that a skewed distribution of employment opportunities across schools has long been a central feature of Japan's highly managed school-work system. The analysis in this chapter has brought this internal stratification to the surface.

The negative consequences of Japan's school-firm networks for students on the lower rungs of the high school hierarchy were quite opaque during the period of high economic growth and labor demand. In the days when Japanese employers' demand for new graduates far exceeded the supply, all but the very least able and least cooperative high school graduates could receive a job placement through the highly institutionalized school-firm network relationships. This deflected attention away from the possible inequalities stemming from how jobs were allocated through these networks. But the recessionary economy in Japan coupled with employment restructuring and educational upgrading in the past decade and a half produced a smaller economic pie and a dramatic decline in the number of "good" entry-level jobs for high school graduates. This has led many Japanese youth to question the ability of institutionalized job-matching to serve their interests. The disadvantages of having to rely principally on the network ties between one's school and local businesses have become vividly apparent to students at lower-ranking general high schools.

The rapidly increasing numbers of Japanese youth who leave school without a clear work or educational destination are symptomatic of an alienation from a school-work process that no longer serves them well. I have shown in this chapter that youth idleness rates are highly patterned across types and levels of high schools, with graduates from vocational high schools and top academic high schools showing the lowest propensity to be idle. The network analysis demonstrates a striking correspondence between schools with high idleness rates and the small volume of information about job openings flowing to these schools through the traditional firm-school networks. In the Japanese discourse over youths' unwillingness to assume the responsibility entailed by full-time jobs provided within the traditional school-work system, it is important to point out the lack of opportunities available to some youth to utilize these arrangements. How can they use the institutional social capital of their schools when there is almost none left?

Still, Japan's longstanding school-work mechanisms are not completely outdated. The network analysis results in this chapter are consistent with the analyses in Chapter 4 that suggested that school-firm linkages seem to be alive and functioning well between vocational (especially industrial) high schools and firms. To the extent that Japan still has a fair number of manufacturing and construction jobs, employers are continuing to hire from such schools.

New policy measures are clearly needed in order to encourage students at Japanese general high schools to more carefully consider what they want to do in the future, not just in terms of the company in which they want to be employed but in terms of the type of work they would like to do.[15] It may strike some observers as unusual that a country so admired for its stable school-work institutions is now struggling to develop policies and programs that will teach young people how to think about their future work possibilities and the content of different types of jobs. But such policies are clearly needed in order to keep a large number of Japanese youth from falling through the cracks.

[15] Honda (2004). Also see Kosugi (2004).

6

Narratives of the New Mobility

"I think that this period is good because it is forcing Japanese young people to reexamine themselves and think about what kind of work they want to do."

– Principal at a low-ranking public high school

Reliance on institutional social capital to get a full-time job straight out of school worked well for many of Japan's youth throughout the post-war period. A school introduction to a job became a more common way of entering the labor market for graduates of every level of schooling during the post-WorldWar II period. Data from the Social Stratification and Mobility Survey introduced in Chapter 3 showed that a school introduction served the educational nonelite (high school graduates) well: Compared to their counterparts who found their first job through a different route, they were much more likely to land a full-time job in a large firm and to stay in that job for at least the first five years of their working life.

In short, individuals who drew on their school's social capital were more likely than others to be placed into a full-time job in a workplace that became their *ba*, the social location that identified them to the rest of Japanese society, often for a sustained period of time. University graduates' job search was similar in timing to that of high school graduates, with large firms recruiting early in the fall to secure the most desirable seniors for immediate postgraduation employment in the following April. In the U.S. such fervent recruitment activity takes place at the most elite private four-year universities and the most elite law and business schools in the country. But in Japan, it has been necessary for the government to regulate the start of the recruiting year not just for university seniors but for high school seniors as well, because the hiring plans of large firms have been laid out so far in advance. Students' battle for good jobs is waged early in their senior year. And as Chapter 3 elucidated, in the post-war Japanese labor market a man's stable attachment to a firm has been an important vehicle for receiving on-the-job training at the employer's expense and garnering steadily increasing earnings.

Even so, some amount of mobility or job-hopping among workplaces has always existed for Japanese young people, despite international and domestic rhetoric that Japanese workers rarely change jobs. The norma-tive template of employee commitment to one workplace is distinct from a more complex reality: Even in the context of a labor market where job-changing has been viewed with suspicion, a fair number of workers have consistently changed jobs in their twenties before settling into a longer-term job. To be sure, the Japanese youth labor market does not exhibit the high level of "churning" that American labor economists describe for the U.S. youth labor market. Japanese labor economists and sociologists have been surprised to observe that even in the tumultuous economic times since the early 1990s, the proportion of Japanese young people who change jobs within the first three years of leaving school has remained quite stable.

The Ministry of Health, Labour and Welfare reports that a quit pat-tern known colloquially as *shichi-go-san* (seven-five-three) has persisted across time. The pattern is that about 70 percent of junior high school graduates (a very small group at this point in time, given nearly universal rates of advancement to high school), 50 percent of high school gradu-ates, and 30 percent of university graduates change jobs within three years of graduation. A perspective not mentioned by the Ministry is that the seeming stability of the seven-five-three pattern may be paradoxi-cally indicative of a trend toward more frequent job-changing among the least educationally elite (junior high and high school graduates). Why? Because the denominator for such rates is the number of young people who entered full-time employment upon graduation. As I have shown, this is a number that has dwindled markedly in the past decade and a half, especially for the educational nonelite. Instead, the number of youth entering part-time employment, unemployment, or idleness (the state of being a NEET) has increased. This sheds new light on the persistence of 70 percent and 50 percent turnover, respectively, for junior high and high school graduates. Fewer and fewer of them are entering full-time jobs to begin with. So it is rather striking that turnover rates remain as high as they do. These turnover rates are complemented by the increased instability in the youth labor market that is reflected in the numbers of unemployed and idle youth.

It is not completely clear what distinguishes job-changers from their counterparts who remain in their first postgraduation full-time job rather than switching to another one within three years. Somehow or other they are people for whom the initial job match was not a good one. As noted in Chapter 4, one possibility is that some of the young people who make a "successful" job match through their school actually end up being round pegs trying to fit into square holes. In such cases one might argue that the *anshin* or peace of mind felt by teachers in having moved students into jobs is associated with a false sense of accomplishment. On the other hand, perhaps it is more likely for graduates to suffer job mismatches if they find the job on their own, either through using personal social capital (strong or weak ties), or through searching the listings in job magazines or other outlets. We simply do not know for sure.

In many ways, the persistence or even increase in job-changing is not surprising. A striking theme in many of my interviews with high school teachers, especially at low-level general high schools, was their assertion that seventeen- and eighteen-year-olds are socially immature and are not necessarily capable of making well-informed employment choices. In my view, this cultural view is institutionally driven and encouraged. Socialized in an educational system that has traditionally focused students' attention more on fitting into society and, for young men, fitting into a company, young Japanese have not benefitted from having to respond to the same kinds of questions thrown at American youth (questions that can, admittedly, be incessant) about what they want to do with their lives and "who they want to be." In a system fueled by institutional social capital, Japanese young people have been offered little incentive to develop interests and skills to bring to employers in an open labor market, let alone to further develop their particular capabilities over time by seeking new opportunities for moving across companies throughout their working life. Even if the first job doesn't "take," moving multiple times across companies has not been a strategy for establishing an upward earnings trajectory in the Japanese labor market. Moreover, as I showed in earlier chapters, the institutional social capital a young man activates to enter his first full-time job can be a protection against employer exploitation. If new young employees are badly treated and this news gets back to the guidance counselor or homeroom teacher who helped introduce them to the company, the firm's relationship with the school will be threatened.

In an institutional equilibrium where the entry-level labor market plays such a central role, schools have been the proverbial geese that lay the golden eggs or *kin no tamago* – new graduates.

But how about young men who do not land on their feet straight out of school? For men who for one reason or another end up in a poor job match, what are the alternatives to institutional social capital? The Japanese youth labor market has become increasingly fluid since the early 1990s and has come to encompass more and more possibilities besides stable full-time membership in a workplace *ba* – *furītā*, NEET, *haken* (short-term contract employment), *arubaito* (part-time jobs held by students as well as graduates). Because the landscape has become more complex, the strategies of young job-changers merit scrutiny.

In this chapter I relate the detailed narratives of three young men and explore the dynamics that underlie their stories. These three men were among the thirty or so who surfaced from the Youth Survey as individuals willing to be interviewed in greater depth. They have different educational backgrounds, different personalities and inner resources, and a range of employment experiences. Taken together, they illustrate the complex mosaic of strategies young men in the lost generation and beyond are using as they learn to change jobs and take chances in Japan's postindustrial labor market. Their narratives are messy counterpoints to so many of the well-patterned narratives of the postwar generation of men who moved smoothly from school into a *shokuba* or workplace with the aid of institutional social capital. In the narratives unfurled in this chapter, plans were made and didn't work out, or plans were not even made in the first place. As a result, the *ba* of school was not a place to which these young men could return to report and discuss the results of the school's guidance, even in the case of mistreatment by their employer (as in the second narrative I relate here). Instead, these men navigated on their own, and their explorations raise thorny issues that motivate the final chapter of the book.

SATOSHI: A TRADITIONAL ELITE STORY WITH A TWIST

In many ways, Satoshi epitomizes the image of a "successful" young Japanese man. After graduating from a high-performing public high school in 1995, he immediately entered one of Japan's most prestigious private universities. He graduated with an economics degree in 1999 and entered a career-track position in a large Japanese bank, where he worked about fifty hours a week with some additional overtime hours during the busiest times. He had full benefits – a company pension plan, health insurance, and unemployment insurance – and lived in a company dormitory. The main way he acquired the necessary skills for his job was through his training in the company and his experiences working there.

Satoshi has mainly positive memories of his high school days, and can still list the names of about twenty friends from high school. He attended English classes at a private exam-preparation school during his high school years and did not do any part-time work. His high school prohibited students from working and Satoshi has a general understanding that part-time work is prohibited in most Japanese high schools. His confident statement of this as a fact is interesting in itself, as I have discussed in previous chapters that many low-ranking Japanese high schools in fact gave up their efforts at keeping students from doing part-time work in the 1990s. Satoshi's understanding that "students cannot work during high school" reflects his segregated experience in the upper reaches of the high school hierarchy.

Satoshi did hold some part-time jobs during his university years. He worked for a while in a supermarket – a job that he had found through a job-advertising magazine. The store was on the way to his university, so it was convenient for him to work there and make a little extra money. He also worked as an exam monitor in a cram school – a job he had secured by registering for the position and listing the name of the prestigious university he was attending.

The first interview we conducted with Satoshi was in 2005. At that time he expressed a desire to work longer hours and make a higher income. He was then twenty-eight years old. He thought the work he was given in the bank was interesting, and felt like the training the company was giving him was improving his skills and knowledge base. On the other hand, he was feeling that he did not have much of a chance to demonstrate his strengths.

When we asked Satoshi what he valued in a job, he expressed a preference to work for one company for a long time and to experience many different types of work tasks. He valued a high income, interesting work, and good relationships with his colleagues. He expressed a desire to get married when he finds a good marriage partner.

In answer to a question about what he imagined the most important thing in his life would be in five years (family, friends, personal life, the company where he would be working, or the work he would be doing), he replied that it would most likely be the work he would be doing.

Satoshi clearly has led a charmed life. He was born to highly educated parents and attended a top public high school and one of Japan's most prestigious universities. Satoshi's father is a professor at a public university, where he has spent his entire working life. His mother is also a university graduate and is a full-time housewife. Satoshi has two siblings, an older brother and a younger sister. Even though Satoshi graduated from university during the economically difficult years of the late 1990s, he landed a job in a major bank. In many ways, Satoshi seems to be very similar to the well-educated men in the cohorts that immediately preceded him.

But Satoshi is different in one key respect: When we re-interviewed him ten months later, he had quit his stable career-track job. Satoshi's new job is in a large Japanese trading company. Although his first job after university was a very good one by most standards, his remarks during our first interview had revealed that he did not feel that he was able to stretch his abilities and challenge himself. He stayed at the bank for six years and then began to search for another job that might suit him better. As he puts it, "I searched for a job in the normal way ... on the internet." After interviewing for another job and getting it, he informed his employer and then switched jobs. Once again he moved into a company dormitory. His job satisfaction is currently very high. As he says, "I often work overtime. But I am really satisfied with my job now, so I don't mind working overtime. Whether I can come home early or not is not really an issue."

What is significant about this portrait of a "typical" young successful Japanese man in his late twenties? What sets him apart from so many elite Japanese men of the 1970s and 1980s is that when he decided that his stable job in banking did not quite suit him, he went about looking for a new job that would be more challenging and a better fit to his talents. His income increased with the job change. The company to which he moved is less traditional than the first one he worked for. During his training period in the company his salary is tied to his age, and later it will become more dependent on performance than on seniority. Satoshi's reference to the Internet as the "normal" way of conducting a job search shows how he has adapted new technological tools to pursue his goals. Even his part-time jobs during university were found through relatively new job-search methods – job-hunting magazines and a registry for helpers at a cram school. Although he had many friends in high school and remains in contact with a number of friends from his main seminar at university, he has neither relied on strong nor weak personal ties in his job searches so far.

Satoshi has a great deal of human capital, comes from a well-educated family, and is actively pursuing what he wants to do – following a trajectory that is unconventional only in the sense that he is willing to take a chance and move out of his comfort zone to find a more challenging work environment with greater risk but also greater rewards. He has figured out the tools with which he can navigate a course through the "external labor market" that has developed in Japan in recent years – the labor market that exists outside of the firm-internal labor markets such as the one where he started his career.

THE BROADER VIEW: MOBILITY PATTERNS
IN THE LOST GENERATION

Satoshi was one of a number of young men interviewed in my research, based on the sample of nearly five hundred young men that my Japanese colleagues and I surveyed in 2005 (the Youth Survey discussed in Chapter 3). For the first time in my research career, I hired a small number of research assistants to conduct these in-depth interviews of a small number of "informants" rather than doing the interviews by myself. I reasoned that Japanese men in their late twenties, particularly ones with nonelite educations (Satoshi was an exception in this regard among those in my in-depth interview pool), were likely to be more open and relaxed with a laid-back female Japanese interviewer of about the same age as themselves or a male American interviewer of a similar age. So the reference to "we" in my description of the interview with Satoshi refers to the interview experience as recorded and transcribed by the interviewer I sent to talk with Satoshi.

The Youth Survey of nearly five hundred men provides a picture of what was encountered by the men who left high school, two-year training school, or university in the mid-late 1990s and entered the troubled labor market at the time. The educational composition of the sample is, happily, very similar to the statistics based on the national sample of young men surveyed in the 2005 Social Stratification and Mobility (SSM) Survey, also discussed in Chapter 3.[1] By the time they were in

---

[1] About 36 percent of men in the sample did not go on for further education after high school. (A small number of these – about 3 percent – in fact did not finish high school at all.) Approximately 23 percent went to two-year training schools or some other type of advanced training school, and 41 percent went to university. The corresponding figures for the "lost cohort" surveyed in the SSM are strikingly similar (in Table 3.2, Chapter 3): 35 percent of high school graduates did not go on to higher schooling, 4 percent

their late twenties, about 11 percent of men in the Youth Survey had not held any full-time job since leaving school. The probability of not ever having worked full-time was highest among those who had attended two-year training schools (18 percent) and lowest among high school and university graduates (10 percent). This difference was statistically significant, meaning that both high school and university graduates were significantly more likely than other men to have had at least some full-time work experience by their late twenties.

Satoshi is an example of the university-educated young men who have done well in the labor market despite the rough economic climate. He represents young men with large amounts of human capital and "cultural capital," what sociologists refer to as the demeanor and ways of behaving that denote comfort with being in the upper middle class (Bourdieu 1986). His clear intelligence, strong goals, and quiet self-assuredness are guiding him down a path slightly different from many of the men who preceded him in Japan's corporate landscape. In my mind's eye I contrast him with a middle-aged employee in a major Japanese bank who told me years ago that "Being in a large company is like bathing in warm water – it's not very challenging, but on the other hand, it's cold when you get out."[2] The similarity between that description of work and the way Satoshi described his first job is striking. But Satoshi's solution was to find a better alternative, and he marshaled his inner resources to do so. In that way, his choices are emblematic of a new way of life among some young Japanese men.

Among men in the Youth Survey, university graduates were much more likely than men of other educational backgrounds to have worked only in full-time jobs since leaving school. Sixty-three percent had done so, compared to just 50 percent of high school graduates and even fewer graduates of two-year training schools. Again, these figures are very close to those produced from the SSM Survey. Eighty percent of male university graduates had held only one or two jobs since leaving school – a figure about 20 percent higher than for high school or two-year training school graduates.

The next narrative is from Koichi, an example of a graduate from a two-year training school who had the good fortune to land in a full-time job when he graduated. But unlike Satoshi, his good fortune soured within a short period of time.

---

did not graduate from high school, 19 percent went to two-year training schools, and 43 percent went to university.

[2] I quoted this bank manager in a previous book (Brinton 1993).

KOICHI: FROM A CHARMED LIFE TO A STORY OF NEAR-DEFEAT

Koichi's story represents a dramatic departure from Satoshi's. Like Satoshi, he has been interviewed twice for my research. The first time we talked with him, he was twenty-seven years old, living with his parents and not working. He had had five different jobs, including the part-time job he had held in high school. Koichi was not very optimistic about his future and felt that the world was pretty much leaving him behind. He expressed the view that society is getting more and more complicated and that it is becoming harder to know what to do or how to fit in. All in all, it seemed life was not going very well for him.

Koichi graduated from a general high school in 1996 that is in the middle of the academic quality hierarchy in one of Yokohama's school districts. His classmates went in a variety of directions after graduating – some to university, some to two-year training schools, and some directly into jobs. He wasn't particularly close to any of his teachers, but he reported having had several close friends in high school and finding school to be moderately enjoyable. Koichi had sort of assumed he would go to university once he graduated. But during his final year of high school he became interested in cooking and decided it was really enjoyable. So he decided to go to a two-year training school that specialized in cooking. After graduating from the school, he got his first full-time job.

On paper, the job was a good one. He was hired as a full-time employee at a small food-manufacturing factory for a well-known Japanese company whose products are sold in the basement level [the food department] of many famous Japanese department stores. The product the company makes is easily identifiable, so it is not a name I will mention. As he puts it, "It's a very famous company, a very large company. They have counters in xx and xx department stores. So I thought it was a trustworthy company." The job seemed well suited to his interests, too. But once Koichi started working at the company, things did not go as he had expected. Within two months, he quit.

What went wrong? As he puts it, "Everything totally fell apart around me." Why? "There was only one reason: The work hours were obscene. I had to go to work at 7 AM and I would work until 3 AM. Plus, they didn't give me any days off per week – only about two days per month. At first they told me that I could have two days off a week. Once I started working, they told me it would be every other week. But we were so busy that I couldn't rest. I didn't even have time to sleep." Koichi said that often when they finished work the trains had stopped running for the night, so someone in the factory would take him home. But once he got home, he had to go back to work at 7 AM. "So there was almost no time to sleep. At the company, during the breaks [a one-hour break at lunchtime and a 30-minute break in the afternoon], I would eat as fast as I could. There was barely any time and I sometimes just ate the edges of xx [the food product that he was making]. Then I would take a quick nap. At 6 PM we would punch out. Then after a thirty-minute break, we would start working again until our boss would tell us we could rest. It was endless. And there were no overtime wages."

Koichi explained the event that pushed him over the edge and was the immediate reason he quit: "The reason I quit was that one of my co-workers who entered the company at the same time that I did committed suicide. He was in the same situation as I was. In that type of working condition, people can go really crazy. He killed himself, and I received a phone call. It was on my day off. I said I would go into the company right away. I went in, and I told them that I wanted to quit. You would think that they would accept it, right? I mean, it was a crazy situation – a person had *died*! But they said, 'You still have a future here. Please stay and work. We don't have enough people now. Please don't quit.' The head of the factory, the section head, the boss ... all of them tried to keep me. But there was nothing they could do." The food brand was becoming more and more popular and the company's factories were under pressure to produce more products. Ironically, when Koichi quit his job at the factory, the company was short-handed but was not hiring regular employees.

At face value, Koichi's was a "good job." After all, he was working as a full-time employee for a name-brand company and using the skills he had learned at the postsecondary school he had attended. After he left the company, he fell into a depression. As he explained, "It was like ... just this one time in my life, I became a social isolate (*hikiko-mori*). I couldn't leave the house or see anyone. I couldn't go anywhere. I was scared of working, too – especially of having a full-time job. I was like that for three or four months. Now [several years later] I can laugh and talk about it, but I wasn't like this at the time. You know, it was the first job I had ever had, and I failed. And the way I failed was terrible. I lost my co-worker."

Later in the interview, Koichi said sadly to us, "My co-workers and I all gathered when the person died. But after that, I didn't contact them. I just couldn't. You know, he didn't have to die. Maybe he was weak ... ."

The Ba *of Adolescence: Responsibilities of the School.* Several things
are striking about Koichi's story of how his work life had begun. First of
all, his employer did not adhere to the conditions that had been promised.
As a result, Koichi and his coworkers were perpetually exhausted. Having
gotten the job after graduating from a two-year training school, Koichi
did not have recourse to the institutional backup of his high school that
was described in previous chapters. There were no teachers waiting in the
wings to make contact with the employer and ask what was going on.
Instead, he was more or less on his own. His experience contrasts sharply
with what might have happened in an earlier time period, when this type
of job might have been filled by high school graduates recommended by
the school to an employer. In that circumstance, Koichi would have been
able to go back to his high school homeroom teacher or to one of the
guidance department teachers and tell them that the job conditions were
not what the employer had promised on the job announcement that had
been sent to the school.

During my discussions with high school teachers at low-ranking high
schools in Kanagawa prefecture, we had talked a lot about the relationships between schools and companies and the types of responsibilities
that schools feel toward students. The following comment by a teacher is
particularly applicable to stories like Koichi's:

There are some cases where the job does not match the description on the job
announcement. This is illegal. For example, perhaps the company states that the
person doesn't have to work on Saturdays and Sundays, but actually, they do
have to work on Saturdays. Or perhaps the job is not at the company itself but
at an affiliated company. In these cases, we say to the graduate 'it is okay to quit'
or 'go ahead and quit.' Sometimes this happens within one month and if we have
another company who needs someone, we can place the graduate there. Or we
might say to the graduate, 'after you find another job and interview and get it,
then go ahead and quit.' We help graduates in this way. We do the best we can
to provide this kind of help if the graduate comes to us. We also tell the public
employment security office about it.

I have shown in previous chapters that the high school-work system
exerted social control over high school students. But this teacher's comments show eloquently how the high school-work system exerted social
control over employers as well. It is important not to overlook this point.
As Japanese students and graduates increasingly get jobs on their own –
jobs to which they are not introduced by their schools – the employers
that hire them are no longer under schools', or even public employment
security offices', radar screens. Young people are increasingly on their

own. If the high school-work system were still functioning well, the school guidance department teachers might help the graduate if it turned out that the working conditions were not what the employer had written down. In this way, high schools exercised social control not just over their students but also over employers. Employers could acquire a bad reputation if they submitted job opening forms to the public employment security offices and to high schools that did not accurately represent the working conditions at the company. In addition, most of the guidance teachers with whom I spoke sorted through the job announcements sent to their school and separated out any that looked suspicious in terms of stating work conditions that were not good or work requirements that sounded strange. Often the teachers would put these job opening forms in a separate file and not even show them to students.

What is the appropriate level of supervision over young people's work trajectory? Have Japanese teachers been too controlling in "protecting" young people? Why not let high school seniors take their fate into their own hands? On the other hand, is it a good thing that high schools have exercised this kind of social control over employers? There is obviously a case to be made for both sides. But the fact is that as school-employer ties have declined and more young people have taken on part-time jobs during high school and entered the labor market on their own, Japanese employers have been subject to less social control by schools. The school's role as a stakeholder in the future of young people has been gradually usurped. Young people are fending for themselves.

One consequence of this shift in control out of the hands of schools and more fully into the hands of employers is that if graduates "fail," their only recourse is to blame themselves or their employer. Koichi blamed himself – "You know, it was the first job I had ever had, and I failed." In fact, he even blamed his co-worker who had committed suicide, saying "maybe he was weak." It is striking that Koichi blamed himself for quitting the company and even attributed his co-worker's death, at least in part, to personal characteristics. The working conditions he described seem intolerable, no matter how much the content of the job corresponded to his interests.

Koichi's attribution of blame to himself and to his co-worker rather than to external circumstances echoes his attitudes about what leads to success in life. Despite his difficult experiences, Koichi is like Satoshi in feeling that effort is more important than luck in determining success in life. Also, like Satoshi, he does not believe that life requires people to do dishonest or inappropriate things to get ahead. Despite his difficult initial work experiences, Koichi has held on to the fundamental values he holds dear. But this has happened at a significant personal cost.

Personal Ties, Personal Decisions. After falling into a depression and becoming a borderline social isolate for four months, Koichi was able to rouse himself out of his depression and get a part-time job working the night shift at a convenience store. One of his friends was doing this, so he found a job at a different store and worked there for about four years. He says that during the first six months or so, he felt like he was doing it to get reintegrated back into society. Gradually, he started to feel better: "While working at the convenience store, I had a moment where I started to think, 'I'm okay now.' I was getting physically healthier, and I was able to sleep again." Once his confidence and health were restored, he began to think about what he wanted to do next. He did not want to continue working at the convenience store for a long time, but he felt that if he quit without another job in hand, he wouldn't be able to move forward with his life. Around that time, a branch of a retail-clothing store opened up near his neighborhood. He was able to get a full-time job there and quit the convenience store. The pay was okay (the yen equivalent of about $1,600 per month, plus benefits and health insurance), the overtime hours were only four or five per week, and he had two days off every week.

At this point Koichi was able to begin thinking again about the kind of work he really wanted to do over the long term. "I was wondering what I should do, and how I could live. I was exploring what kind of job I wanted to do for the long-term. You know, I felt that as long as I could move forward gradually, it's okay." He got a job at a real estate office that handles rental contracts; then, after one year, he left the job. The other people who had entered the company at the same time also eventually quit, partly because the salary fluctuated so much. Just before he quit, he interviewed with a railway company that a friend worked for and liked. But he did not pass the third interview, which disappointed him. So he went to the public employment security office and was able to find a job, this time in a construction consulting company that advised construction firms on landing government contracts. That company had a policy that overtime work had to be less than thirty hours per week, but "Usually it would go over the limit. But at least I could get paid for 28 hours of overtime work or so, so it was okay." Koichi saw things about the construction industry and its relationship with the *yakuza* (Japanese gangsters) and the government that were hard for him to accept. So he left the job after working there for a little more than a year.

Like Satoshi, Koichi has not relied directly on other people to help him find jobs. Instead, he has used "Hello Work" (the employment security office) and job advertisements in magazines. Koichi does not have the amount of human capital, the socioeconomic background, or the upper middle-class cultural resources that Satoshi does. But he has not been beaten down by circumstances. He has thought hard about what he wants in his work life, and he has been able to get psychological support from some of the people closest to him. For example, he sought a job at a convenience store because one of his friends had worked in one and he learned from that person that the job was not too difficult (this was after he quit the food manufacturing company). Later, he interviewed at the railway company where a friend works. And importantly, his parents supported him psychologically while he recovered from the trauma of his job at the food-manufacturing factory. In fact, his parents had offered to help him pay for a motorcycle license, which seems to be one of the things that got him to go out of the house and break the vicious cycle of staying at home day after day, feeling bad about himself. Over time, his parents had gently encouraged him to get another full-time job at a company where he could work for a long time.

Koichi's parents did not require him to contribute financially to the household. Instead, they told him that if he contributed then they would save the money for him anyway and give it to him when he moved out. What seems to have saved Koichi is the combination of a supportive family and his own inner ability to move beyond his terrible initial work experiences and go forward and explore different jobs to see what he really wanted to do.

When we interviewed Koichi ten months later, he was in his fifth and current job, working for a company involved in environmental concerns. He is very satisfied with the job. To him, the working conditions, the salary, his co-workers, and the work hours (two days off per week) are fine. As he says, "I'm confident that I can keep doing this job. I feel I can do this for the rest of my life. I found a job about which I can feel this way."

Koichi is thoughtful about his work experiences in life so far. As he puts it, "It took me time to find a job that suited me. But you can't quit a job right away, right? You know, people think it's strange. So I tried to stay in most of my jobs [except the food manufacturing factory] for at least a year. Now I've finally found a job that suits me very well. I don't feel that it's because of my own improvement or anything, but rather because of my experiences doing different types of jobs. If I had entered this company without those experiences, I might have thought it was not perfect for me. But because I know what didn't work for me in the past, I can see that this is the best fit for me so far. In that sense, I feel it was good that I had these experiences. I did sales, customer service, worked at a convenience store, and so forth. Some people can find their perfect job without trying out different kinds of jobs, and some people can't."

HIDEKI: WITH A LITTLE HELP FROM HIS FRIENDS (AND WEAK TIES)

Hideki has had yet a different set of experiences and has used other strategies to find satisfying work than either Satoshi or Koichi. We first interviewed him in 2005 when he was thirty years old. Hideki graduated from a low-ranked general high school from which very few graduates went to university; many more went to two-year training schools or tried to enter the job market. Hideki remembers a large number of friends – about fifty – from his high school days, and he is still in contact with about fifteen friends from middle school. He was active in soccer club throughout his high school years. He did not do any part-time jobs during high school except for short-term jobs during the summer and winter breaks. But his first job after graduating was part-time. We asked him about the circumstances that had led to this, and he explained what was going on at home and in his own thinking during high school.

Hideki's father is a university graduate. Throughout Hideki's childhood, his father and uncle ran a small software company. But when Hideki was in his late teens, his father closed down the company: "It was in the middle of the recession. There was no business, and no point in continuing. So before the company went into the red, he closed it down. After that, he took a job as a driver in the carrier business." Hideki continued: "My parents came to the end of their rope back then. I had been thinking about going to university but we had not talked about it much. I decided on it rather late – around October or November of my senior year in high school. We talked about it and found out how much it would cost. But when I understood my parents' financial situation better, I said that if that was the situation, I wouldn't go to university. After all, it wasn't that I wanted to study something in particular. I realized that going to university would cause a lot of financial problems for my parents. But I was not using the career guidance at my high school for job-hunting either. In a way, everything was too late."

For these reasons, after graduating from high school Hideki took a part-time job in a small company that overhauls vending machines.

He found the job through a job search magazine. After two years the company asked him if he wanted to work full-time. He thought about it seriously but decided that the company was not stable enough and that the work was not what he wanted to do over the long term. "When the company suggested that I become a full-time employee, I thought about a lot of things. I also consulted with my friends. When I seriously thought about what I wanted to do, I sort of thought I wanted to do aircraft maintenance. A friend of mine referred me to a job in the airport. But when I got there, I discovered that the job was not at all what I expected – it was a job at the counter of a travel agency! But anyway, I thought to myself: 'Since it is a job at the airport, there may be other opportunities here as well.' Rather than having nothing, I thought it was better to take this job and see if I could make some connections through the job."

Hideki's easygoing, extroverted nature and his practical approach to life were particularly clear in the second interview we had with him. He had worked at the airport travel counter for six months. During that time he was talking to one of the more senior employees at the job, discussing the fact that he wanted to work on the airfield doing things related to aircraft maintenance. As he told us, "I did not live near the airport. But my co-worker did, so I asked him if he could bring 'help wanted' ads to me from his local newspaper. I thought there might be more job ads for positions in the airport in that newspaper than in the one where I lived. I found my current job that way. When I saw the ad, I told him about it and he said that I should call them right away and ask about the job. We'd been talking about that sort of thing for a while." So Hideki quit the travel agency job and moved into the job of airplane mechanic. The company hired him as a contract worker and one year later, he was able to become a full-time employee. The company has provided quite a lot of training and he feels like he has been able to develop many skills.

Hideki's current job is therefore the third one he has had since leaving school. He is a full-time employee in a medium-sized company that services airplanes. Hideki works about forty-five hours a week and makes the equivalent of about $30,000 a year. It is not a high salary, but Hideki likes his work. He feels that he is able to develop and use his abilities and has been able to do interesting work so far. When we asked him what he values most in his work life, he said that it is the opportunity to do interesting work and to have good relationships with his colleagues. The other things he values in a job are possibilities for promotion and a higher income, a convenient commute, and little need to worry about becoming unemployed.

Hideki feels fortunate in many ways. Among his friends, he doesn't know anyone else who has been able to become a full-time employee after starting out in a part-time job after graduating from school.

After seeing what his father went through, Hideki does not have a desire to be self-employed. He respects his father: "He supported us by running his own business. I think he was paying his employees as much as he could so that they could eat for all those years. In that respect, he had a lot of responsibilities. It is amazing that my own parent was doing that." Reflecting on his parents' situation during those years, he says, "They didn't show it much, but I think it was tough for them."

Hideki is unusual in that he got married at a fairly young age (twenty-five) for men in his cohort and already has two young children. He and his wife and children live in an apartment. He expresses satisfaction with all aspects of his life so far. Just like Satoshi and Koichi, Hideki does not think it is necessary to do dishonest things in order to get by, and he too feels that effort is more important than luck in order to succeed in life. Unlike what Koichi said when we interviewed him the first time, Hideki does not have the feeling that life is leaving him behind.

In terms of whom he says he would rely on in times of need, Hideki is like many of the other young men we interviewed – he would turn first to his family for help in trying times such as when he is ill, has financial problems, or has problems with other people. But unlike most of the other young men in my research, Hideki says that his friends would be the ones he would be most likely to talk to if he were feeling down.

What does Hideki's story illustrate? And how do we "connect the dots" across the stories of these three young men? Hideki, the high school graduate, got a slow start on planning his next steps after high school, and did not use his schools' guidance department for his initial job search. But of the three men, Hideki is the most extroverted and adaptable. When a job situation did not work out for him, he talked to friends and consulted with co-workers to get information and advice. He utilized a combination of strategies in job hunting, including asking his co-worker to bring in job advertisements from the local newspaper. This contrasts with Satoshi, who used the Internet to make the one job change he has made so far. It also contrasts with Koichi, who has used a variety of resources to manage his pathway in the labor market. Koichi relied on his empathetic parents for financial and psychological support during a several-month long period when he was not working and was on the verge of becoming a serious social isolate. In his job searches, he has relied on job advertisements, on encouragement from friends who have had positive work experiences, and on the public employment security office. None of these young men have held just one job since they graduated.

How can we interpret the ability of these three very different young men to adapt to the changed employment environment in Japan and to eventually land on their feet? Do their experiences constitute evidence that the lost generation will thrive, even though the security of the school-work transition system and the promise of stable employment have more or less dissolved? This is the question I consider in the final chapter.

7

The Future of the Lost Generation

"So far, one of the strong points of the Japanese system has been that the manufacturing labor force gets so well trained. But now the needs of industry are changing and the employment system is changing, so education needs to change, too."

– High school teacher in Yokohama

"The working conditions of part-time jobs have become worse and worse. People have to work almost as hard as full-time workers but even so, the pay is very low."

– Teacher in the guidance department at a vocational high school, commenting on current working conditions for young people

"The crisis of youth" (*wakamono kiki*). Proclaimed in boldface type, this is the phrase that ran across the cover of Japan's weekly magazine *Tōyō Keizai* in early 2009. The cover story was accompanied by a photo of a grim-faced young Japanese man in a business suit. Other phrases on the magazine cover amplified the gloomy message: "Average monthly overtime hours are 150. The percentage of young people in their early twenties who are in irregular work is 43. More than 50 percent of workers are dissatisfied with their workplace." The list goes on. Inside the magazine, statistics and stories of Japanese young people's uneasy job situation fill the pages in discouraging detail. Comparative statistics for other OECD countries appear in colored graphs but do little to brighten the depiction of Japan.

In this book I have used numbers to illustrate the employment situation of the lost generation and have added the voices of Japanese high school teachers, officials at public employment security offices, employers, and young men themselves to articulate what is happening "on the ground." These varied viewpoints collectively demonstrate how young people's employment has been closely linked to the existence of a strongly segmented Japanese labor market that demarcates the boundary between jobs designated for new graduates and jobs designated for everyone else. Young graduates have alternatively benefited and chafed against the restrictions of having an entry-level labor market of their own, just as they have benefited and chafed against schools' and employers' assumption that they are naïve about the world of work and must be shepherded into it by watchful adults.

Japan's segmented youth labor market and the assumptions it implies about young people are two sides of the same coin. The inextricable connection between the two sides of the coin brings us full circle to the sociological insight with which I opened this book: Social institutions are not just the structural underpinnings for individual lives. They bear an intimate connection to the way people formulate their identity and navigate in society writ large. As the Japanese school-work system has crumbled, nonelite young men have increasingly been required to exercise greater initiative and new types of skills in making their way into stable employment than their fathers needed to demonstrate. Young men in the social generation dubbed Japan's "lost generation" have had to negotiate their identities at a historical moment when previously stable institutions have begun to crumble. These institutions were precisely the ones around which the identities of the men in the previous social generation – the men who are the fathers of the lost generation – had been molded.

Japan simultaneously completed its passage to a mature postindustrial economy and endured a massive economic recession beginning in the 1990s. In the process, one implicit social contract was abandoned and another was more or less maintained. Which contract was broken? It was the implicit understanding that young men who graduated from school and moved into the workforce could earn a spot in the Japanese middle class for themselves and eventually for their family. Such a lifestyle had been open even to high school graduates, not just to the educational elite who graduated from first- or second-ranked universities. This social contract with the young was broken in the 1990s in order that society's implicit contract guaranteeing secure employment to middle-aged breadwinners could be upheld. It has been a bittersweet trade-off.

Would it have been better if the social contract with middle-aged men hired during Japan's high-growth period had been broken? Better if more of them had lost their jobs, and lost as well the economic well-being and sense of identity they derived from the *ba* of their workplace? To claim that this would have been less destabilizing to Japanese society would be a hard case to make. Choosing between job loss and instability for current versus future breadwinners is a thankless task for employers and governments. Rather than engaging in this thought exercise, this chapter concludes by stepping back and placing the changes in the Japanese youth labor market and its institutions in comparative perspective to see what implications exist for Japan itself and for other countries facing difficulties in incorporating their young nonelite men into positions that set them on the path to economic stability. In doing so, I hope to bring to the surface some of the labor market dynamics that are so taken-for-granted in Japan (and by scholars of Japanese society) that they tend to remain under the radar screen.

The first part of the chapter critically examines the advantages and disadvantages of the segmentation of the Japanese labor market into jobs for new graduates on the one hand and jobs for everyone else on the other hand. It can be argued that this highly regulated labor market segmentation and the postwar school-work system that supported it have both contained the seeds of their own demise. Bracketing off part of the labor market for new school-leavers worked well in Japan's expanding economy throughout much of the postwar period. But this segregation presumed a continued demand on the part of employers for young full-time workers, and presumed as well the ability of employers to be able to pay an ever-increasing wage bill as their current employees aged. Moreover, it conditioned Japanese young people to rely on institutions to shepherd them from the *ba* of school into the *ba* of the workplace and to rely on the workplace to provide skill training. This contrasts with the demands for autonomy placed on young people in many other postindustrial economies, especially the U.S. I argue that facile claims by both Japanese and foreign commentators that the Japanese labor market is becoming more and more "Americanized" threaten to trivialize the impact of Japanese labor market change on individual lives. In doing so, such claims trivialize the difficulties faced by individuals in adapting to rapid social change. They also unrealistically simplify the complexities and pitfalls entailed in arguing for the relevance or "exportability" of school-work institutions across national and cultural boundaries.

In these final pages I consider the types of attitudes, behaviors, and cultural underpinnings required for the operation of a vibrant external labor market – a labor market characterized by competition for jobs across age groups and sexes, and characterized by the mobility of workers across different jobs and companies throughout their life course. If this is the direction in which Japan is moving, it is illustrative to compare the Japanese labor market with one of the most mobile of postindustrial labor markets, the U.S., with its lack of employment protection and absence of long-term implicit contracts between employers and workers. Such a comparison implies neither a positive nor a negative judgment of the mechanisms in the American labor market. It requires only the recognition that an open and flexible labor market necessitates attitudes and predispositions on the part of workers that are strikingly different than what Japan's segmented labor market has heretofore required of individuals.

The second part of the chapter builds on the first by looking at the consequences of institutional change and economic recession on patterns of inequality in Japan's lost generation. I close with thoughts on the broader implications to Japanese society of an aging lost generation.

IMPLICATIONS OF SEGMENTED VERSUS
OPEN LABOR MARKETS FOR NEW GRADUATES

The smooth operation of the Japanese school-work system was closely connected to the highly segmented nature of the labor market. While much has been written about Japan's "dual labor market" – the duality of well-paid, stable jobs in large firms versus lesser-paid, more unstable jobs in small firms – other aspects of segmentation in the Japanese labor market are not as commonly remarked upon. The designation of some jobs as open only to new high school graduates, others as open only to new university graduates, some jobs open only to men and some only to women (although such designations are now formally illegal), and some jobs designated for mid-career hires has created a highly delineated set of pathways and specific slots for certain types of people to fill. Furthermore, it has reinforced the necessity for young people to graduate "on schedule" because after all, April 1 is the day that new full-time jobs in Japan commence.

These points were brought home to me as I interviewed Japanese high school teachers in the course of doing the research for this book. Many teachers expressed great surprise to learn that most of their "taken-for-granted" rules of the game with regard to the labor market simply do not apply in the U.S. More than a few teachers expressed genuine amazement that the American labor market is not partitioned at least into a segment for new graduates and a segment for everyone else. They were also very surprised to learn that there is no standard calendar for recruitment and hiring activities and no set date each year when graduates begin their new jobs. From their vantage point, the American labor market sounds like a veritable free-for-all.

The high school-work transition model that served Japan so well during the period of rapid economic growth rested on the coordination between schools and employers in moving young men into full-time jobs. The Ministry of Health, Labour and Welfare and the local public employment security offices tightly controlled the application process for full-time postgraduation jobs. High schools and employers cooperated with the process. In the workplace, many employers took over the task of developing new workers' human capital. Occupational preparation in school was not the key to the system. Rather, the keys were school-employer communication and cooperation. Intense communication and the forging of stable recruitment ties were driven, on the one hand, by schools' appointed duty to facilitate the transition of adolescents into full-time jobs and, on the other hand, by employers' desire to smoothly integrate new young workers into an existing workforce to which they would develop a strong attachment. Many employers worked from an assumption that alumni from the same school would naturally reproduce a harmonious and stable workforce. Preparing young people to think about the type of work they wanted to do was not really necessary – the employers who hired them straight out of school would see to that.

Under the Japanese school-work system, many parents essentially turned the guidance of their youth over to high schools. In my research, neither the Youth Survey nor in-depth interviews gave much evidence of sustained parent-adolescent communication about work and life goals. As one teacher at a low-ranked general high school put it:

When students are sophomores, we talk with them about what 'working' is. For the juniors, we explain what you need to do in order to get a job. Then when the students are seniors, the decision is right in front of them, so we talk concretely about what kinds of employees companies are looking for....It's not that any of this is a big headache for us, but it just kind of seems like discussions like this don't happen much at home, between parents and kids. I think one reason is because many fathers are working long hours and are not at home very much. There doesn't seem to be much communication at home. Parents rely on the school to take care of their kids' future.

Also telling is the fact that among the two-thirds of personnel officers in my Employer Survey who agreed with the system of having the school serve as the intermediary between high school seniors and themselves, by far the most common reason employers gave for their agreement is that high school seniors are minors and cannot make decisions about post-graduation employment on their own. Personnel officers emphasized that adolescents are young and unworldly, a view also frequently expressed by high school teachers in my interviews with them.

But while the school system continued to treat them as young and unworldly, many Japanese young people in the past decade and a half became tangled in a web of contradictions as employers began to hire them as students into low-paid, part-time jobs with neither benefits nor insurance. The demarcation between student and worker became increasingly blurred in the lived experiences of more and more young people. Even as students began learning about the world of work through part-time jobs, they were generally advised by their teachers not to mention this on their applications for postgraduation jobs lest prospective employers view it as a strike against them. After all, in the highly standardized life course model on which Japan operated for the past few decades, it was not normatively acceptable for adolescents to simultaneously hold the roles of "student" and "worker." The hallmark of the "modern" Japanese life course of the 1960s to 1980s was young people's orderly transition from student to adult – from student to *shakaijin* (social person). As illustrated in the opening pages of this book, for men this translated into a meaningful inversion of the syllables and Chinese characters for *sha* and *kai* into *kaishain* or "company person."

The contrast with the organization of the labor market and adolescents' experience of education and work in European countries with apprenticeship systems is jarring. In apprenticeship systems such as those in Germany, Austria, and the Netherlands, many adolescents begin experiencing the world of work through the context of the educational system. This early experience of work is marked by an occupational focus. Both of these elements – the combination of school and apprenticeship experiences, and the emphasis on occupational preparation – have been brought up in recent educational debates in Japan as possible directions in which the country should go.

As I recounted in Chapter 1, in my interviews at Japanese high schools in the past few years it was striking to hear the concept of internship raised for the first time. Grasping the idea as a familiar one from my reading on apprenticeship and internship systems in Europe, I questioned teachers more, only to realize that what they were referring to as student "internships" were often no more than one- or two-day trips to view a given company. Even so, the labor market changes of the 1990s and the early twenty-first century have forced educational policymakers in Japan to recognize that schools increasingly need to prepare students to think about what they want to do and what their particular skill set will be.

An unusual event that happened to occur as I was completing this manuscript brought home to the Japanese public in full force the fact that they can no longer take for granted young people's access to full-time, stable jobs where employers will offer years of training and job security. In December 2008 a number of prominent Japanese companies abruptly cancelled the employment promises they had made to graduating seniors due to start work on April 1. Public outcry was immediate and dramatic. As usual, concern centered not so much on the effect this had on Japan's nonelite (high school graduates) for whom employment offers had been cancelled. Instead, outrage focused on how companies could possibly do this to Japan's young elite – the graduates of first- and second-ranked universities in particular. Emblematic of the general reaction were the comments of a middle-aged woman who called into a Japanese talk show soon after the announcement, angrily blaming the companies for "ruining these young people's lives."

The strongly segmented nature of the Japanese labor market by age and experience in the decades preceding the 1990s contrasts even more markedly with the U.S. than with most European countries. The U.S. arguably represents the most unregulated of labor markets among postindustrial countries. Young American high school graduates compete head-to-head with middle-aged workers and with workers at different educational levels – the explicit age, educational, and gender segmentation of the Japanese labor market is absent. As an example, in his book *What Employers Want* the labor economist Harry Holzer reports the results of his 1990s survey of the hiring practices of three thousand employers in four large metropolitan areas in the U.S. As in Japan, the industries that recruit the highest proportions of noncollege-educated workers are retail sales, service, and manufacturing. But only about 20 to 30 percent of the Americans hired into these jobs in the 1990s were under age twenty-four. Depending on the city, another 30 to 60 percent were age twenty-five to thirty-four and an additional 25 to 45 percent were over age thirty-five. Furthermore, Holzer found that referrals from current employees and referrals to the employer by his or her acquaintances together accounted for up to 50 percent of new hires. In short, even in the labor market for low-skilled jobs – jobs open to workers without a university education – "weak ties" play an important role in the U.S. This led Holzer to conclude that American noncollege graduates with few personal contacts in the work world are likely to have a harder time finding jobs than those with contacts.

Holzer also found that prior work experience played an important role in the American low-wage labor market. Nearly three-quarters of employers in his survey required applicants to have previous work experience. Nearly three-quarters also required letters of reference, preferably from prior employers. While young people are clearly at a disadvantage vis-à-vis other workers in this respect, a significant body of social science research documents many American adolescents' active participation in paid work from ages as young as thirteen. Estimates are that at least 80 percent of American students now engage in part-time work at some point during their high school years (Mortimer 2003). As a result, by the time they apply for their first full-time job after leaving school (including dropping out, graduating from high school, or completing a higher level of education) most American young people have a variety of work experiences to list on their vitae. And unlike Japan, it is generally an advantage – not a disadvantage – to list such experiences. It demonstrates to an employer that a young person took the initiative to find paid employment and was responsible enough to show up for work over a period of time. Work experience also shows that a young person can function well in environments other than the limited *ba* of home and school – he or she can interact smoothly and competently with "strangers," surely a prerequisite of success in the ballooning postindustrial service sector.

Most of the paid work done by young middle-class American adolescents through the end of middle school is informally-arranged work for neighbors or family friends, such as babysitting, snow shoveling, yard work, or pet sitting. Such informal opportunities to work for pay often depend on the level of trust that exists in a neighborhood and in a community – trust on the part of adults that young people will try hard and will act responsibly, and trust on the part of young people that the adults who hire them will be fair in terms of payment and work conditions. The common reliance on weak ties is striking, as is the interconnectedness of the adults that help set up this work for young people. The interconnectedness is a good example of what the late American sociologist James Coleman called "social closure" (Coleman 1988). Figure 7.1 illustrates the social closure that exists when adolescents, their parents, and the adults who hire these adolescents are connected through bonds of trust. Informal social control over the working conditions and terms of employment is enforced via these trust relationships.

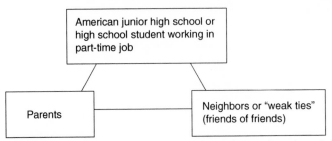

FIGURE 7.1. Social Closure through Personal Ties: American Adolescents' Part-Time Jobs.

The informal social control that operates in the social closure apparent in many middle-class and upper-middle class American adolescents' early work experiences can be compared to the similar but more formal social control that Japanese high schools were able to exert over employers during the period of high labor demand for high school graduates in the 1960s to 1980s. As I discussed in prior chapters, if employers did not uphold the working conditions they had specified on their job opening announcements for new graduates, young people sometimes went back to their high school and told their former teachers about it. The teachers could call the employer and talk to him or her, and could also call the public employment security office to tell them that the employer did not treat workers in the way specified on the job announcement. Figure 7.2 illustrates how we can think about this type of interconnectedness. It is not so much a case of informal social closure as a case of what could be termed institutional social closure, consistent with the importance of institutional rather than personal social capital in Japan.

Here, the Japanese high school graduate is not isolated in the sense of being connected only to the employer. Instead, the graduate may still feel a sense of connection to his high school, whose guidance department initially introduced him to the employer. There are channels of communication between the high school and his employer, between the high school and the public employment security office, and between his employer and the public employment security office. This structural situation is nearly ideal in terms of the amount of information and social control over exploitation that exists. But in contrast to the American situation depicted in Figure 7.1, it is exercised through institutions rather than through ties among individuals.

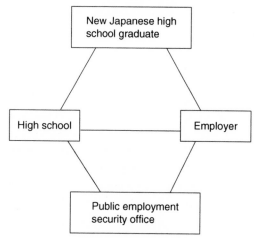

FIGURE 7.2. Institutional Social Closure: Japanese High School Graduates' Traditional Job-Hunting Process.

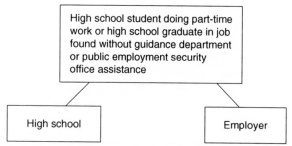

FIGURE 7.3. Lack of Social Closure for Japanese High School Students or Graduates Not Using Institutional Social Capital.

Both of these situations contrast with the present situation of Japanese high school students who do part-time work and with the situation of high school graduates who find jobs on their own. These are the circumstances that became more and more prevalent in the lost generation and, without further intervention, will probably continue for the coming cohorts. Here, high school students doing part-time work are connected to their school (albeit sometimes tenuously) and also to an employer, but the school and the employer do not have any communication with each other (Figure 7.3). So the student's relationship with the employer exists beneath the radar screen of the school as well as the public employment security agency. A similar situation exists for Japanese high school graduates who get jobs without going through their school's guidance department.

If social control through institutional social closure (communication across institutions, as was traditionally the case in Japan) is virtually non-existent, then each institution involved needs to be subject either to legal control or to the informal social control exercised by society. The situation shown in Figure 7.3, where institutional closure does not exist, is precisely the type of situation where the exploitation of workers is most likely to occur. While I have purposely not used this term at any point in the book, stories like Koichi's in Chapter 6 – where the employer did not abide by the employment terms that had been laid out, instead demanding longer and longer work hours – certainly bring this expression to mind. As more and more young Japanese workers have been relegated to various forms of contingent employment, the necessity of regulating their work conditions through the enforcement of labor law and through informal social norms has become critically important for twenty-first century Japan.

BEYOND THE JAPANESE CASE?

The research laid out in this book shows that as Japan has moved into the position of being a postindustrial economy – an economy with a large service sector and a much smaller manufacturing sector – the high school-work system has faltered. Industrial high schools continue to be recruiting targets for Japan's remaining manufacturers and engineering and construction firms, but graduates from general high schools receive little interest from employers unless these graduates are willing to take dead-end sales or service jobs. Strikingly, among a sample of twenty-one-year-old high school graduates surveyed by the Japan Educational Association in 2007, just 50 percent of employed general high school graduates were regular employees compared to nearly 80 percent of vocational high school graduates. This difference reflects the fact that the proportion of new high school graduates entering full-time office or sales jobs declined by nearly two-thirds between 1970 and 2007 (from 34 to 12 percent). Instead, new high school graduates became more concentrated in manufacturing, construction, and other blue-collar jobs (increasing from 31 to 47 percent). The proportion in low-level service sector jobs increased as well, from 4 to 15 percent (Japan Institute of Labour Policy and Training 2005).

Higher rates of advancement to university have translated into a labor pool of university graduates from which employers can draw when they have openings in more "high-end" jobs such as those in finance, insurance, commercial services, and information technology. The Japan Institute of Labour Policy and Training conducted a survey in 2005 of companies that had hired university graduates but no high school graduates during the previous year. Among these companies, by far the most common reason cited was that they could fill their labor needs entirely with university graduates. Tied for second place as the most cited reason was that they could not devote enough time to training high school graduates, and that they utilize part-time, *arubaito*, and dispatched workers. As a result, the bulk of high school graduates from general high schools as well as those who go on to two-year training schools have been relegated to an ever-more marginal position in postindustrial Japan.

Given these developments in recent years, how generalizable to other postindustrial economies is Japan's greatly admired school-work system of the 1960s to 1980s? Like Japanese employers in the early twenty-first century, it is likely that employers in most sectors of other postindustrial economies have little incentive to seek rich information from nonvocational high schools about the trainability and future productivity of their graduates. This is so for two reasons. First, most of the jobs for which high school graduates still qualify in postindustrial economies are similar to those that now exist in Japan: low-end service sector positions that involve little training investment by employers. Gone are the days when high school graduates can qualify for service-sector jobs that might constitute rungs in internal labor market ladders. Because employers' interest in carefully screening entry-level applicants for low-end service sector jobs is limited, they do not have a strong reason to form recruitment partnerships with high schools. Second, because countries such as the U.S. have a much less stratified secondary school system than Japan's, high schools themselves can serve only a minimal screening function for employers who want to save on recruitment costs by choosing high school seniors based on the school they attended.

Even so, there is a positive lesson that can be learned from the recent history of Japan's school-work system. The minority of schools in the U.S. and elsewhere that equip students with vocational knowledge and skills could benefit from taking cues from the Japanese school-work model about stronger communication and partnership efforts with manufacturers and other employers who seek a high-quality blue-collar labor force. The empirical findings in this book suggest the durability of links between vocational schools and employers even in Japan's postindustrial landscape. Many postindustrial economies, including the U.S., retain a small but robust manufacturing sector and it is here that the example of the Japanese system retains its relevance.

IMPLICATIONS FOR THE FUTURE OF JAPAN'S LOST GENERATION

Rising Inequality and Young Men's Economic Marginalization. Hand-in-hand with increased rates of unemployment and part-time employment among young Japanese men has come increasing economic inequality and the specter of a rigidifying social class structure in the new generation. The high-growth era in Japan had led to the achievement of "basic equality," in the words of Hara Junsuke and Seiyama Kazuo, two prominent sociologists of inequality,[1] with the vast majority of Japanese citizens having access to a standard of living that included sufficient food, decent housing, a wide range of household appliances, and the opportunity to attain at least a secondary education. Consistent with this, opinion polls taken in the 1970s and 1980s showed that close to 90 percent of Japanese people considered themselves to be in the middle stratum of society, leading to Murakami Yasusuke's famous coinage of the term "the new middle mass society" (Murakami 1980).[2]

While economic inequality (*kakusa*) had certainly existed in the 1970s and 1980s, it was masked in the daily experiences of many Japanese because standards of living had increased so much and for so many during the high-growth era.[3] The economic floor had risen high enough that even though people at the bottom were worse off than those at the top, they were much better off than the people at the bottom had been in the prior few generations. As Yamada Masahiro pointed out, this helped keep the hope for a better life alive and well among many of Japan's least economically well-off in the 1970s and 1980s (Yamada 2006).

But by the late 1990s several leading Japanese sociologists and labor economists sounded the alarm bell that inequality in Japanese society was

---

[1] See Hara Junsuke and Seiyama Kazuo, *Shakai kaisō: Yutakasa no naka no fubyōdō* (*Social Stratification: Inequality in an Affluent Society,* 1999). An English translation of the appeared as *Inequality Amid Affluence: Social Stratification in Japan* (2005).
[2] This article was revised and published in English (Murakami 1982).
[3] See Kelly (1993). For a view thirty years earlier, see Vogel (1963).

on the rise. Suddenly, inequality became more evident than in the high-growth period when everyone had become "middle class." Important books arguing this point included, among others, Tachibanaki Toshiaki's *Nihon no keizai kakusa: Shotoku to shisan kara kangaeru*, Satō Toshiki's *Fubyōdō shakai Nihon: Sayonara shochūryū*, and Kariya Takehiko's *Kaisōka Nihon to kyōiku kiki: Fubyōdō saiseisan kara iyoku kakusa shakai e*.[4] One of the principal facts underlying the claim of increased economic inequality was that the standard measure of household income inequality, the Gini coefficient, had increased in the 1980s and 1990s. The documented increase in income inequality came as a shock to many Japanese. A 2006 report from the OECD (Organization for Economic Cooperation and Development) showed that Japan's Gini coefficient had changed from being slightly below the average for OECD countries in the mid-1980s to slightly above the OECD average by 2005. Moreover, the rate of relative poverty in Japan had become one of the highest among OECD countries.

The reasons behind these phenomena soon became hotly debated in the Japanese press and among Japanese academics. It is clear that one of the reasons for the Gini coefficient's increase is compositional: The share of Japanese households with older people has increased, and there is greater economic variation in this age group than in others. So as the proportion of households composed of people over age sixty increased (from 25 percent of all households in 1990 to 33 percent of all households in 2000), household inequality likewise increased. Another reason is that the income difference by age became wider in Japan with the postwar spread of "lifetime employment" and seniority wages to more workers. This means that, in general, households headed by middle-aged and older workers now tend to have higher incomes than those headed by younger workers who are only at the beginning of their lifetime earnings trajectory (given Japanese employers' use of seniority-based pay principles).

If economic inequality across households and individuals in Japan is strongly related to age, then might we expect Japan's current generation of young people to naturally improve their economic circumstances as they age, following in their parents' footsteps? Not necessarily. One need only return to the figures on youth unemployment and part-time employment on the previous pages to cast doubt on this optimistic scenario. More importantly, the gap in economic life chances among young

---

[4] See Tachibanaki (1998), Satō (2002), Kariya (2001). All three books became bestsellers in Japan.

people is increasing and is likely to become even wider as they age. This is creating the possibility of a level of inequality between the "haves" and "have-nots" that Japan has not experienced for several decades.

Rising Inequality Among the Young. When the Gini coefficient is calculated within age groups in Japan, the only age group that shows widening inequality is people under age thirty-five. The increase in inequality has been particularly large among people under twenty-nine years old. As many Japanese scholars as well as the 2006 OECD report suggest, there appears to be increasing rigidity in the "dual structure" of the Japanese labor market – a stark duality between full-time workers with good wages and working conditions, and workers in smaller companies and marginal jobs (part-time positions, dispatched labor, and other types of contingent work).[5] The quote from a perceptive high school guidance department teacher at the beginning of this chapter illustrates this dichotomy.

The number of unemployed Japanese youth has doubled since the early 1990s. The number of *furītā* (young people who move among temporary jobs, often with spells of nonemployment) was estimated to have reached more than two million by 2005. And the number of NEET (youth who are not in education, employment, or training and who are not actively looking for work) has also increased dramatically. Meanwhile, in contrast to these groups, some Japanese young people continue to get "good" jobs that are relatively stable. An important question underlying this bifurcation is whether the reproduction of social class is increasing for the younger generation.

In the shadows of a widening gap between young people who moved smoothly into full-time jobs in the 1990s and young people who did not, the intergenerational transmission of economic and social status may be increasing. It is quite possible that as economic inequality widens within the under-thirty-five age group, the divisions among socioeconomic classes are rigidifying. Why? Recent data show that more and more, the Japanese young people who are doing poorly in the labor market tend to come from households in the lower socioeconomic brackets.

Social Class and NEET. A recent research project of Genda Yūji's is one of the first to use hard data to explore the social class backgrounds of young Japanese who are NEET (Genda 2007b). As explained in earlier chapters, NEET are distinct from the unemployed and also from *furītā* (young people who move among jobs and in and out of the labor force). Unlike young people who are formally classified as unemployed,

---

[5] See also Brinton (2009).

NEET are not searching for employment. The formal definition used by the Japanese government includes unmarried individuals age fifteen to thirty-four who are not in school, not employed, and have either stopped actively looking for work or have never actively sought it and do not express a desire to work. Consequently, NEET generally have less employment experience than *furītā*. As Genda points out, much of what we know about the lives of NEET is based on empirical studies of a hundred or fewer young people, which makes it difficult to understand who NEET are and what their lives are like. Nevertheless, the in-depth research of the Japan Institute of Labour Policy and Training's (JILPT) Kosugi Reiko has suggested that a high proportion of NEET are junior high school graduates and high school dropouts. And since there is a strong relationship between social class background and education in Japan, as in other postindustrial societies, it is likely that a high proportion of NEET are from lower-class households.

Genda investigated the prevalence and characteristics of NEET using proprietary micro-level data from the 1992, 1997, and 2002 *Basic Survey of Employment Structure (Shūgyō kōzō kihon chōsa)*.[6] He estimated that there were 687,000 NEET in 1992, and that ten years later this number had reached 844,000, representing nearly a 25 percent increase. A disproportionate number (more than 70 percent) of NEET are men, and nearly three quarters of NEET are noncollege graduates. Disturbingly, more than one-third of NEET report that they have never held a job. The numbers of NEET who say that they would like to work but are not searching for a job has increased by more than one-third since 1992.

Perhaps the most striking finding of all is that NEET are increasingly likely to come from poor households (households with a total income of less than 2 million yen). NEET have been severely criticized in Japanese society and by the government for lacking the desire to work, with the underlying assumption being that NEETs' reliance on economic support from their parents makes it possible for them to be very picky about the type of work they do. In contrast to this view, promulgated by Yamada's "parasite singles" argument, Genda's analysis shows that while youth in households with high incomes are indeed somewhat more likely than those from middle-income households to become NEET, this trend has diminished over time. By the early twenty-first century the probability

---

[6] The micro-level data were based on large samples of jobless youth (around 10,000 in each of the three years.)

that youth from middle-income households would become NEET had declined, countered by the rising probability for youth from low-income households.

Implications of Rising Youth Inequality. Why should a widening gap between the economic haves and have-nots in Japan's younger generation be of concern? After all, a devil's advocate might well point out that the rising wage gap in recent years between young Japanese university and nonuniversity graduates is simply mirroring the pattern that developed two decades ago in countries such as the U.S. and Great Britain.[7] And why worry about the possibility of greater social class reproduction in Japan? Might one not argue that this, too, simply renders Japan a more "normal" postindustrial society? An optimist might further point out that the levels of social unrest among youth that are evident in so many other postindustrial societies seem hardly to have appeared in twenty-first century Japan. After all, there is little evidence in Japan of participation in youth gangs and criminal activity, phenomena in the U.S. that likely stem in part from young male joblessness and feelings of hopelessness. While crime rates are rising in Japan, they remain very low compared to many postindustrial societies and the age patterns of Japanese crime belie any connection to young men's employment difficulties.[8] As far as social protest is concerned, young people in France marched on the streets in the spring of 2005 when a revision of labor law made their employment less secure. But there has been little evidence until very recently of young jobless Japanese taking to the streets to march in protest over the fact that so many of the jobs available to them are short-term, low-wage, and lacking in the job security that their fathers were promised when they entered the labor market a quarter of a century ago.

Even though the consequences of new work patterns and rising inequality among young men may be different in Japan than in other countries, the possibility that they are just as severe for society and for individuals should not be dismissed. There are signs that Japan is developing a different pattern of negative consequences. The bifurcation of work

---

[7] The literature on widening wage inequality in the U.S. and Great Britain in the 1980s is extensive. See for example Blau and Kahn (2002), Juhn, Murphy, and Pierce (1993), and Freeman and Katz (1996).

[8] Reported rates of theft, burglary, assault, consumer fraud, and other crimes are low in Japan compared to other OECD countries. Even so, a higher percentage of people in Japan than in most other OECD countries report feeling unsafe on the street after dark. See Van Dijk, Van Kesteren, and Paul (2008).

hours, with some young people working extremely long hours in "good" jobs and other young people working very low hours in "not-so-good" jobs, seems unusually severe in Japan (Genda 2007b).

Moreover, just because Japanese young people are not dealing with joblessness and feelings of hopelessness by marching in the streets in protest or by engaging in criminal activity, we cannot necessarily conclude that the repercussions of joblessness and lack of hope are insignificant. The more common response among Japanese young people has been to turn inward and blame themselves, questioning their own abilities and losing their self-confidence. Isolating oneself from society crystallizes the phenomenon of *anomie* (alienation and uncertainty) made famous by the classical French sociologist Emile Durkheim. In the most extreme cases in Japan, this *anomie* leads to a retreat into the status of *hikikomori* (extreme social isolate), a lashing out at the authority figures inside one's own *ba* – especially parents and teachers – or the ultimate retreat of suicide. Notably, these extreme cases seem to be concentrated among young men, precisely the group that has been the most severely affected by economic recession and employment restructuring over the past decade and a half.

It is important to be cautious in positing causal connections among the many phenomena and trends occurring among young Japanese, and it would be a mistake to assert a direct connection between unemployment and severe forms of social withdrawal such as *hikikomori* and suicide. The relationships among these phenomena need to be studied carefully before conclusions can be drawn, and it is not at all clear that the data necessary for such an endeavor even exist. Nevertheless, none but the most careless of observers could deny that a web of social problems was engulfing many young Japanese men by the first decade of the twenty-first century.

Young male university graduates struggled to gain a toehold in the Japanese labor market of the 1990s and the early twentieth century. Young women at all educational levels also struggled. Many middle-aged and older men struggled to keep their jobs or to change jobs. But young men without university degrees and from households with low incomes arguably waged the hardest battles. Historical demographic research on a range of societies has demonstrated that when a society denies entry into full-time employment for young men, more and more young people will delay marriage, delay childbearing, and delay in many other ways the transition to adulthood. It goes without saying that Japan has come to represent a contemporary case in point.

CHALLENGES FOR THE LOST GENERATION

Domestic assertions in Japan of the Americanization of the labor market
are almost uniformly accompanied by a set of negative connotations having to do with young people's greater proclivity to move across jobs and
their supposed lack of commitment to companies and to the very idea of
hard work. Americanization is also taken to signify higher rates of unemployment or outright nonemployment than late twentieth-century Japan
experienced prior to the bursting of the economic bubble in the 1990s
and the crippling world financial crisis of 2008 and 2009. But these are
assumptions and characterizations that belie the impact of the "flexibi-
lization" of the labor market on Japanese young people's identities. The
bursting of the bubble economy is not just an economic transformation
that mimics a similar phenomenon in other countries. To be sure, it needs
to be understood within a global, comparative context, but it also needs
to be interpreted within the recent historical context of Japan itself – a
context that had been characterized by extreme labor market segmentation and strong life course orderliness for the generations that immediately preceded the lost generation. To locate labor market flexibility and
the rapid expansion of unstable part-time employment within Japan's
recent historical past is to focus attention on what the wrenching transformations of the 1990s and beyond signify for the present and future
lives of Japan's young people, especially the nonelite.

To wit, a society such as Japan's that has been based on individuals'
stable attachment to a *ba* has required people to have a different interpersonal orientation than a society based on the presumption that people
will move across multiple settings throughout their life, carrying their
skill set with them and interacting with a succession of new co-workers
as they enter different workplaces. The highly orchestrated Japanese
school-work transition system assumed that young people would receive
little occupational preparation in school, and in fact it did not require
young people to think deeply about what type of work they wanted to
do. Schools matched new graduates to firms, not to occupations or jobs.
The system also reinforced the tendency in Japanese society for individuals to rely on institutional social capital instead of forming and utilizing
interpersonal ties, especially weak ties.

As the demarcated labor market in Japan for new high school graduates has begun to merge with a broader labor market of job searchers of
different ages, new graduates have lost some of the constrictions as well
as the comforts of a protected labor market space. This necessitates the

acquisition of new skills on the part of young Japanese school-leavers to compete not just with other new graduates but also with mid-career job-changers and with an ever-larger group of underemployed workers of different ages.

A Keidanren survey in 2004 asked employers who hired new graduates (from any level of education) into white-collar or technical jobs to articulate the biggest gaps between their expectation of new graduates and what they actually observe. The answers were illuminating. The three main deficits employers reported seeing in young people concerned "the ability to express one's point of view lucidly after fully taking into account the other person's questions and opinions"; "having the experience of striving toward one's own goals"; and "making creative and independent judgments based on one's own experiences and thinking."

If Japan is transforming into a society that requires individuals to move across *ba* with greater initiative and confidence, to formulate independent judgments, and to forge a broad array of weak ties rather than strong in-group ties, what does this portend for young people's ability to adapt? As I illustrated through the detailed portraits of three young men in Chapter 6, many Japanese young people are grappling with how to find meaningful work and tolerable work conditions in the new economy. They are using many methods of finding work. In doing so, they are charting new territory compared to the terrain that many of their fathers traveled. Those with strong egos, many inner resources, and an adventurous spirit can make their way through the changed labor market environment. But many others appear to be struggling with a persistent sense of failure that debilitates and isolates them from their more "successful" peers and from broader social contact.

Like Koichi, some young people wonder why they themselves are not strong enough to survive the working conditions one must seemingly endure in a "good job." One could reasonably ask why Koichi should feel badly about himself, rather than his employer feeling bad about the way employees were being treated. The fact that Koichi was not able to form a stable attachment to one workplace *ba* early on in his career might tell us more about the circumstances he encountered in the workplace and about his lack of recourse than about the faults in his own character. Just as many young Japanese are criticized for not wanting to work hard or for being too picky about work, why has it been hard for so many in Japan to see that the other extreme – being willing to work to the point of exhaustion – should not also be grounds for criticism and reproach? If the first category of behaviors is taken as a signal that individuals'

identities are not attached enough to their workplace *ba*, might not the
second category of behaviors signal that individuals' identities are too
attached to their workplace *ba*? While the second category of behaviors
does not lead society to view individuals as maladapted or abnormal, the
effect of extreme attachment to one *ba* on a person's identity and sense
of well-being may be almost as detrimental as the effect of having a very
weak attachment or no attachment to a *ba*. In an ironic twist, it may be
that weak attachment to a *ba* and extreme attachment to a *ba* are actually two sides of the same coin. That is, a culture that encourages and
valorizes a strong attachment and reliance on *ba* is a culture that offers
few incentives for individuals to trust acquaintances and strangers or to
develop the capability to form accurate judgments about who does and
does not merit trust.

Among working men in the Youth Survey, 45 percent work eight
hours per day or less and 55 percent work more than eight hours per
day on average. Of these 55 percent, more than two-thirds report that
they work at least ten hours per day. Genda Yūji reports the results of a
Japanese government survey that asked unemployed workers why they
had left their previous job. While prime-age workers (ages twenty-five
to fifty-four) were most likely to cite involuntary reasons such as firms'
bankruptcy or layoffs, workers under age twenty-five were most likely
to say they had left their job because working conditions were not what
they had anticipated (Genda 2001). One might regard this as a reflection
of the pickiness and fickleness in the younger generation, and for some
proportion of cases this would no doubt be an accurate characteriza-
tion. But looking at this statistic from a different viewpoint, one might
interrogate the working conditions that young people are rejecting. This
would lead to a different sort of inquiry and a different set of government
policies. Such policies would aim to enforce reasonable working hours
and conditions instead of attempting to shame young people into feeling
like they must make the choices their fathers made – choices that often
led to tremendous personal sacrifice and exhaustion during Japan's high
economic-growth period in the 1960s–1980s.

While the failure to find a satisfying full-time job with adequate working conditions and wages is an unhappy outcome for individual young
men, there are of course larger implications for Japanese society as well.
The government is correct in worrying that small cohort sizes and the
fact that so many young people are contingent workers means that fewer
and fewer people are paying into the pension system. Also at the top of
the government's list of worries for the past decade and a half have been

the increasing rates of delayed marriage or nonmarriage and the very low birth rate. While Japanese men in their twenties and early thirties are in the process of navigating the uncharted territory of the external labor market, most of them are living with their parents and are partially or fully financially dependent on them. My research suggests that most of these young men want to be settled in relatively stable jobs – at minimum, in full-time jobs rather than part-time temporary jobs – before they take on the responsibilities of marriage and parenthood. The relationship between becoming a full-time employee and being able to marry is a common theme in interviews with young Japanese males. This suggests that the Japanese government would do well to consider that public policies to address youth labor market problems might have the side benefit of addressing one of the causes of the low-fertility crisis.

Japanese society and employers need to figure out ways of utilizing and nurturing the skills and capabilities of young people, including those in the lost generation who have become more socially mature and responsible by engaging in new ways of searching for work after graduating from school. Many of these individuals have taught themselves and one another how to use the public employment agency, job magazines, and the Internet. They are newly engaged in talking to other people about what they find to be satisfying and unsatisfying in working life. It may be that fewer individuals in the lost generation than in the prior generation are willing to tolerate what they view as inhumane work conditions for the sake of basing their identity on long-term attachment to one *ba*. More and more Japanese young people are learning how to maintain a sense of identity and self-respect as they move across workplaces. They are not Japan's present failures. They are Japan's future hope.

References

Aoki, Masahiko. 1988. *Information, Incentives, and Bargaining in the Japanese Economy.* Cambridge: Cambridge University Press.

Ariga, Kenn. 2005. "From Golden Eggs to Rotten Apples: Changing Landscape of the Market for New High School Graduates in Japan." Discussion paper no. 80, *21st Century COE, Interfaces for Advanced Economic Analysis.* Kyoto: Kyoto University.

Blanchflower, David G., and Richard B. Freeman. 2000. "Introduction and Summary." In *Youth Employment and Joblessness in Advanced Countries,* edited by David G. Blanchflower and Richard B. Freeman, 1–16. Chicago: University of Chicago Press.

Blau, Francine D., and Lawrence M. Kahn. 2002. *At Home and Abroad: U.S. Labor Market Performance in International Perspective.* New York: Russell Sage Foundation.

Bourdieu, Pierre. 1977. *Outline of a Theory of Practice.* Translated by Richard Nice. Cambridge: Cambridge University Press.

——. 1986. "The Forms of Capital." In *Handbook of Theory and Research for the Sociology of Education,* edited by J. Richardson, 241–58. New York: Greenwood.

Breen, Richard, and Marlis Buchmann. 2002. "Institutional Variation and the Position of Young People: A Comparative Perspective." *Annals of the American Academy of Political and Social Science* 480: 288–305.

Brinton, Mary C. 1988. "The Social-Institutional Bases of Gender Stratification: Japan as an Illustrative Case." *American Journal of Sociology* 94: 300–34.

——. 1992. "Christmas Cakes and Wedding Cakes: The Social Organization of Japanese Women's Life Course." In *Japanese Social Organization,* edited by Takie Sugiyama Lebra, 79–107. Honolulu: University of Hawaii Press.

——. 1993. *Women and the Economic Miracle: Gender and Work in Postwar Japan.* Berkeley: University of California Press.

———. 2000. "Social Capital in the Japanese Youth Labor Market: Labor Market Policy, Schools, and Norms." *Policy Sciences* 33: 289–306.

———. 2005. "Education and the Economy." In *The Handbook of Economic Sociology, 2nd Edition*, edited by Neil Smelser and Richard Swedberg, 575–602. Princeton: Princeton University Press.

———. 2009. *"Nihon no rōdō shijō no nijū kōzō o anwa suru tame ni hitsuyō na koto"*(Measures Required to Lessen the Japanese Labor Market's Dual Structure). *Business Labor Trends: Special Issue on Stabilizing Irregular Employment* 4: 14.

Brinton, Mary C., and Takehiko Kariya. 1998. "Institutional Embeddedness in Japanese Labor Markets." In *The New Institutionalism in Sociology*, edited by Mary C. Brinton and Victor Nee, 181–207. New York: Russell Sage Foundation.

Brinton, Mary C., and Zun Tang,. 2010. "School-Work Systems in Postindustrial Societies: Evidence from Japan." *Research in Social Stratification and Mobility* 28: 215–232.

Brown, Clair, Michael Reich, Lloyd Ulman, and Yoshifumi Nakata. 1997. *Work and Pay in the United States and Japan*. New York: Oxford University Press.

Chauvel, Louis. 2006. "Social Generations, Life Chances, and Welfare Regime Sustainability." In *Changing France: The Politics That Markets Make*, edited by Pepper D. Culpepper, Peter A. Hall, and Bruno Palie, 150–75. New York: Palgrave Macmillan.

Chiavacci, David. 2005. "Transition from University to Work under Transformation." *Social Science Japan* 8: 19–42.

Chinhui, Juhn, Kevin M. Murphy, and Brooks Pierce. 1993. "Wage Inequality and the Rise in Returns to Skill." *Journal of Political Economy* 101: 410–42.

Clark, Jon, ed., 1996. *James S. Coleman*. London: Falmer Press.

Coleman, James S. 1988. "Social Capital in the Creation of Human Capital." *American Journal of Sociology* 94: S95–120.

———. 1990. *Foundations of Social Theory*. Cambridge: Harvard University Press.

Dustmann, Christian, and Uta Schoenberg. 2008. "Why Does the German Apprenticeship System Work?" In *Skill Formation: Interdisciplinary and Cross-National Perspectives*, edited by Karl Ulrich Mayer and Heike Solga, 85–108. New York: Cambridge University Press.

Esping-Andersen, Gösta. 1977. "Hybrid or Unique? The Japanese Welfare State between Europe and America." *Journal of European Policy* 7: 179–89.

Freeman, Richard B., and Lawrence F. Katz. 1996. *Differences and Changes in Wage Structure*. Chicago: University of Chicago Press.

Fukuzawa, Rebecca Erwin. 1994. "The Path to Adulthood According to Japanese Middle Schools." *Journal of Japanese Studies* 20: 61–86.

Garon, Sheldon. 1990. *The State and Labor in Modern Japan*. Berkeley: University of California Press.

Genda, Yūji. 2000. "Japanese Labour in the 1990s: Stability and Stagnation." *Oxford Review of Economic Policy* 16: 85–102.

———. 2001. *Shigoto no naka no aimai na fuan* (A Vague Sense of Job Anxiety). Tokyo: Chūō Kōron Shinsha.

———. 2003. "Who Really Lost Jobs in Japan? Youth Employment in an Aging Japanese Society." In *Labor Markets and Firm Benefit Policies in Japan and the United States*, edited by Seiritsu Ogura, Toshiaki Tachibanaki, and David Wise, 103–34. Chicago: University of Chicago Press.

———. 2007a. "Jobless Youths and the Neet Problem in Japan." *Social Science Japan Journal* 10: 23–40.

———. 2007b. *A Nagging Sense of Job Insecurity: The New Reality Facing Japanese Youth*. Translated by Jean Connell Hoff. Tokyo: International House of Japan.

Granovetter, Mark. 1973. "The Strength of Weak Ties." *American Journal of Sociology* 78: 1360–80.

Hara, Junsuke and Seiyama Kazuo. 1999. *Shakai kaisō: Yutakasa no naka no fubyōdō* (Social Stratification: Inequality in an Affluent Society). Tokyo: University of Tokyo.

———. 2005. *Inequality Amid Affluence: Social Stratification in Japan*. Melbourne, Australia: Trans Pacific Press.

Hashimoto, Masanori, and John Raisian. 1985. "Employment Tenure and Earnings Profiles in Japan and the United States." *American Economic Review* 75: 721–35.

Hertog, Ekaterina. 2009. *Tough Choices: Bearing an Illegitimate Child in Japan*. Stanford: Stanford University Press.

Hillmert, Steffen. 2008. "When Traditions Change and Virtues Become Obstacles: Skill Formation in Britain and Germany." In *Skill Formation: Interdisciplinary and Cross-National Perspectives*, edited by Karl Ulrich Mayer and Heike Solga, 50–81. New York: Cambridge University Press.

Holzer, Henry J. 1996. *What Employers Want*. New York: Russell Sage Foundation.

Honda, Yuki. 1999. *"Kōkō kigyō-kan no 'jisseki kankei' no henka"* (Changes in the Relationship between High Schools and Companies). *Kikan Kyōiku Hō* (Educational Law) 121: 30–33.

———. 2003. "The Reality of the Japanese School-to-Work Transition System at the Turn of the Century: Necessary Disillusionment." *Social Science Japan* 25: 8–12.

———. 2004. "The Formation and Transformation of the Japanese System of Transition from School to Work." *Social Science Japan Journal* 7: 103–15.

———. 2005a. "'Freeters': Young Atypical Workers in Japan." *Japan Labor Review* 2: 5–25.

———. 2005b. *Wakamono to shigoto: 'Gakkō keiyū no shūshoku' o koete* (Young People and Employment in Japan: Beyond the 'School-Mediated' Job Search). Tokyo: Tokyo University Press.

Ishida, Hiroshi. 1993. *Social Mobility in Contemporary Japan*. Stanford: Stanford University Press.

———. 2000. *"Kōtō gakkō no shūshoku shidō to kōsotsusha no shūshoku"* (High Schools' Job-Hunting Guidance and the Job-Hunting Process of Graduates). In *Jakunensha no koyō/shitsugyō nado ni kansuru sōgōteki na chōsa kenkyū* (Comprehensive Survey Research on the Employment and Unemployment of Youth). Tokyo: Sanwa Sōgō Kenkyūjo/Koyō Nōryoku Kaihatsu Kikō.

Iwata, Katsuhiko. 2004. "Diverse Working Conditions among Non-Standard Employees: JIL Research Report and Policy Implications." *Japan Labor Review* 1: 77–91.

Japan Institute of Labour Policy and Training. 1989. Seinen *no shokugyō tekiyō ni kansuru kokusai hikaku kenkyū* (A Comparative Study of Youths' Work Adjustment). JIL Research Report No. 86. Tokyo: JILPT.

——. 2005. "*Shinki gakusotsu saiyō no genjō to shōrai: Kōsotsu saiyō wa kaifuku suru ka?*" (The Present and Future Situation of New Graduate Hiring: Will the Hiring of High School Graduates Recover?). JIL Research Report No. 28. Tokyo: JILPT.

Kalleberg, Arne L., and James R. Lincoln. 1988. "The Structure of Earnings Inequality in the United States and Japan." *American Journal of Sociology* 94: S121-S53.

Kariya, Takehiko. 1988. "Institutional Networks between Schools and Employers and Delegated Occupational Selection to Schools: A Sociological Study of the Transition from High School to Work." PhD Dissertation, Northwestern University.

——. 1991. *Gakkō, shokugyō, senbatsu no shakaigaku* (Sociology of Schools, Jobs, and Selection). Tokyo: Tokyo University Press.

——. 2001. *Kaisōka Nihon to kyōiku kiki: Fubyōdō saiseisan kara iyoku kakusa shakai e* (Stratifying Japan and the Crisis in Education: From the Rise of Inequality to a Society of Diverging Aspirations). Tokyo: Yushindō.

Kariya, Takehiko, and James E. Rosenbaum. 2003. "Stratified Incentives and Life Course Behaviors." In *Handbook of the Life Course*, edited by Jeylan T. Mortimer and Michael J. Shanahan, 51–78. New York: Kluwer.

Kariya, Takehiko, Shinji Sugayama, and Hiroshi Ishida, eds., 2000. *Gakkō, shokuan to rōdō shijō: Sengo shinki gakusotsu shijō no seidōka katei* (Schools, Public Employment Offices, and the Labor Market: The Process of Institutionalization of the Labor Market for New Graduates in the Postwar Period) Tokyo: Tokyo University Press.

Kariya, Takehiko, Shinji Sugayama, Hiroshi Ishida, Yumiko Murao, and Y. Nishimura. 1997. "*Shinki gakusotsu rōdō shijō no seidōka katei ni kansuru kenkyū*" (Research on the Process of Institutionalization of the Labor Market for New Graduates). *Shakai Kagaku Kenkyū* 49: 123–200.

Kelly, William W. 1993. "Finding a Place in Metropolitan Japan: Ideologies, Institutions, and Everyday Life." In *Postwar Japan as History*, edited by Andrew Gordon, 189–238. Berkeley: University of California Press.

Knack, Stephen, and Philip Keefer. 1997. "Does Social Capital Have an Economic Payoff? A Cross-Country Investigation." *The Quarterly Journal of Economics* 112: 1251–88.

Koike, Kazuo. 1988. *Understanding Industrial Relations in Modern Japan.* New York: St. Martin's Press.

——. 1999. "White-Collar Workers in Japan and the United States: Which Are More Ability Oriented?" In *The Transformation of the Japanese Economy*, edited by Kazuo Sato, 173–205. Armonk, NY: ME Sharpe.

Kosugi, Reiko. 2004. "The Increase and Background of the Jobless Youth: An Examination of the Jobless Youth in the Transition from School to Working Life." *The Japanese Journal of Labour Studies* 46: 4–16.

———. 2008. *Furītā to iu ikikata* (Escape from Work: Freelancing Youth and the Challenge to Corporate Japan). Translated by Ross Mouer. Melbourne, Australia: Trans Pacific Press.

Lifson, Thomas B. 1979. *An Emergent Administrative System: Interpersonal Networks in a Japanesse General Trading Firm*. Cambridge, MA: Cambridge Graduate School of Business Administration, Harvard University.

Lucas, Samuel R. 2001. "Effectively Maintained Inequality: Education Transitions, Track Mobility, and Social Background Effects." *American Journal of Sociology* 106: 1642–90.

Mannheim, Karl. 1952. "The Problem of Generations." In *Essays on the Sociology of Knowledge*, edited by Paul Kecskemeti, 276–322. London: Routledge & Kegan Paul.

Masahiro, Yamada. 1999. *Parasaito shinguru no jidai* (The Age of Parasite Singles). Tokyo: Chikuma Shinsho.

Mayer, Karl Ulrich. 2004. "Whose Lives? How History, Societies and Institutions Define and Shape Life Courses." *Research in Human Development* 1: 161–87.

Mayer, Karl Ulrich, and Heike Solga. 2008. "Skill Formation: Interdisciplinary and Cross-National Perspectives." In *Skill Formation: Interdisciplinary and Cross-National Perspectives*, edited by Karl Ulrich Mayer and Heike Solga, 1–18. New York: Cambridge University Press.

Ministry of Education, Culture, Sports, Science, and Technology. 2009. "*Heisei 21 nendo gakkō kihon chōsa sokuhan.*" (Summary of Basic School Statistics). Tokyo: MEXT.

Morgan, Philip S., Ronald R. Rindfuss, and Allan Parnell. 1983. "Modern Fertility Patterns: Contrasts between the United States and Japan." *Population and Development Review* 10: 19–40.

Moriguchi, Chiaki, and Hiroshi Ono. 2006. "Japanese Lifetime Employment: A Century's Perspective." In *Institutional Change in Japan*, edited by Magnus Blomstrom and Sumner LaCroix, 152–76. London: Routledge.

Mortimer, Jeylan T. 2003. *Working and Growing Up in America*. Cambridge, MA: Harvard University Press.

Murakami, Yasusuke. 1980. "*Shin-chūkan taishū seiji no jidai*" (The Age of New Middle Mass Politics). Chūō Kōron, December.

———. 1982. "The Age of New Middle Mass Politics: The Case of Japan." *Journal of Japanese Studies* 8: 29–72.

———. 1984. "Ie Society as a Pattern of Civilization." *Journal of Japanese Studies* 10: 281–363.

Murata, Shoji, and Sam Stern. 1993. "Technology Education in Japan." *Journal of Technology Education* 5: 29–37.

Naganawa, Hisao. 1999. "From School to Workplace: Changes in the Labor Market for New Graduates." *Japan Labor Bulletin* 38: 5–10.

Nakane Chie. 1970. *Japanese Society*. Berkeley: University of California Press.

O'Toole, James, and Edward E. Lawler III. 2006. *The New American Workplace*. New York: Palgrave Macmillan.

Ochiai, Emiko, 1996. *The Japanese Family System in Transition: A Sociological Analysis of Family Change in Postwar Japan*. Tokyo: LTCB International Library Foundation.

OECD. 2009a. *Jobs for Youth: Japan*. Paris: OECD.
——. 2009b. *OECD Employment Outlook 2009*. Paris: OECD.
Okano, Kaori. 1993. *School to Work Transition in Japan: An Ethnographic Study*. Philadelphia: Multilingual Matters.
Osterman, Paul. 1999. *Securing Prosperity: The American Labor Market: How It Has Changed and What to Do About It*. Princeton: Princeton University Press.
Portes, Alejandro. 1998. "Social Capital: Its Origins and Applications in Modern Sociology." *Annual Review of Sociology* 24: 1–24.
Raftery, Adrian F., and Michael Hout. 1993. "Maximally Maintained Inequality: Expansion, Reform, and Opportunity in Irish Education, 1921–75." *Sociology of Education* 66: 41–62.
Rosenbaum, James E. 2001. *Beyond College for All*. New York: Russell Sage Foundation.
Rosenbaum, James E., Stefanie DeLuca, Shazia Miller, and Kevin Roy. 1999. "Pathways into Work: Short and Long-Term Effects of Personal and Institutional Ties." *Sociology of Education* 72: 179–96.
Rosenbaum, James E., and Takehiko Kariya. 1989. "From High School to Work: Market and Institutional Mechanisms in Japan." *American Journal of Sociology* 94: 1334–65.
Satō, Toshiki. 2002. *Fubyōdō shakai Nihon: Sayonara shochūryū* (Japan as an Unequal Society: Farewell to the Time of the Mass Middle-Class Society). Tokyo: Chūō Kōron Shinsha.
Solga, Heike. 2002. "Stigmatization by Negative Selection: Explaining Less-Educated People's Decreasing Employment Opportunities." *European Sociological Review* 18: 159–78.
Song, Jiyeoun. 2008. "Global Forces, Local Adjustments: The Politics of Labor Market Deregulation in Contemporary Japan and Korea." PhD Dissertation, Harvard University.
Swidler, Ann. 1986. "Culture in Action: Symbols and Strategies." *American Sociological Review* 51: 273–86.
Tachibanaki, Toshiaki, ed., 1998. *Wage Differentials: An International Comparison*. London: Macmillan.
Tachibanaki, Toshiki. 1998. *Nihon no keizai kakusa: Shotoku to shisan kara kangaeru* (Japan's Economic Inequality: Income and Property). Tokyo: Iwanami Shoten.
Thelen, Kathleen. 2007. "Contemporary Challenges to the German Vocational Training System." *Regulation and Governance* 1: 247–60.
Tōyō Keizai. *Japan Company Handbook*. 2007. Tokyo: Tōyō Keizai, Inc.
Tsurumi, Patricia. 1990. *Factory Girls: Women in the Thread Mills of Meiji Japan*. Princeton: Princeton University Press.
Upham, Frank. 1987. *Law and Social Change in Postwar Japan*. Cambridge: Harvard University Press.
Van Dijk, J., Van Kesteren, and P. Smit Paul. 2008. "Criminal Victimisation in International Perspective: Key Findings from the 2004–2005 International Crime Victims Survey and European Survey on Crime and Safety." WODC.
Vogel, Ezra F. 1963. *Japan's New Middle Class*. Berkeley: University of California Press.

Watanabe, Shin. 1987. "Job-Searching: A Comparative Study of Male Employment Relations in the United States and Japan." PhD Dissertation, University of California-Los Angeles.

Woolcock, Michael. 1998. "Social Capital and Economic Development: Toward a Theoretical Synthesis and Policy Framework." *Theory and Society* 27: 151–208.

Yamada, Masahiro. 2006. *Shin byōdō shakai: 'Kibō kakusa' o koete* (The New Inequality in Society: Overcoming the 'Gap in Hope'). Tokyo: Bungei Shunju.

Yamagishi, Toshio. 1999. *Anshin shakai kara shinrai shakai e* (From a Society of Security to a Society of Trust). Tokyo: Chūkō Shinsho.

———. 2003. "Trust and Social Intelligence in the United States and Japan." In *The State of Civil Society in Japan*, edited by Frank J. Schwartz and Susan J. Pharr, 281–97. New York: Cambridge University Press.

Yamagishi, Toshio, and Midori Yamagishi. 1993. "Trust and Commitment in the United States and Japan." *Motivation and Emotion* 18: 129–66.

Index

absences from school, 91–3
academic high schools. *See* general high
    schools
adult education, 17
adulthood, transition to, 9–11, 13–14, 18
advancement rates, university, 47, 102,
    177
age: at first childbirth, 16; at first marriage,
    15–17; employment and, 22–3, 28–9,
    172, 179–80;
    of students, 17
Age Discrimination Act (1975), 17n16
Americanization, 184
anomie, 183
anshin, 2, 19, 31, 87–8
Aoki, Masahiko, 40
apprenticeship systems, 38–40, 171–2
arubaito. *See* employment, part-time
attachment. *See also* ties, personal: stability
    of 184–6; to family, 31n19; to schools,
    64, 89–94, 145–6; to social structures,
    31n19; to workplace, 11, 19, 50, 64,
    66, 88, 163, 186
attendance, 91–3
Austria, 171

ba. *See also* ties, personal; ties, school-
    employer: decline in centrality of,
    31–2, 64–5, 88–9, 94–6; definition of,
    2–3; importance of, 4, 14, 18, 31–2,
    184–6; in United States, 4; of schools,
    64–5, 94–6; of workplace, 39, 61–2,
    65

Basic Survey of Employment Structure,
    181
benefits, employment, 135–6, 172
births, 16, 48, 97, 187
blanket recruitment, 48, 68
blue-collar jobs, 27, 48, 66–8, 134n12,
    176–8
bonus systems, 136
Bourdieu, Pierre, 9
Brinton, Mary, 35, 51–4

capital, types of, 53–4, 155. *See also* social
    capital
career paths, 12, 74
Chauvel, Louis, 10
class. *See* social class
clerical jobs, 134–5
cohort, 9–10. *See also* generations
Coleman, James, 8, 173
colleges. *See* higher education
commercial high schools, 40, 80, 138.
    See also vocational high schools
company person, 171
comparative statistics: on government
    spending, 40–1; on job training,
    37–41, 171; on labor markets, 20, 23,
    26–7, 172; on vocational education
    enrollment, 37–8;
    on wages, 67
competition between schools, 81–2, 91,
    94–5, 140–4, 158
comprehensive technical schools, 40.
    See also vocational high schools

CPSIA information can be obtained at www.ICGtesting.com
Printed in the USA
268897BV00001B/8/P

9 780521 126007